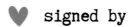 

truth matters
love wins

truth matters
love wins

A Memoir of Choosing Faith over Fear in the Face of False Accusations

Alexandra J. Kuisis

gatekeeper press
Columbus, Ohio

Disclaimer: This book reflects the author's present recollections of her experiences over time. Some names and identifying characteristics have been changed, some events have been compressed, and some dialogue has been recreated. While no official court documents were used to recall this re-telling, personal notes taken in real time, personal journal entries, personal correspondence, and detailed written summaries from friends and family also present in the courtroom each day were.

Truth Matters, Love Wins: A Memoir of Choosing Faith over Fear in the Face of False Accusations

Published by Gatekeeper Press
2167 Stringtown Rd, Suite 109
Columbus, OH 43123-2989
www.GatekeeperPress.com

The editorial work for this book are entirely the product of the author. Gatekeeper Press did not participate in and is not responsible for any aspect of the editorial work.

Library of Congress Control Number: 2021933841

ISBN (paperback): 9781662910371
eISBN: 9781662910388

Dedicated to the truth tellers

***

Also, for my mother, with love

Contents

A note from the author

Sometimes when we look back in reflection on the other side of an intense period of struggle, we can tend to downplay or paint it in a different light: it wasn't *that* big a deal, it wasn't *that* much of a hardship. To do so here would be misleading to the reader as well as disrespectful to myself, because my story was categorically disruptive in a way that created real trauma. That said, it is important to note that the injustices of my situation were comparatively mild to what many other defendants face and if not for the socioeconomic privilege I was born into, they could have been much worse. For women of color, they routinely are.

A Black person is five times more likely to be stopped without just cause than a white person, and the imprisonment rate for African American women is two times that of white women. Compared to observably similar whites, Black people are more likely to be searched for contraband, more likely to experience police force, more likely to be charged with a serious offense, more likely to be convicted, and more likely to be incarcerated.

I am neither a criminal justice scholar nor a social justice expert, but you don't have to be to understand what the studies, statistics, and historical data clearly show – the criminal justice system in the United States is not only broken, but it is also glaringly unjust and systemically racist.

Change is needed and possible. One way to help is to support non-profit organizations working to reform criminal justice systems, policies, and procedures in the United States.

• **Proclaim Justice** is a non-profit dedicated to winning freedom for victims of wrongful convictions. Learn more and donate at: http://proclaimjustice.org/ Please note: 5% of this book's proceeds will be donated to Proclaim Justice.

- **The Innocence Project** is a non-profit that works on exonerating the innocent through DNA testing and reforming the criminal justice system to prevent future injustice. Learn more and donate at: https://www.innocenceproject.org/
- **The Criminal Law Reform Project** from the American Civil Liberties Union (ACLU) seeks to end harsh policies and racial inequities in the criminal justice system. Learn more and donate here: https://www.aclu.org/issues/criminal-law-reform
- **The National Bail Out** collective is a Black-led and Black-centered collective of abolitionist organizers, lawyers and activists building a community-based movement to support our folks and end systems of pretrial detention and ultimately mass incarceration. Learn more and donate at: https://www.nationalbailout.org/
- **The Bail Project**™ National Revolving Bail Fund is a critical tool to prevent incarceration and combat racial and economic disparities in the bail system. Learn more and donate at: https://bailproject.org/

Additional Reading:
- M. Alexander, *The New Jim Crow: Mass Incarceration in the Age of Color-blindness*, New Press, 2010.
- B. Stevenson, *Just Mercy: A Story of Justice and Redemption*, Spiegel and Grau, 2015.
- D. Cole, No Equal Justice: *Race and Class in the American Justice System*, New Press, 1999.

Prologue

"Three things cannot be long hidden: the sun, the moon, and the truth." – Gautama Buddha

1979 - Milwaukee, Wisconsin

I am four years old and waiting. My parents are going out to dinner with friends from church tonight so one of the many babysitters who watches us on a rotating basis is coming to spend time with me and my baby sister, who will likely sleep the entire evening. This babysitter plays a special game with me, a game I'm instructed not to talk about, so I don't. I'm a really good rule follower. Plus, the babysitter told me I'll get in trouble if I say anything and although I'm an insatiably curious kid, I'm not someone who intentionally goes looking for trouble.

I already know how the night will go. After my parents leave, this babysitter will pull off the blue plastic lid from the tiny tub of Vaseline she always brings and instruct me to dip my small fingers in soft yellow jelly as she pulls her pants down and lies across my bed. Then she'll tell me where and how to touch her. She'll make it seem like I have an important role, something only I can do, and I will believe her, even though the game is confusing to me.

When I'm sent to wash my hands after the game is over, I'll wrinkle my nose in quiet disgust at the sour smell as I patter down the hall to the bathroom at the top of the stairs. I don't have the slightest inkling of how this secret will create utter havoc in my life 40 years from now, and I can't yet realize how this game is going to alter the quality of every decision I make going forward.

How can I? I'm four.

My parents don't find out because I do not tell them, even after this babysitter is long gone from our lives, even after I come to understand that it had never been a game at all.

1998 - Boulder, Colorado

I am 23 years old and happy to be here. I've only lived in this city for a week, but my rickety '89 gold VW Golf has already conked out on me a handful of times. Maybe it doesn't like the altitude, maybe it feels out of place in this land of BMWs and Range Rovers. In any case, I'm in good spirits and hoping for the best as I drive my sister, Mona, to the train station in Denver, 45 minutes away. She's been helping me get settled in my new life a thousand miles from the home we shared as children, and now she's heading back to Wisconsin to finish her college education. I completed mine in the spring and surprised family and friends alike by choosing to re-locate to Boulder as my next move.

We're cheerfully gabbing about my exciting fresh beginning, laughing as the gold Golf rumbles its way down Highway 36, one of my carefully-crafted mix tapes serving up artists like Dar Williams, Jewel, and the Indigo Girls as the backdrop of our ride.

There is a brief pause in our conversation, each of us lost in our own thoughts as we take in the mountainous views against the blue sky of August. Ani DiFranco is singing a song I've heard a thousand times before; lyrics about waiting for truth are wafting in the background. As the song nears its end, I snap to attention, suddenly hyperaware that my intuition is using the final line to deliver a message from my inner child somewhere deep inside my soul: *"I will wait for you."*

At this point in my life, I still have not shared the story of my childhood abuse with anybody, but in that moment the message couldn't have been clearer: healing will happen for me in Colorado. This I know for absolute sure. But what I don't know, what I cannot even begin to guess, is the amount of hell I'll have to go through to get there.

Chapter 1

"False words are not only evil in themselves, but they infect the soul with evil." – Socrates

September 1, 2016 - Colorado

The doorbell interrupts our sun-drenched, back patio laughter around 4:30 in the afternoon.

My husband and I exchange a quizzical glance. *Now what,* I wonder.

James and I live in a tiny city near Denver, on a nice enough block at the west end of a gentrifying neighborhood. After renting the place for the past four years – the same four years we've been married, which are actually the only four years we've known each other – we purchased the house from our former landlord just a few weeks ago.

Our tiny, red brick house isn't much, but we've had fun with our landlord's generous permission to channel our inner DIY weekend warriors and spruce the place up over the years with things like paint colors, privacy fences, and garden beds.

Inside, our home décor is primarily a combination of maps, picture books, and trinkets from our travels. As an avid record-keeper and dedicated memory collector, I have long enjoyed amassing mementoes of my personal history, and it's a habit I have enthusiastically expanded to my married life. Our walls display framed photos of our newlywed adventures in places both nearby and faraway; a bulletin board displays every ticket stub to all of the concerts, movies, and events we've attended together.

Feathering our nest has become a favorite pastime, as has fixing it. Now that we own the house, we are finally able to have brand new windows installed, a treat that's coming next week. I can't wait – I'm weary of feeling a breeze through the closed window pane as we snuggle under a blanket on the couch.

We're just a few houses away from a thoroughfare with a bus stop, and just a few blocks north of Colfax Avenue, the most notorious street in Colorado. Between the random colorful characters who wander through our neighborhood and the fact that neighbors across the street use the police to facilitate their mutual dislike for one another, we have come to expect the unexpected around here.

For example, last year a woman rang our doorbell, and when I answered the door, she tried pushing past me into my house. When I refused her entry, she mouthed, *"Help me,"* and glanced back at the disheveled couple lingering at the end of our driveway. At her request we phoned the police who ended up arresting her for an outstanding warrant, which she knew about but didn't care. She just wanted away from those people. She thanked us repeatedly and told us she felt guided to our particular door.

Then earlier this summer, two police officers knocked on our front door, asking for me by name, following up on a complaint that I was running an unlicensed daycare out of my home. It was baffling because I wasn't (nor had I ever), and after a few moments of friendly conversation, the officers dismissed it and apologized for bothering me. I didn't think to ask who had lodged the complaint until they were gone, and although it sat a bit funny in the back of my mind, I chalked it up to the bizarre energy that seems to cloak our end of the block.

So when the doorbell rang today, *now what*.

I'm certainly not expecting anyone. Carys, one of my dearest childhood friends, is in town visiting from Wisconsin, and we are 20 minutes away from leaving to meet other friends for an outdoor concert. We just have to change clothes, and that won't take long at all. My new chambray pinstripe sundress with the red embroidery across the chest (and pockets!) is already hanging on the hook in the bathroom, ready to go.

James goes to answer the door, and Carys goes downstairs to her guest room. I stay on the back porch for a moment longer gathering dirty dishes to bring inside as the bees and butterflies flit in the sunlight around our flower gardens.

My husband's raised voice echoes through the house as I walk inside. I drop the dishes off beside the sink and head to the front door to see what all the fuss is about. There are police officers on our front stoop, asking for me. I roll my eyes.

Now what.

A female bounty hunter, two officers, and a man clad in blue jeans and a bullet-proof vest are waiting on my doorstep. Sounds like the beginning of a joke, but no.

"What is this about?" I ask.

They are talking over one another. Snippets of their sentences are landing in my brain but I can't piece them together in a way I understand. *A felony charge... sexual misconduct... a minor.* No one knows details, they are just here to get me.

"Ma'am, you need to come with us..."

"... on behalf of the city of Denver..."

"... no choice in the matter...."

"The house is surrounded..."

They tell me I won't be coming back home tonight; they don't care that I'm on my way to a concert with an out-of-town friend. I do not have the option of coming in tomorrow morning to discuss this. This is happening, and it is happening now.

"You want to talk to who sent us? Come with us. Or, we can take you straight to the jail. That is your only choice right now."

My head is swirling. I rack my brain, come up empty. None of it makes sense. None of it fits.

Obviously this is a weird mistake just like the accusation of the unlicensed day care was. *Are they connected*, I briefly wonder?

Obviously we can get to the bottom of it, because this thing they are suggesting is preposterous.

There has been no sexual misconduct, not by my hand. Not once. In fact, my entire career thus far has been dedicated to empowering, educating, and protecting young children; both of my university degrees are in early childhood development, and I'm even specifically trained in body-safety practices for young children. This is a misunderstanding, just like the daycare accusation a few weeks ago.

It does not occur to me yet that sometimes kids lie.

My husband is still arguing with them. Our confusion is clashing with their aggression and in that moment, a voice in my head instructs me to take a breath, remain calm, and just go.

"*Go,*" this inner voice whispered, "*go take advantage of this opportunity to get a glimpse of what the inside of this system is like. It'll be fine, just go.*"

I haven't always trusted this inner voice of mine, but repeated experience has led me to realize it has my best interest in mind, so when the voice tells me to go, I assume that as usual, it knows something I don't, and I decide to listen. This is so me, to be immediately searching for a deeper meaning or bigger purpose mere nanoseconds into a confusing or troubling situation.

I try to hush my protesting husband. I mouth, "I'm so sorry!" to Carys when she appears behind James in the doorway with a confused and concerned look on her face, and I turn to the officer as I say, "Ok yes, let's go. Let's go get this figured out."

I protest when they handcuff my hands behind my back. "Are the handcuffs really necessary? You haven't placed me under arrest, and I am coming with you willingly," but they have no choice, they say. I am led by my elbow to the bounty hunter's car, which is parked all the way at the other end of the block.

"Don't worry, I doubt anyone is watching. Most neighbors aren't home right now," she chirps brightly as we all make our way down the sidewalk and I hate her for it.

The handcuffs hurt as we ride to the detective's office, and I can feel a state of bewildered shock seeping into the crevices of my breath. Despite conventional wisdom dictating you should never speak to the police without a lawyer present, I opt to, anyway. I truly believe this is imminently solvable. I'm thinking I might even be able to still make the concert.

"Have you ever been arrested for anything before?" the bounty hunter asks me casually.

"No."

"I can tell. You don't seem the type."

I don't have the mental bandwidth to unpack her statement. My mind is racing on the drive to the detective's office. I'm flipping through my mental rolodex of all the children I care for, trying to determine where this mix-up could have been born. Nothing is landing. We arrive, and the bounty hunter leads me to a small, white, sterile concrete room. Handcuffs off, jewelry off, handcuffs back on, but one wrist only this time, attached to the bench where I sat. She clangs the door shut behind her when she leaves, taking my stuff with her in a huge Ziploc bag. I slowly inhale the stale air in an effort to steady my nerves and glance around at the unwelcoming sharpness of the tiny room, my brow furrowed, my eyes involuntarily filling with tears, the way they do when I am overpowered by emotion. Right now, I'm scared.

I cry a bit, in this first moment of alone.

What. Is. Happening?

A man opens the door and I sit up as I take another deep breath.

"Hello," the man says, "I'm Detective Sherbert and I'm working this case. I understand you want to talk to me?"

I nod, and the bounty hunter unchains my handcuff.

I follow the detective to a room where he places me under arrest, reading me my rights. I have nothing to hide and am desperate for information.

We begin.

"Do you know what this is about?" he asks.

"No."

"You really don't have any idea?" He glances up at me and raises an eyebrow.

"No, I really don't. It's why I'm sitting across from you right now, to find out. They said you would tell me."

He tells me his job is to clarify, and that he shoots straight – "I don't beat around the bushes," he assures me, and I feel slightly alarmed at his confident misuse of the phrase. It reminds me to be extra careful with my words. I'm glad this is being recorded.

"What," he wants to know, "comes to mind when I say sexual assault on a child?"

"That it's a terrible, horrible thing," I say. "A terrible thing to have happen and a horrible thing to be wrongly accused of. I don't understand why anyone would point something so ugly and decidedly untrue at me."

"Let me ask you this. Do you know a Loretta?" he asks.

Are you fucking kidding me, I think to myself and I almost laugh out loud.

"I actually know more than one Loretta," I truthfully respond.

"Oh," he looks puzzled. "I didn't know. I thought maybe you knew just one."

My left eyebrow arcs a bit as I study him. Is he joking? *Why would you know everyone I know?*

I send a quick prayer up for guidance and steel myself for what feels like the most important, most baffling conversation of my life.

What. Is. Happening?

When he clarifies the Loretta he is talking about – "Loretta X...she says she used to think of you as a second mother," – the complexity of the situation at hand flashes in front of me.

Oh dear one, I think, *what have you done?*

"It isn't true," I tell him, because none of these accusations are. It *is* true that I know Loretta X (and her mother, Ivy, and her dad, Angus, and her sister, Rose, and her brother, Slater), and I have for over sixteen years now. But these accusations? No. These are ugly: dirty and devastating and decidedly false.

"Well, here's the thing," the detective replies, "I've been doing this a long time and she has some pretty detailed stories. I mean, in all my years…"

I don't even need to hear what they are, these stories, these "details" he mentions; no matter what she is saying, it won't be true because nothing criminal has ever transpired in any of those sixteen years.

"Your information isn't correct," I tell him, "*I* was a victim of sexual abuse as a child, not a perpetrator of it."

"Are you calling her a liar?" he cocks his head at me. "Because if what you say is true, that means she's lying."

"Well," I say slowly, "I know she's not telling the truth. Maybe she got confused. Maybe she's misremembering. Maybe it's a ploy for attention. Maybe it's a transference from a trauma she's experienced in the past few years since I've last seen her. Maybe it's a casual fib that got away from her, but with god as my witness, sir, it's definitely not the truth."

He obviously has no proof – I know this because there was no crime – and I point this out to him.

"But why would Loretta make something like this up?" he asks me.

"I'd like to know that, too," I answer. "I'd be curious to look her in the eye and ask her that very same thing."

My mind is furiously working to add these new layers of information into the mix. Now I think it's less a mistake and more a set-up. It's been over three years since I've seen anyone from the X family, and what has happened to Loretta in those three years feels significant in ways I can't pinpoint. I don't bother to ask the Detective about this. He won't know, that much is obvious. But the questions still hang there. Has Loretta become malicious or mentally ill? Is she doing this out of spite or as a cry for help?

I don't see many other options, because what the detective is implying is an outright falsification of facts, a gross disfiguring of something that was joy-filled and solid and pure. These accusations are nonsensical, preposterous, and absurd.

They are also going to turn into felony charges against me carrying life in prison as their consequence.

I answer his questions truthfully, even as my stomach is churning and my skin feels prickly with alertness. I maintain my innocence with every breath. *Yes, I lived in a few different places during the 2008-2010 timeframe being examined, and yes, she visited me in every one of those places and yes, sometimes the visits included overnights, but abuse? Never.*

"I didn't do this," I tell him. "I am innocent."

"You know," the detective replies with a sarcastic smirk, "there is not one guilty person in prison because everybody there is innocent, too."

His mind is made up. He is not listening to me. When we finally finish the conversation over an hour later, nothing I've said has mattered. He takes me back to the original room I'd sat in and handcuffs me to the bench once again.

Now what?

Almost immediately, a different detective offers to take me over to the jail, says he is leaving anyway. So again I undergo the handcuff shuffle until my hands are cuffed in the front.

"It's easier to sit in a car this way," he smiles at me.

I thank him, but I do not smile back.

We drive to an underground parking garage, and I am delivered to jail.

In the dank entryway vestibule, I do as the intake officer directs. I put my hands on the cold wall and spread my legs to get patted down as the two detectives make small talk while they watch. I take my ballet flats off to show my bare feet, I walk through the metal detector. I stand where they tell me to stand, I spell my

last name when asked, I pronounce it for her when she wonders
how with a smile.

"It's Lithuanian," I say. I'm on auto-pilot.

The detectives leave the same way we arrived while I am
ordered through heavy, metal doors on the opposite wall.

I wait in the designated female corral of the big, open room,
which is divided from the men's side by the simplistic kind of rail-
ing that queues the line at theme parks. I see a line of holding
cells along the back wall of the big room, some of which are filled
with people either passed out, or pounding on the windows while
flipping off and cussing out the surrounding police officers. I'm
amazed at their bravado.

There are televisions bolted in various corners and entertainment shows are on; carefully crafted people sharing irrelevant
details about other people's personal business, and I feel almost
woozy with the stark realization that life is chattering on out there
no matter what happens to be going on in here. Metal chairs are
bolted to the floor, and I sit. The clock on the wall reads 6:30pm.

I am the only one on the female side, while the male side is
packed to the rims. I am stoic. I keep my arms crossed over my
chest. I keep my long, blond hair hanging a bit in front of my face,
not tucked behind my ears as usual. I am careful not to make eye
contact with anyone, no matter how many times I am called to or
jeered at.

"Smile, girlie!" someone calls to me from the men's side. Other
men laugh.

Another voice: "What's a pretty little something like you doing
here? Need a friend?" More laughter.

My stomach turns. I might be sick. Oh please, not now,
not here.

"That's enough," a guard calls.

I regret not grabbing a sweater but am grateful I had the
presence of mind to insist I bring my glasses. It's still summer

outside but borderline chilly in here, and I'm wearing a light, loose peach-colored tank top blouse, summer linen capris, and ballet flats. I feel vulnerable, exposed and very underdressed.

By now the Thursday night football game is on the television and the Denver Broncos are playing the Arizona Cardinals. I am grasping for comfort, and I find a small degree here because Arizona is where my beloved late grandparents lived for decades. Just seeing the word "Arizona" on the screen fortifies me, like my grandparents' spirits are somehow here with me now.

I use the football game as a distraction to my situation, but everything distracts me from the game. People getting paperwork, getting photographed, getting fingerprinted, getting sent to medical, chatting each other up, laughing away (that was mostly the officers,) and I'd be willing to bet I am the only sober person in holding. Men of all ages, colors, and sizes are stumbling, yelling, slouching over in drunken stupors. I am so grateful to be sequestered off from them all, even if just by a rail.

When it's my turn, I get paperwork, take a mug shot with my glasses and one without, ink and roll my fingerprints, and get sent to medical, which amounts to a round and friendly grandmother-ly-type lady asking me about my health and lifestyle habits.

"Do you have AIDS?" No.

"Are you an active heroin user?" No.

"Are you, or have you ever been, an alcoholic?" No.

On and on it goes until I am sent back to my chair. I sit some more.

On television and in the movies, they often portray the idea that you get to make one phone call when you are arrested, but that is not the case here tonight. There are two pay phones at my disposal on the female side of this big room, and I call James collect around 8:00 p.m. As soon as I say, "Baby?," he launches immediately into, "THIS IS A BIG FUCKING DEAL. IT'S SO SERIOUS, BABY. YOU CAN GO TO PRISON FOR THE REST OF YOUR LIFE. DO NOT TALK TO ANYONE."

I'm four hours into this disaster and already making unadvisable decisions.

"Too late, babe. I already did talk to someone. And guess what? It's Loretta who did this." I spit out her name. "The detective wants me to take a polygraph in the morning."

"What a bitch," he says, and I cringe a little, because this is Loretta we're talking about, the same girl I used to lovingly praise for her "overflowing heart."

He assures me he's on it, making phone calls, calling in favors, basically working to move heaven and earth. He has called my sister to fill her in, knowing she'll tell my parents. I am so grateful for him, and I tell him so.

I love you.

I love you.

We hang up.

I watch a heavily tattooed young man walk up and instigate a fight with a very drunk old man who could barely hold himself upright. I watch Tattoo Man bump chests with, then push Drunk Old Man on both shoulders. I watch about seven cops descend faster than you can say, "Uh oh." I watch the aggressor get thrown against the wall, his shoes and socks stripped off before he gets pushed into one of the holding cells. Almost immediately, he lies down and falls asleep, which makes me wonder if he did it just to get into one of the rooms.

As the kerfuffle dies down, the grandmotherly-type lady from medical walks by, leans down, and says merrily into my ear, "When stuff like that happens, I always like to look the other way. There are at least forty-six cameras on you right now and the last thing you want is to be called into a deposition."

I glance up at her. "Thanks for the tip." It feels like a kindness.

The clock on the wall says 10:00 p.m. The football game ends and a sitcom I've never seen before starts. I sit and stare dully at the antics of Mike and Molly on the screen, then I call James again at

10:30 p.m. He tells me not to take the polygraph. He and Carys have been frantically doing research and have discovered a substantial amount of controversy around both the reliability and the accuracy of these types of tests. He tells me he's pushing for an early court time. He tells me he has a bails bondsman ready to move. He tells me he's in the process of setting up a meeting with a lawyer. He tells me we'll handle this, that we'll do whatever it takes. He tells me he loves me. We say our goodnights, our see you tomorrows.

I sit some more.

It is one o'clock in the damn morning when they finally call my name. I have been sitting here in this hard, plastic chair for over six hours. It has been nine hours since the doorbell rang; I could have gone to the concert and still had time left to wait.

Another woman arrived just a few minutes ago. She is either very drunk, very drugged, or both, her body draped across multiple chairs, her eyes drooped shut. She smells terrible. She and I are put in a concrete room together with dim lights. A female officer tells us to strip all the way down and change into the provided yellow and white striped short-sleeved V-neck tops and long bottoms, white granny panties, white cotton over-the-head sports bras, white tube socks, and orange foam soccer sandals. We bag up the clothes we arrived in, hand them over to the female officer hovering at the door, and grab a black mesh zip pack that I later learn contains a towel, two flat sheets, a wool blanket, and a spoon. Jail accessories.

In an elevator, up a floor, and down a hall. I'm sent left, the other woman goes right. I am relieved when we split up; I didn't want to be in a room with her, so I see this as a silver lining.

I am taken across a dimly lit expansive room and sent inside a small cell. It is dark and I choke on my breath as the smell of stale urine smacks me in the face.

"Stay here. A mattress is coming." The heavy door slams, and I stand in the darkness clutching my pack. When a thin, plastic mattress is placed on the bottom bunk a few minutes later, I curl up in the sandpaper sheets under the stiff blanket best I can. I draw my hair over my mouth and nose to mask the smell, and quickly resign myself to the fact that it is never going to actually be completely silent. I can hear doors slamming, the murmur of voices, an occasion holler.

It is 2:00 a.m. I fall asleep from sheer exhaustion.

At 5:00 a.m. the door is kicked open, and the lights blind me with their full and sudden brightness.

"Do you want to eat?" the female guard shrieks at me by way of good morning.

I stand up, grab my glasses from the top "bunk" and take the offered tray, setting it down where my glasses had been. I am still squinting.

"Coffee?"

"Please."

"Give me your cup."

I scramble around my pack. "I don't have a cup."

"I'll bring you back a cup next round."

Door slams. The door next to mine is kicked open.

Breakfast is bleak. I gobble down a small, dry apple as I wearily survey the rest: a small bun, a tray compartment of Cocoa Puffs cereal that I initially think is dog food, a smaller tray compartment filled with tiny paper packets of salt and pepper, a cardboard carton of milk, and a few sugar packets. I take a few sips of the milk. I leave the rest.

I look around my surroundings at what I couldn't see in last night's darkness. There isn't much to see. A stainless steel toilet with no lid and no seat sits directly underneath a sink that also serves as a water fountain, a small, square, stainless steel "desk" with a small shelf protruding from the wall, a circle stool bolted to the wall, and two heavy duty slabs of steel attached to the long wall that serve as bunks. Under the bottom bunk, there are two rectangular boxes.

My tray is collected shortly thereafter (no coffee, no cup, no mention of either, and I'm certainly not going to bring it up), and the lights suddenly turn off again without warning. I curl back up in the dank darkness and doze back into fitful rest.

I wake a couple hours later to the same deafening click of my door opening, and I start to hop out of bed, putting my glasses on my face as I sit up.

"Stay there," a female guard orders.

I do as I'm told.

A man with a clipboard and an identification badge pops his head in and asks me a few questions, including what cell phone provider I use, then tells me I'll be in court at 10:00 a.m. that morning.

"Great," I say, "Thank you, sir."

He steps back, and as the guard is closing the door, I ask her, "Can I have some toilet paper, please?"

"Next rounds," she replies, slamming the door behind her.

Great.

I've had no water since I've been here, and I haven't relieved myself yet this morning. It's time, and in a move that clearly demonstrates I definitely think I'll be out of here in a matter of hours, I use the corner of the bottom sheet to gingerly pat myself dry after I go.

Moments later, my door is popped open again, and this is the first time it doesn't startle me. Nobody is there, but a guard motions me forward from her position at the main desk. As I push open the door, she calls, "Bring your blanket, your bag and your cup—I've got a new towel and new sheets for you."

"I don't have a cup. There was no cup. The breakfast guard said she'd bring one but she didn't."

"Here's a cup. You're getting a new room. Didn't you smell it in there?" she wrinkles her nose and looks at me, waiting for an answer.

"Oh, I smelled it," I reply emphatically, "It smelled horrible."

"Why didn't you say something?" she asks, and tears involuntarily spring to my eyes.

My voice breaks a bit as I reply, "I don't know how this is supposed to be."

She half smiles at me, sympathetically. "If ever anything is dirty or broken, please tell us. We'll get it taken care of. Ok, up you go. 213." And she buzzes the door open.

Room 213 smells drastically better than the first floor room but is identical in its sad presentation in every other way.

I toss my sheets and blankets on the bottom bunk, leaving my small assortment of jail accessories – my towel and bag and spoon and now, a cup – on top. My copy of my processing papers are folded neatly and tucked snugly in the single breast pocket of my yellow-striped top.

I climb to the top bunk, sit cross-legged, and close my eyes. I start to meditate.

I'm grasping for things to think about that make me feel better, so I decide that this move to a brighter, cleaner, better vantage point room is somehow significant, a step in the right direction. I breathe slowly. I discover "Bob Barker" imprinted across the bottom of my shoe and decide it's another small sign; I'll come to learn it's the name of a prison supply company, but in the moment, I am reminded of the host of The Price is Right game show, which has always reminded me of my grandpa and the hours we'd spend watching it together. There's grandpa again.

I pray. *Spirits around me, hear my prayer; keep me in thy loving care; be my guides in all I do, bless all those who love me, too.*

What else feels good? I want a small glimmer of hope to noodle on, instead of absorbing any more of the soul-sucking energy of these walls.

I decide to think about what is within my control, and I visualize a courtroom scene in my head, hearing the words, "not guilty" spoken over and over until I can see and feel and hear that outcome so clearly in my mind's eye that there's no way the universe isn't scrambling to make it so. This is a big one, though, so I understand the monumental levels of patience and strength I'll need to tap into while the Powers That Be do their thing. All in perfect divine timing, I remind myself.

I mentally plead with Loretta to come clean, to tell the truth, to admit she got it wrong, she made it up, she's confused or joking, or was misheard or misunderstood or whatever the case may be. I mentally plead with Ivy to come to her senses – I send her "you're an educated woman, please be smarter than this, you know better than this" vibes, but we were best friends for so many years that I know all too well how little she trusts herself, how easily her intuition is thwarted by her insecurities.

My door clicks open again. I have an "official call," I'm told.

The guard sends me to a dark, concrete vestibule to wait alone, saying someone will retrieve me momentarily. I wait as the minutes pile up, and a voice over a speaker eventually instructs me to step out into the same long hallway I walked down last night, where another guard motions me towards him and puts me on an elevator by myself, button already pressed. The doors close and the elevator moves, but when the elevator stops, the doors don't open. I stand still as a statue, my eyes rapidly scanning the small box I am in. *At least the lights are on,* I think. I do not make a sound.

"Just a sec, hon," comes a friendly female voice from the speaker a few moments later.

When the doors finally open, I step out to a dimly lit lobby with chipping linoleum floors and no windows. There is no one waiting for me, so I stand there and wait as more minutes tick by. A passing officer happens to glance up from his list as he walks by, startles a bit when he sees me and says, "Well, hello there. Where did you come from?"

I tell him my name and about the official call, and he shakes his head as he consults his list.

"No, I don't see you here. You're not on my list."

I don't belong here.

He sends me back up the elevator, where the hallway officer sends me back down the hall to where I started, and the female guard sighs an exasperated sigh when I tell her the sequence of events. Again I am sent to wait in the vestibule.

When I finally get to the room where my "official call" is waiting, I find it's the polygraph detective. I had already guessed this was the case, and I already knew I wasn't going to take the polygraph, but I also already understand the value of being out of that suffocating cell, so I'd kept that information to myself.

I explain to the polygraph detective that I haven't met with a lawyer yet, that I'm still processing this totally unexpected, very unfamiliar, and quite unwelcome turn of events, and I'm not actually going to take his test.

He tries one time to change my mind. "Whether you have a lawyer or not, it's just you and me in the room during the test so a lawyer doesn't really matter." When I reaffirm my position, he dismisses me, giving me his card. I am sent back up the elevator and back down the hallway.

There is a new female guard at the desk who asks my name when I return, then asks without irony if I want some "free time." I immediately accept, despite not knowing what she means. I soon learn that each inmate gets exactly one hour each day to spend time outside of their cell. One hour a day.

I take my free time in the common area and use the phone to call James again. He says he and Carys are there, at the courthouse. It is 9:45. Court is at 10:00, but I've been told it's running late. Carys has to leave at 11:00 to catch her flight. She's hoping to at least see me one more time.

Court begins at noon. Carys is gone, but James is there.

He and I stare at each other across everything, each calmed by the other's presence. The judge does not read my charges out loud – a kindness, considering - and I am given a $50,000 bond for release, with an additional condition of wearing a GPS anklet monitor.

A public defender I met not 10 minutes ago does my talking for me. In our 30 second conversation prior to appearing before the judge, he tells me to expect the situation to cost me about $30,000 and a year of my time, both of which end up being gross underestimations. I balk when he says this – *but I didn't do this! I don't belong here!* – and he shakes his head impatiently. "That doesn't matter right now," he says.

I do not yet understand the criminal justice system is part business, part game.

After I face the judge, I am returned to wait in room 213.

It is almost 1:00 p.m. It's only been 20 hours since the doorbell rang, but it feels much longer than that.

I have a better vantage point of my surroundings from this second-story room than I did on the first floor, and I take a moment to take it all in. There is an empty concrete warehouse vibe; a vast two-story square room has a guard's station in the corner near the thick double doors, with cells like mine lining both levels of the three remaining walls. Tucked into another corner is a small open room with showerheads and waist-high dividers creating six tight shower stalls. In the square room's main center area are a few round metal tables with attached stools bolted to the floor. On the same wall as the guard's station is a row of pay phones, where your only option is to call collect.

I begin to study some of the other women locked up in the other cells. From what I can see of the other two walls of inhabitants, we are a mix of Black, white, and Hispanic women ranging from our 20's to our 60's. A few rooms are empty, but one room has two girls in it. I never find out why. Most rooms hold only one person, and it looks like some of them have been there awhile. I see books, t-shirts, deodorant, lotions, a box of Ritz crackers, a jar of peanut butter all lining top bunks. I see children's drawings and photographs adhered to the walls.

The first woman to draw attention to herself stands in her door on the first floor holding one of her shoes like a phone and laughing maniacally into it as if she's hearing something hilarious. When she's not doing that, she shouts tirades of disgust into the air.

I wait some more. So much waiting. It feels like wasted time.

Around 5:50 p.m., the door buzzes open and the guard calls to me, "Leave your stuff there. We just need you to sign your bond."

So I go to them, and I sign, and her eyes get wide when she reviews it: "You need a pre-trial? Oh, shit." She looks at the other guard. "Fuck! They're not there anymore today, are they? And, oh no, it's a holiday weekend, too." She looks at me, "It might be Tuesday before you can leave." Today is Friday.

"*No.*" My voice is measured but direct and again my naïve privilege shows as I assume I have a voice in this. "No, please. I can't…."

She sighs and picks up the phone, then says, "Yeah, so if she has a pre-trial… are they here on weekends? Oh, they are? Great!"

She hangs up. "It'll be first thing tomorrow morning."

I ask desperately, "Can I *please* call my husband? He's been here all day, we thought I was going home tonight."

She hesitates, sort of shakes her head in annoyance, then picks up the phone in front of her: "What's his number?"

She puts him on speakerphone and does most of the talking. I sneak in a few words here and there, and collectively, we determine that the pre-trials start at 9:00 a.m.

James says he'll be there at 8:00 a.m.

I love you.

I love you.

I climb back up the stairs to Room 213.

It is 6:15 p.m.

I go to bed for the night.

A ruckus wakes me at 2:00 a.m. Someone below is wailing her contempt for the police while methodically pounding on her bunk window. I hear the officers initially try to convince her to calm down, and when it doesn't work, they just ignore her. She screams and moans and her sorrowful anger echoes through the huge room. Eventually I either get used to it or she simmers down, because I fall back asleep.

At 5:00 a.m. the fluorescent lights snap on brightly and the door is kicked open to announce the arrival of breakfast. I chew half a flavorless orange and one bite of undercooked biscuit before climbing back into the lower bunk and falling back into a dreamless sleep.

My eyes fling open again at 8:00 a.m. and I am practically crawling out of my skin, I'm so ready to get out of here. I pace the room, I meditate, I do some push-ups, some jumping jacks, some lunges. I watch the minutes tick by, then I watch the minutes turn into hours. So much for "first thing."

At 11:30 a.m., I motion through my window to the guards below, different women than the ones I spoke with last night.

"Yeah?" one calls back without moving.

I raise my voice and practice advocating for myself through a jail cell door.

"I posted bond yesterday at 3:00, and last night at 6:00, they told me I'd be released at 9:00, but now it's almost noon, so…"

"I'll look into it."

I pace back and forth. It's after 12:00 now. Is pre-trial like a bank with only morning hours on a Saturday? I sure hope not.

I find a happy place in my mind. *Not guilty not guilty not guilty.*

My door finally clicks open but when I step out, she tells me to stay there. I am in fact on the list of bonded, she says, and it's not unusual for pre-trials to happen after court, so I just need to wait a while, but it "should be" sometime today.

Oh my lord, please yes, please let it be sometime today. If it's not today, it's Tuesday.

I can't stay here until Tuesday. I mean, obviously I don't have any actual say in the matter, but I've eaten an apple and part of an orange, two bites of rice and a few chews of biscuit. I'm still in a haze of confusion, deprived of even basic details about what I'm up against. I can't stay here.

I thank her for the information, and politely add, "When it's my turn for free time, may I please use the phone?"

"Sure," she says cheerfully.

I know I can, but I like giving the guard the opportunity to feel like she's in charge.

I go back to studying the other inmates. The woman directly across from me looks younger but has one of the settled-in looking bunks. Sometimes it feels like she's trying to catch my eye, but I am diligent in my self-imposed "no eye contact except with authority" rule and fastidiously skirt any interaction.

I watch her request free time. The guards say yes, but when it's time for the next free time, the guard is occupied with aiding the nurse and isn't at the desk to buzz the woman across from me out of her room right away.

The woman across from me can see the guard helping the nurse, but rather than wait for the nurse to finish, this woman starts to bang on her door and yell, "Helloooo? Helloooooooo?" getting louder and louder, banging faster, then slower, then furiously. I stand silently at my door with a neutral face, watching everything through the door's window. The guard and the nurse finish and start walking down the hall.

As they pass my room, the guard gestures to me and calls down to the desk, "Let her out for free time, instead."

My door pops open, and I'm out like a flash. I hear the guard say, "Quiet wins every time."

I immediately call James, and he asks me exactly what I want to ask him: *What's going on? What's happening? What have you heard?*

"Baby," I tell him, "I'm locked up in a room talking to no one except for this one hour when I get to talk to you. I know nothing about anything."

We spend half of my allotted free time on the phone so I can spend the other half in the outside area which isn't actually outside at all; it just has some open ventilation at the top of the concrete walls. I run, because I can't do that in my room. Yoga, I've done; bodyweight exercises, I've done; walking meditation, I've done. But running is what I do now. Not a lot, because I hate running, but I run anyway. I lunge, and I side shuffle, and I stretch a little, and then it's time to go back into my cell.

Before I do, the guard tells me to start asking questions if I haven't heard anything by the end of business hours. This tip feels like another kindness, but it doesn't make me feel any better.

I lie in my bed and close my eyes. *Not guilty, not guilty, not guilty.* I start to doze again, but the nanosecond my door clicks, I jump up, hopeful.

And praise all that is holy, it's finally time.

I'm being released alongside a woman named Belle who has been in her holding cell for a week; she smiles and calls "Praise Jesus!" the whole way down the hall. We take the elevator down a floor, and into the same room where I declined yesterday's polygraph with the police. We're told to sit on the bench, and it is Belle's turn first.

I can't help but smile as she praises Jesus when she is given her personal belongings, praises Jesus when she signs her papers, and praises Jesus when she goes into a small room to change back into her own clothes. It's my turn next, and when I'm handed my bag, I almost weep. If they are giving me my clothes back, I reason, this must actually be happening.

I sign what I need to sign and kiss my wedding ring as I change into my clothes, although I'm told not to put the ring on yet since I'll be going through a metal detector, and I think, *on the way out of jail, too?*

Belle is released, but I have to meet with a pre-trial officer because of the GPS condition of my bond, so I sit back down in the room with the bench, and wait for another pre-trial-bound inmate to come through. Always waiting. I make small talk with the two police officers who are working the release desk in the meantime.

"Everything seems to move pretty slow here," I say, "Feels a bit disjointed and disorganized."

"Oh, this system is a joke," one officer matter-of-factly replies.

"It's frustrating even for us," the other officer chimes in, "I can only imagine how frustrating it feels for folks on your side of things. And you're right, 'disjointed' is a good word for it."

I have to ask. "Have you ever eaten the food here? I was shocked at how awful it was. Like, lacking-in-basic-nutrition levels of bad."

"Oh, it's terrible. It's not much better in the staff cafeteria, to be honest."

They are kind even if their perspectives are disheartening.

It's not long before someone else comes, and we are collected by the pre-trial officer, walking down hallways, around corners, and finally through a door leading to a mostly empty main lobby area. James is not there, but I know that he can't be far and it won't be long until I will see him. I follow our leader around another corner, where he instructs us to put our personal belongings into a small locker, explaining we'll retrieve them after pre-trial consultations.

As we continue through the lobby, I see James has just returned and is getting settled in a seat facing away from me, looking towards the door I'd just come through. He has headphones on and I'm not even sure it's allowed, but I can't help myself.

I shout-whisper, "Baby!" in his direction and watch the sound of my muted voice penetrate the barrier of the headphones. His head jerks up, his body turns as he rises to standing, and he yanks his headphones out. We make eye contact and my heart soars. I gesture to him that I'll be right back.

Pre-trail means sitting in a chair listening to the conditions of my bond, including how to manage the GPS tracking unit. I gape when he presents it. The apparatus is large and clunky and burdensome, and he has trouble finding the "right fit" when he puts it on my ankle.

I ask if they are familiar with modern-day technology. "You do know how small trackers can be these days, right?" But convenience is not a priority here.

I will be charged $11/day while I wear the device, in addition to the $30 they bill me to be arrested. I am instructed to plug the unit in once every 24 hours—not doing so is a violation of my bond agreement. While he tells me it can take up to an hour and a half to fully charge, I soon learn that 3-4 hours for a charge is more typical.

I ask if I need to wait in the chairs for the other person to complete pre-trial, but no, I can finally leave this godforsaken place. I retrieve my belongings from the lockers, thank the pre-trial man, and run directly into my husband's open arms. I bury my face in his chest, and he squeezes me tight. We kiss and kiss again, and I say to him, "Let's get the hell out of here." We hold hands as we walk to the truck.

I call my sister, Mona, on the way home, and we cry together, but we also share the sentiment that it will all be okay when it is all said and done. After all, I'm the one telling the truth here. I'm the one with truth on my side.

That has to matter. Mona advises me to write down every last detail I can think of from the past few days as soon as I get home, and I do. James has found a lawyer for me, and I'll meet him tomorrow.

In the meantime, I've got to figure out how to untangle Loretta's web of lies. I begin at the beginning.

Chapter 2

"There are friends. There is family. And then there are friends that become family." –Unknown

August 2000 - Colorado

It'd practically been love at first sight.

I met Loretta in a small town outside of Denver, Colorado, at a tiny but distinguished daycare where I'd recently been hired as one of three teachers in the infant classroom.

I'd graduated from university with a degree in early childhood education only two years earlier, and much to my mother's chagrin, turned down a few job offers to follow my heart's high romantic hopes a thousand miles west.

Those high romantic hopes were dashed before I even left home, but I decided to go anyway. I fell in love with Colorado almost immediately. For two years, I'd been happily patching together three part-time jobs – two nanny families and the Kids' Corner at a fancy health club – but a personal health scare made medical benefits a new priority for me, so I was thrilled to be offered this full-time position at the daycare.

I continued babysitting on a regular basis for both my nanny families, and I kept a weekly shift at the health club, too, because the benefit of the free membership was just too valuable to release.

Loretta was a six-month-old bundle of honey brown curls and laughing blue eyes when she entered into my infant classroom. An alert and observant baby, she loved to cuddle and snuggle and was a complete joy to be around. Her parents were new parents, and this was already the second daycare Loretta had attended in her short life – the first had been a stop-gap measure for a few months while they waited for our school's waitlist to move.

It was cute the way you could tell neither Ivy, Loretta's mom, nor Angus, Loretta's dad, were entirely sure what they were doing, often by their own admission. One day, Angus dropped Loretta off only half-dressed, in just a turtleneck onesie snapped over a pair of tights. Typically, there'd be an accompanying jumper or dress or pants or bloomers to complete the outfit, but not that day, which we teachers all found impossibly adorable. Even Ivy had rolled her eyes and laughed when she picked Loretta up later that day, asking, "Did she not arrive fully dressed this morning?" It was because of that day's outfit that I became completely endeared to little Loretta.

Babysitting for classroom families was an encouraged practice at the daycare, and as I'd done with the other nine families in our room, I extended an invitation to babysit for Loretta. Her parents happily took me up on it, and a friendship both inside and outside of the classroom was born.

This friendship grew as my bond with Loretta deepened. She loved me, and, like most of the kids I cared for, I loved her right back. Loretta repeatedly and insistently chose me among the three classroom teachers, and in turn I easily and gladly became the most consistent caregiver in her world. I changed most of her diapers, fed her most of her bottles, and rocked her to sleep multiple times per day, five days a week. I kissed boo-boos and flew the airplane of peas into her tiny, open mouth. She was always in the stroller I was pushing or the wagon I was pulling. She lit up when I entered a room and cried when I left. She took her first steps to me; both of my co-teachers watched it happen and we all cheered for Loretta's milestone, but we did not mention a word of it to Ivy or Angus. That's the unspoken rule of daycare: never tell the parents when their babies do their firsts for you.

"We're kindred spirits," I half-jokingly mused. We just clicked.

When she aged out of my classroom and into the next, and then the next after that, those teachers sought me out to share fun Loretta anecdotes or ask for quick advice on how to handle a Loretta-related situation. Sometimes I was called in to help her fall asleep at naptime if she was particularly squirrely or sad. When she fell on the playground and Ivy tried to comfort her, Loretta wriggled out of her grasp to find me for comfort instead, which made Ivy laugh.

"I'm glad she has you," she'd say.

The validation felt nice but wasn't new. After all, my reputation as a baby whisperer was already long-established by then. I was known for my talent of "speaking fluent toddler." Neither fussy babies nor tiny people tantrums fazed me.

When the tiny-but-distinguished daycare celebrated a milestone anniversary, the local newspaper came to do a feature story. A reporter and a photographer spent a crisp, sunny morning observing all the classrooms and hanging out on the playground during outside time at lunch. Of all the photographs they took that day, it was a picture of Loretta and me that made the cover of the section. I'm wearing a brown sweater, and she's in a navy jacket; I'm holding her while she laughingly pushes my upside down glasses onto her own face. Our mutual adoration became public record, broadcast for the world to see.

There was no way of knowing then that our demise would eventually be of public record, too, albeit in a very different way.

Her parents paid me exorbitantly for babysitting, offering a beer anytime I came to their house, just like they did with anyone who came over. They hosted big Sunday night dinners and encouraged the daycare teachers to participate in popular weekly cruiser bike rides around town. They lent me a cruiser bicycle to use for the rides, then ended up giving it to me as a birthday present. They were an easy family to fold into, especially for someone like me who has a predisposition for connection and community and was living far away from home.

Angus liked to rock climb but Ivy didn't; would I like to go with him, instead? Sure! Fun! Ivy liked to shop but Angus didn't; would I like to spend a day at the outlet mall with her and Loretta? Yes! Absolutely! I'd only lived in Colorado for a couple years and was always actively looking to widen my friendship circle. They seemed easy to be around. They were both numbers people, working in financial roles, and Ivy offered to do my taxes for me, an offer I happily took her up on. I became the pal neither of them seemed to have in each other while modeling how to be the parent figure neither of them claimed they knew how to be to Loretta.

May 2002

A couple of years after I met Loretta, I hit a bumpy personal patch in the form of a disturbed ex-fiancé following me around looking to make trouble, and Loretta's parents kindly extended another generous offer. In January, they'd had another baby, a girl they named Rose, and our friendship had grown even closer since Rose started in my classroom a few months prior.

"Move in with us," they said, "Come lick your wounds and get a clean break from that whole ugly situation. You can have the front bedroom with the floral wallpaper. Just until you get your legs back under you."

No rent, no utilities; I'd only be expected to help parent the girls. *I am so lucky.* I moved in.

Forms were filled out and filed with the school; I became the emergency contact. Each week there were days I brought the girls to school with me and days I brought them home again. Two car seats took up permanent residence in the backseat of my car. Loretta was often given a choice about which car she wanted to ride somewhere, and she always picked mine. I became a fixture for birthday parties, trick-or-treating, snow days, vacations, and pancake Sundays. I took my turns gently bouncing a screaming baby Rose up and down the hallway in the middle of the night. I snuggled under a blanket on the covered front porch with Loretta during thunderstorms; "We're so cozy," she'd squeak.

"Parent meeting!" Angus periodically called, summoning Ivy and I to the dining room to compare schedules and calendars and logistics for the week.

I changed diapers and organized closets and helped with the monstrous mounds of laundry that seemed to permanently occupy their basement floor. I spent multiple weekends watching the girls while Ivy tagged along with Angus on his work trips; it was one of their perks, free babysitting, and they relished it. I house-sat when they all flew south to grandma's for Thanksgiving. In return, I was given a place to live and food to eat, and I was appreciated, which is one of my favorite feelings to feel.

"*We are thrilled to have an Early Childhood expert living under our roof!*" their annual holiday letter declared that year.

They were originally from the south, and I traveled to a beach house with them on their dime for the 4th of July that year. Loretta sat on my lap on a lounge chair during the gorgeous beachfront fireworks show that stretched for miles along the beach both directions. I watched all the kids so Ivy and Angus could go out with their local friends. I met Ivy's pals from childhood, high school, and college. I met both Ivy and Angus' parents, Ivy's sister and Angus's brothers. They mused over which buddy to set me up with, but nothing ever came to fruition.

Back in Colorado, Angus traveled constantly for work; plus, he had different hobbies and interests than Ivy, so Loretta, Ivy, Rose and I became our own girl gang of sorts.

"You know, people probably think you're my wife," Ivy laughed often when we were out in public, handing off crying babies and whiny toddlers to one another.

I laughed, too, because it was probably true. The four of us looked and acted like a family. I had become a part of their family.

"Alex?" Loretta asked one day from the backseat, "How come you don't have any kids?"

Ivy glanced at me with a raised eyebrow from the driver's seat: "*Good luck with this one,*" her expression said.

"Well, I just haven't gotten to that part of my life yet. Once I meet –"

Loretta interrupted me, "I know why! Because you have us!"

Ivy laughed.

I shrugged with a smile.

"That I do, my dear. I do have you."

***

On a day off from the school, I had a lunch and ice skating date with four-year-old Jane, one of the little girls I'd nannied for when I first moved to Colorado. I took her to the school to show her where I worked. We saw Loretta, and I introduced the two of them. Loretta scowled at Jane as she threw her whole self at me in a bear hug.

"This is my Alex," Loretta said, eyes on Jane.

Jane was two years older than Loretta and smiled at the younger girl kindly.

"Maybe she can be both of our Alexes."

"No." Loretta's tiny voice was firm, and her grip tightened around my neck, "*My* Alex."

I laughed it off. It didn't strike me as worrisome. I didn't think of it as inappropriate. It didn't send any warning signals. It didn't yet look like a pattern.

I applied and was accepted to graduate school in the same town as the daycare, so after just over a year of living at Ivy and Angus's house, I moved out when Loretta was three and Rose was a year and a half. Ivy and Angus both helped me lift the heavy stuff into my new place, and then they adopted Guacamole, the cat my new roommate Alice was looking to re-home.

August 2003

I no longer lived there, but I was still at Ivy and Angus's house on a regular basis, still bringing the girls home from school on occasion, and still carting around two car seats in my car. Alice often came to Sunday night dinner with me. She liked the chance to visit with Guacamole and soon grew fond of Loretta and Rose, too. She loved that they came to visit and didn't mind when they spent the night.

Slumber parties were a fun, new development. "Can the girls sleep at your and Alice's place Friday night?" Ivy had asked one day, "I would consider it a personal favor. Angus and I need the together time."

I checked with Alice – *of course, of course* – and collected Loretta and Rose from their classrooms that Friday, each with a Disney princess backpack containing their nightgowns, tooth-brushes, pull-ups, and favorite stuffed animals. We built our own personal pizzas for dinner, played Candyland, used my costume jewelry for dress-up, and enjoyed ice cream in front of the electric fireplace before reading bedtime stories, all three of us curled up in a row in my queen-size bed. It was a win for everyone, and before long we did it again, and then again after that. Soon, each girl kept a nightgown and toothbrush at my and Alice's apartment.

Because Angus was an avid bike rider, I was invited to accom-pany the family on a camping trip to Moab for one of his team races in October. Given the choice, both Loretta and Rose chose to share my tiny tent with me, while Ivy and Angus enjoyed the giant tent by themselves. One afternoon, Loretta, Ivy, Rose, and I explored Arches National Park. Ivy and Rose meandered around together while Loretta and I explored the rocks, and I explained to the best of my limited knowledge how the arches came to be.

"I think I know why you know so much about these rocks," she told me, her three-year-old blue eyes sparkling, "I think it's because you used to be the king of this place."

Everyone called me "King Alex" for the rest of the weekend.

***

"So, I have a strange question for you," Ivy said one day after the Utah trip, and my ears perked up. Any time Ivy started a conversation with that, something intriguing was bound to follow. It was her go-to phrase at the beginning stage of an idea.

"My buddy Mika and I have decided to run the Disney World half-marathon in Florida this January," she said that day. "You want to come, too?"

"A half-marathon? We don't even run," I answered.

"I know, but it's Disney. I want the bling. We'll bring the girls. It'll be fun."

That's about all the convincing I'd needed. It *did* sound like fun, and I *do* enjoy a challenge, and if Ivy could run it, well, I certainly could, too.

We made fun vacation plans around the race. My parents drove down from their home in Atlanta, and we got adjoining hotel rooms, while Ivy, Mika and the kids stayed elsewhere. We ran the race, and it kicked my untrained, race-ignorant butt six ways to Sunday. I hobbled for weeks afterwards.

We went to Disney World while we were there. Both Ivy's and Angus's parents joined us for the day, and we all gathered around a park bench at dusk so a kind bystander could take our group photo rife with mouse ears and twinkling lights.

We looked like one big, happy family.

We repeated the same half-marathon the following year without Mika.

This time around, my parents rented a big vacation house with a humid domed pool room for us, Ivy, Angus, the kids, plus my sister and her husband from Wisconsin, too.

I actually trained for this run, proudly shaving 23 minutes off my race time. We went dancing that night.

"We're so lucky," Ivy and I said. "It's so rare to make close friendships like this as adults." Ivy was neither close nor in regular touch with her actual sister, and she often joked with Mona and me that she'd decided she was going to be our sister going forward, instead.

May 2005

I finished my Master's degree in Instruction and Curriculum with an emphasis on Early Childhood Education and followed a first grade teacher job offer to Denver, 45 minutes away. The bump in salary allowed me a spacious, seventh-floor apartment right in the heart of lower downtown – "Lodo" to the locals – with mountain views and a balcony for watching the sun set over them, which quickly became my new favorite hobby.

Alice also moved to Denver and lived just a few blocks from me on the other side of Coors Field, where we got season tickets to watch the Rockies play baseball. We were practically joined at the hip, living our very best single gal lives.

My one-bedroom place boasted a "den," a room with a closet but no windows, which I turned into my office. I outfitted the room with a brand new queen-sized futon and told Loretta and Rose the futon was for them. I'd bought it just so they'd have their very own place to sleep when they stayed with me, instead of continuing to cram into one bed like we had to in my last apartment.

"Good luck with that," Ivy teased me when I told her of this plan. "I doubt it'll work. They are not going to want to sleep without you."

She was right. The girls came over for their first sleepover and initially seemed jazzed when I showed them their room. We unpacked their things, swam in the pool, had dinner, and the two girls took a bath together with my supervision before pajamas, stories, and bed.

Within ten minutes of tucking them in, they were both climbing into my bed with me, like *haha that was a fun game, but we're not actually going to sleep over there, you silly goose.*

I didn't fight it. I knew Ivy was okay with and even encouraged co-sleeping. I knew co-sleeping was a perfectly normal, natural experience from a historic, biological, anthropological, and even evolutionary perspective. I knew that studies repeatedly show that bed-sharing with family, which we all absolutely considered each other to be, does not lead to any negative outcomes for children; in fact, co-sleepers often exhibit better outcomes in relation to behavioral and emotional maturity. So even though I slept terribly with five- and three-year-old sleep acrobatics happening on either side of me, it so rarely happened – once every few months, maybe – that it didn't seem like a hill to die on.

In November, my mom had a work conference in Denver. Both she and my dad came for the conference then stayed for my birthday and Thanksgiving, which we happily celebrated with Loretta, Ivy, Angus, and Rose at their house, along with Ivy's parents and Angus's parents.

One big happy family.

Ivy stayed overnight at my Lodo apartment sometimes, too – she took advantage of my new, prime location to plan occasional nights out downtown for us. It was in this apartment where she first asked me to smoke marijuana with her. She never had and knew I sometimes did.

"I want the experience of it," she said, "I want to know what it's like so I can talk intelligently about it with Loretta and Rose one day."

So one night we sat on my fluffy, suede sectional and passed a packed pipe between us.

She didn't want Angus to know. She didn't think he'd understand her reasoning, and she didn't want to navigate his judgment.

May 2006

When my teaching contract became a casualty of the No Child Left Behind budget cuts, I soothed the sting by deciding to sell almost everything I owned and move to Hawaii for a massive change of pace. This was the dawn of social media, and an old acquaintance with romantic potential had recently reappeared in my life. He lived in Hawaii now, and his flirtatious encouragements to visit evolved into direct encouragements to join him.

"We need teachers in Hawaii…" he said, again and again, "and I've not stopped thinking about you since we met all those years ago. Come be with me."

I believed him because I wanted to, and I fast-tracked the planning process. Even a call from him weeks later with the disappointing news that he'd slept with someone else, that perhaps I should not come after all, did not deter me from my new plan. It felt bigger than him by then.

So for the second time in my adult life, I moved ostensibly to feed my sense of adventure, but actually to be closer to a man who didn't necessarily want me around. And just like the first time when I'd moved to Colorado, the potential romance fizzled before I even stepped foot in my new home.

In retrospect, I can easily find gratitude for these men both for lighting the fire of movement under me *and* not staying in my life afterwards, at points when I would have willingly tried to make the unworkable work for the sake of a romantic tale to tell.

I'd been keeping a public blog about my personal adventures for a couple years at this point, and my blog readership grew as I continued to write openly and often about my adventures, heartbreaks, and island experiences, because with big risks comes raw emotion, and people are fascinated by both. Ivy read my blog, and I read hers. We instant messaged any time we were both online. I talked to Loretta, Ivy, and Rose on the phone constantly. There was a three-hour time difference between us now and my phone sometimes rang at 4:00 a.m., because Loretta wanted to call before school.

"It's okay, Mama," she reportedly assured Ivy, "Alex won't mind."

She was right. I didn't mind. It filled my cup to hear from them, no matter the hour.

After some initial interviews, I decided not to pursue a class-room teaching position – I could tell my time on the island would be finite, and I did not want to commit to 40 hours a week in the same four walls or to the extra work time during evenings and weekends that teaching required. Instead, I signed on with a nanny agency that partnered with the vacation resorts along the coast of the island during the busy tourist season. It amounted to babysitting for wealthy families on vacation, and I was all about it.

It wasn't quite tourist season yet though, so my time on the island also included a short-term, full-time nanny gig for an adorable 10-month-old baby, and a short stint as assistant crew on a dolphin-tour boat for which I harbored mixed emotions. Swimming with wild dolphins in the ocean is undoubtedly magical but cleaning a boat that size is not. I quit two weeks later.

Once the agency gig got going, though, it was everything I'd hoped it would be and more. I got my first real taste of being in charge of my own schedule, as I could accept or decline jobs as I chose. The more I accepted, the more they called. I accepted most of the jobs.

I was the help, but the differentiation didn't make the experi-ence of becoming a semi-permanent fixture at the Four Seasons less luxurious. I got paid to play in the pools and walk strollers along ocean paths and order room service and read books on the lanai while babies slept. I lunched next to movie stars and spent New Year's Eve at the same small, private beach party as Diane Von Furstenberg, the famous fashion designer. Some families I worked with one time, some families for weeks on end. One family took me out to dinner on their last night, sending me home with grocery bags of leftover food and bottles of leftover wine. I always received rave reviews.

Eventually, I made friends with some locals and we camped on black sand beaches, volunteered at the Iron Man World Championships, and drove up to the observatory on the top of the dormant volcano, Mauna Kea, for a New Moon party where we brought a dinner spread to eat in the back of the car, bundled up to wander around in the surprisingly chilly air, and took turns looking through the smattering of telescopes pointed at various planets – I gasped at the visible level of detail I could see on Saturn's crisp, clear, colorful rings.

I learned to snorkel. I hiked to hidden beaches. I attended my first surfing competition and my first luau. I sang karaoke every Wednesday when the cruise ships would dock in the harbor and all the entertainment staff would come sing their hearts out with us. I had a romantic fling with an island native. I experienced my first earthquake, an exhilarating 6.7 rocker that woke me up in a state of confusion as picture frames flew off the shelves around me, and my bed bounced across the floor. I took meditation classes that focused on getting in touch with the divine feminine at the community center down the hill. I helped Loretta with her first-grade homework over the phone each week. I started to see hearts appear in nature, everywhere. Hearts in clouds, rocks, shadows, seaweed.

I took myself to Hawaii Volcanoes National Park and hiked to the crater of Mt. Kilauea with an offering for the volcano goddess, Pele. Island folklore suggests Pele is the spirit who accepts or rejects outsiders who move to Hawaii. Sometimes, moving there is one hard knock after another. You can't find housing, you buy a lemon of a car, you lose job after job – one woman told me she felt like she couldn't fully breathe on the island, so she broke up with her girlfriend and moved back home to the mainland after only a few weeks. Conversely, some people have everything practically fall in their lap, like I did. I'd been looked after since the moment I arrived, and I was grateful. I wrote about it all in detail on my blog.

But.

For all its beauty, history, and charm, Hawaii was clearly not my settle-down-and-do-forever spot. As the months passed, I came to have a deeper understanding of the phrase, *"Lovely place to visit, wouldn't want to live there."* I didn't regret the move, but I missed the mainland too much to ever seriously consider staying. My boss cried when I told her I was leaving.

April 2007

I missed Denver with every fiber of my being and thought moving back was a no-brainer, but then an interesting situation presented itself and gave me pause.

Oh look, something shiny!

A family I'd worked with at the Four Seasons – the family who took me out to the fancy dinner on our last night together –called from Santa Barbara, California.

"I remember you saying you were planning on leaving the island, and I hung onto your number. I hope you don't mind," Santa Barbara Mom said to me, "You, of course, remember 10-year-old Susie and 6-year-old Otto, yes? Well, their grandmother has decided to step back a bit from helping with our childcare needs, so we are looking for a new nanny. We asked the kids what kind of nanny they would want, and they said, 'Someone like Alex in Hawaii,' so I figured I'd start by calling Alex in Hawaii. Are you interested?"

Turns out, I was.

And so it was with a July 1st start date set in California that I bid adieu to island life in May and took myself back to Colorado for a brief respite. I had an invitation to stay with Loretta, Ivy, Angus, and Rose during my visit, and I happily accepted. Loretta and Rose had a new baby brother by then, Slater, and Ivy paid me to watch him for the six weeks I was there.

"You and Slater need bonding time," she insisted, "since you won't be helping to raise him the same way you did the girls."

On the way to dinner my very first night back, Ivy recounted the snarky attitude mutual acquaintances gave her when she mentioned I was back in town staying with them.

"...so she asks who will be watching Slater before we put him in daycare, and you should have seen the sour look on her face when I said your name," she laughed from the front seat, and I wondered why she felt compelled to tell me this. It was a quirk of hers I had not missed, this habit of pointing out who didn't like me and why. My time in Hawaii had given me just enough perspective to recognize that if not for the girls, I would likely be loosening my grip on my friendship with Ivy, because I had begun to realize as we'd gotten closer over the years that I honestly didn't really like her very much. She could be thoughtful and generous, but she could also be quite unkind when she was feeling insecure, which happened a lot. I often felt I had to brace myself for her passive-aggressive commentary and her seemingly incessant need to keep me small.

"That's funny," I said distractedly from the backseat as I smiled at baby Slater in his car seat next to me.

She fully turned around in her passenger seat to meet my eye. "Yeah," she said, "It really was hilarious. She does *not* like you."

The guest room I used to live in was now where seven-year-old Loretta and five-year-old Rose slept, so I was put in a concrete corner room in the basement with a tiny window and a full bed, which I begrudgingly shared with both girls every night, as they would not even entertain the idea of sleeping in their own beds.

What they would do is both sleep next to me every night for six weeks, which meant for six weeks, I did not sleep through a single night. In the mornings, Ivy would come wake the girls up to get them ready for daycare and drop baby Slater into my bed with me. I journaled about my lack of sleep misery; I blogged my exhaustion. I asked other friends if I could come sleep at their house for just one night before I completely lost my mind. Alice came to my rescue, tucking me away in her Denver loft one evening with a cozy bed, earplugs, and an eye mask. I slept for 13 hours straight.

When I moved to California, all my moving expenses were covered by the Santa Barbara family. Ivy asked to come with me on my road trip; she wanted to keep me company, but really, she wanted to check out the family's mansion and my new guest house. After an overnight stop in Las Vegas, we arrived in Santa Barbara around the same time my moving trucks did. Ivy helped me get settled into the one-bed/one-bath and explore the city a little bit, then she returned a couple months later to run a half-marathon at Disneyland in Anaheim with me.

"I have a strange question for you," she said during that trip, and it was soon decided the girls would visit me by themselves for their spring break.

I couldn't wait.

March 2008

I was beside myself with excitement as I drove to the Los Angeles airport to collect the girls for our Spring Break reunion. I had welcome gifts in the backseat and a whole week's worth of adventure planned on the calendar.

I'd been dating a man, Jonathan, for a handful of months at that point, and with Ivy's knowledge and consent, he joined me, Loretta, and Rose for our overnight trip to Anaheim as our fourth to balance out the rides at Disneyland and California Adventure. When we arrived back in Santa Barbara late the following night, Jonathan helped me carry the sleeping girls inside before heading back to his own home.

Most of the vacation was just us girls. We swam in the Santa Barbara family's saltwater pool, visited the miniature horses the Santa Barbara Family kept on their *other* property, visited parks and beaches and yoga studios, played what Rose liked to call "beauty parlor" at home, and watched movies. We held hands everywhere we went.

And of course, we slept like sardines, three to a bed, despite the fact I'd borrowed and set up a large air mattress for the girls to use. They didn't want to, so I endured another week of nightly knees in my back and flailing arms across my face. It felt but a small price to pay for the joy and love they brought to my waking hours. I smiled through and made jokes about my tears when the girls teased me as I put them on an airplane back to Colorado at the end of the week. When I got home, I created a photo book of memories and shipped it off to them in the mail.

A couple months later, personal turmoil escalated in the Santa Barbara family. Tension had been building for a while, and the mom had moved out with the kids to the other house, leaving dad behind on the property with my guest house. I was suddenly caring for the kids in both places, interacting with each parent separately, and getting caught in the middle of a lot of projected emotion.

The whole thing collapsed one Thursday when I received a text from the mom:

"My plans have changed. I need you to watch the kids Saturday night, not Friday night this weekend."

To which I replied:

"Oh no! I actually have plans on Saturday with friends in Los Angeles. We have tickets to a show."

To which she replied:

"You're fired. You have 24 hours to get off our property."

Even the apology her husband delivered on her behalf an hour later with an invitation to "go ahead and take the weekend to move out" felt unnerving to me. My ego was flustered by the sudden pivot, but my heart was a little relieved. As Jonathan once observed, they acted like they owned me from the moment I arrived. I would miss Susie, but that was about it.

I stashed most of my stuff in a storage unit and packed the rest for an extended stay with my sister and her family in Wisconsin. My niece, Talia, was 11 months, and they were as excited to have me as I was to be there.

"It's finally my turn to live with the legendary baby whisperer," my sister laughed. I also got a temporary job subbing at my niece's daycare for the eight weeks I was there.

It was such a wonderful stretch of life. I was asked to cover shifts at the daycare nearly every single day, and I accepted every shift I was offered. I spent my days bonding with my darling niece, and my evenings hanging out with my sister, one of my favorite humans on earth. I ran a quarter-marathon with a pal, visited with old friends, and made a few new ones. I was asked more than once if I'd like to stay and take a permanent position at the daycare.

I was flattered, but I did not. The big question that summer was actually this: should I move back to California and in with Jonathan, effectively advancing our relationship in ways he was asking for, or should I go back to Colorado instead, effectively ending my relationship with Jonathon entirely?

It was a pickle.

The plan had originally been to stay in Santa Barbara for the one year the nanny family initially indicated needing me, but I hadn't accounted for meeting a tall, dark stranger.

Jonathan and I met on a Sunday, my only day off each week. He approached me sitting by myself at a pub watching football, as was my weekly tradition at the time, and he struck up conversation. I'd learn later he was dating someone else during that first conversation, but ended things with her after he left that day, making him single by the time we "ran into each other" a couple Sundays later at the same bar. A gregarious and extroverted person, Jonathan seemed to know practically everybody in town, and this was exciting to me because I was new to town and knew nobody. He was charming and thoughtful, even if he continued bringing me chocolate long after I'd thanked him and asked him to stop. "No really, stop. I don't want any more chocolate, please knock it off. What part of 'no, thank you' are you not understanding? Oh my god, what's with all this chocolate?"

We started dating in November of 2007, four months after I'd moved to Santa Barbara. I had a dream one early December night that we were sitting at a counter in a beachside restaurant while an unfamiliar song played loudly. The following weekend, without knowing of my dream, Jonathan took me to a restaurant on the water where we sat at a counter and he gave me a mix CD he had made for me. The first time I listened to it, I heard the song from my dream. It was Damien Rice's "The Blower's Daughter," and I took it as a sign to see where it would lead despite my lukewarm physical attraction.

When the nanny gig ended prematurely, I wasn't convinced our six-month relationship was reason enough to stay in the expensive city by the sea. My prolonged Wisconsin visit was to act as my buffer zone, a safe place where I could compare the pros and cons of Santa Barbara and Denver without being in either one.

Jonathan came to visit me in Wisconsin the same long weekend my parents visited from Georgia. We gathered for cocktail hour on my sister's back deck to watch the sun set. My niece played in her nearby sandbox while the dogs frolicked in the spacious backyard, a swath of deep green surrounded by thoughtfully-curated, colorful landscaping. Fireflies dotted the evening and tears of laughter rolled down our faces as the stories flowed.

Jonathan and I went ring shopping that weekend; I was choosing California.

But not immediately.

I acquired a new-to-me vehicle during my Wisconsin weeks, and in early July I drove myself to Colorado for a much-anticipated six weeks of immersing myself in everything I loved about the place, including time with Loretta, Ivy, Angus, Rose, and Slater. In fact, that's where I started my visit.

Ivy and Angus knew I was arriving on Friday – or, at least Ivy did – but the girls thought I was coming on Saturday. This was a thing Ivy and I liked to orchestrate, these surprises for the girls. This would not be the first time we'd pulled one off, nor would it be the last.

I called Ivy's phone when I crossed the border of Nebraska into Colorado, then spent the last hour of my drive being passed between Loretta and Rose, chatting with them as girlfriends did, mostly about all the adventures we had planned for when I arrived.

I was still on the phone call, speaking at the moment to Rose, when I parked my car in front of their house and started up the driveway. I saw Rose see me from where she sat on the front porch. I watched her look at the phone in her hand as her voice trailed off, then back to me, the wheels in her head turning. I was grinning ear-to-ear, waiting for it to click.

Meanwhile, Loretta had spotted me from the garage behind the house and came tearing down the driveway, shrieking and screaming, "This is the best day ever! This is the best day ever!" over and over as she flung herself into my open arms. Rose ditched the phone on the porch and joined our bear hug, squealing with excitement.

We are so lucky.

August 2008

When I drove myself back to California six weeks later, I was a blubbering mess. It felt like my heart was actually breaking more with every sob, every mile. A day later, I arrived back in palm-tree-lined Santa Barbara, and I moved into Jonathan's matchbox rental with him until we located a bigger option around the corner a few weeks later.

After a bumpy start in a temp position, I landed a full time position with benefits as the Director of Admissions at a Montessori school. I was proud of myself and could feel my mother exhale from across the country. Finally, a real job.

Not only did I love this job, I was good at it. I conducted campus tours, admissions interviews, assessment testing, and open houses. I happily took my turns for playground duty, drop-off duty, and library duty.

However, the more I tried to filter my love for my job into other areas of my life, the more obvious it became that I was, deep down, miserable. Jonathan and I had very little in common, had trouble communicating with one another, and worst of all, didn't particularly enjoy each other's company. Most of my Friday evenings were spent in bed, reading, while Jonathan went out with his friends. Most of my Sundays were spent the way I preferred – watching football at home, prepping my meals for the week and cleaning our house, while Jonathan spent his Sundays the way he preferred – out drinking with his friends during the day and watching television at his friends' houses in the evening. A couple nights a week and every other weekend, his young teenage kids from his first marriage stayed with us, and while I was on friendly terms with both of them, Jonathan did not invite nor include me in their weekend plans and activities. It was assumed I would fend for myself those weekends.

Santa Barbara has farmers' markets that will knock your socks off and yoga studios that can touch your very soul and beaches that offer solace any day of the year, but I was lonely and disconnected and living with a man who I felt like I barely knew. I discovered he was having an emotional affair with an ex when she overnighted soup to him when he was sick. I emailed her to thank her for her thoughtfulness (and to make extra sure she knew about me), and she wrote me a lengthy, detailed email in response, apologizing all over the place. She had not known about me. When I confronted Jonathan, he told me I had no business reaching out to his friends for anything, and anyway, I was overreacting.

I began to plot my departure from both the city and my relationship; I would leave when the school year was over. In the meantime, I started therapy and anti-anxiety medication, both of which gave me a second wind with Jonathan as life steadied itself a bit. I started laughing again. We started laughing together. I started second guessing my decision to leave.

And then another interesting phone call happened.

This call was from my buddy Alice back in Colorado, who told me about speaking with a new energy-reading intuitive, a psychic medium, which was a shared interest of ours. Alice, Ivy, and I had visited psychic fairs together in the past, speaking with mystics and mediums about our goals, hopes, directions, and dreams.

This intuitive woman's name was Saida, and despite being in a big role at a bank on the east coast, she experienced premonitions, received messages, and took in information that came to her in ways she couldn't fully explain but definitely couldn't ignore. Saida was starting to hone her psychic skill by offering spiritual readings not for money, just for practice. Alice had been referred to Saida for a phone call by a mutual acquaintance.

During that phone call, the story goes, Alice mentioned me in passing, and Saida immediately started receiving messages for me, about me. So much so that Saida backed up the conversation and asked Alice if I would be open to speaking with Saida; Alice was calling me now to find out. I agreed to a phone call with tingly anticipation.

As soon as our call began, Saida shared with me that we were kindred spirits – she had visions of how we'd fought alongside each other in many lifetimes already and she knew we possessed similar abilities. She said mine would blossom during my 40's. I was 34 at the time of the call.

"I know you think you love him," she said of Jonathan, "and as human beings, we have free will, so it is, of course, up to you to decide if you'll go through with marrying him. But hear this: if you marry him, you will need to spend the rest of your marriage reminding yourself, I *chose* this. I *chose* this. I *chose* this."

It was as if she was reading my mind, or at least pages of my journal, because I already knew Jonathan wasn't the right man for me. I'd known it for almost the entire sixteen months we'd already been together. So at that moment, I was speechless.

"Your karma isn't even with him," she continued. "Your karma was with his ex-wife, and that's been resolved now. Frankly, you don't need him anymore in terms of fulfilling your life purpose. As I said, you can choose to keep him around, or you can choose to continue following your divine path. Tell me, have you ever considered living in Colorado?"

I am careful with my answers when I have conversations like this, because while I believe the gift is real, I also believe people without the gift can make a convincing argument just by paying close attention to the words you use, the way you use them, and how you react to different turns of phrase. So, I hold my cards close to my chest because I know the real deal will be able to deliver anyway. I had not mentioned Colorado during our conversation, nor had my personal history with Colorado come up in Alice's conversation with Saida, either.

"The next piece of your puzzle is in Colorado, and so is your future husband. I suggest you consider moving there. Spend a few years getting settled, because your future husband is still sorting out some of his own life circumstances, preparing for you. In a few years, you'll both be ready and that's when you'll find each other. You just need to get yourself to Colorado."

Chapter 3

"Believe nothing you hear, and only one half that you see."
– Edgar Allen Poe

September 2016 - Colorado

One of the many lies this country tells itself is that we have an "innocent until proven guilty" policy in our legal system. There is no such thing.

We do not tell innocent people they cannot go to a concert. We do not put ankle monitors on them to track their movement. We do not require that innocent people ask a judge to take a business trip, nor do we broadcast photographs of innocent people throughout entire states, and into other ones. We do those things to people because we assume they are guilty.

What actually happens in this system is that you are assumed guilty until proven innocent and until massive financial strain is incurred unless you have the time and money to fight for your name to be cleared. In my interview with the detective on the day I am arrested, I point this out to him.

"Sir, this feels like guilty until proven innocent. You're saying I *have* to be here, like right now, today. I mean, I have a friend in from out of town. We have tickets to a concert at Fiddler's Green tonight. We were on our way out the door when the police showed up. And I just… I feel like I'm already being punished for something I didn't even do. Now you're saying I have to go spend the night in jail for – "

He interrupts me. "No. There is no guilty until proven innocent."

"Well," I say, "I'm sure you can see how it might feel that way. If I was being assumed innocent – which I should be assumed, right? I'd be able to go to the concert with my friend. You know what I mean?"

A look of frustration flashes across his face, his forehead crinkles, and his dark eyes narrow. I keep talking.

"Like that's what an innocent, free person gets to do. They get to go to the concert they bought tickets to with their friend who is visiting. And I'll show back up here in the morning, to figure this whole mess out. I'm not going to not come, you know? But I guess that's the thing – you *don't* know that about me. You don't know me at all. I don't know. I don't know how this all works, exactly. But it doesn't seem like I'm being given any benefit of the doubt here. She says one thing, I'm saying it's not true, there's been no investigation or anything, so why are her words, her accusations, all that it takes to literally lock me up?"

He stumbles over his words. "Well, Ms. Kuisis, the fact of the matter is, I've laid everything out to you and the report we have. And the reason I do that is I want to make sure that you don't leave here and say, 'Well, I still don't know why I was there,' or, whatever."

I struggle to make sense of his response. "I know. I know you said all that. But – "

He keeps going. "So it was not… hey, like I said, I didn't beat around any bushes with you. I tell you that this is what, you know, we have."

He isn't making very much sense. He's definitely not answering my questions.

"Sir, I understand why I was brought in, but since I am adamantly and categorically denying all of it, shouldn't I be able to go act as an innocent person until I am proven guilty?"

There is a pause.

"That's not the way it works."

***

It is the Sunday morning of Labor Day weekend 2016. I got home yesterday from my three days in holding, and my dogs were over-the-moon excited to see me when I walked through the door. I dropped immediately to the floor, cuddling them close and crying into their fur as they happily wagged their tails and climbed all over my lap.

Where've you been, Mom?

True to his word, my husband has lined up both a bails bondsman, Ricky, who I am told I will need to phone every three days as a condition of my bond until this matter is resolved, and a lawyer with excellent credentials, who we are on our way to meet.

"How'd you sleep?" my husband asks.

"Like a rock," I say. It's a perk of a clear conscience.

I pick at the skin around my fingernails as we drive east on 6th Avenue. I am innocent, but that doesn't make me not nervous.

I am brand new to the criminal justice system, and the lawyer has trouble finding my name in the database.

Even the system knows I don't belong here.

"Let me tell you, I don't need your case," the lawyer is saying now, "and if I decide to represent you, and if you decide to hire me, you'll need to meet me halfway. You'll need to show up to our meetings, be forthcoming with me, show up to your court dates as expected, and pay money up front. Those sorts of things."

I nod. "Sure. Of course." *I am so out of my element.*

"You'll need to cooperate with me, listen to me, and trust that I'll have your best interests in mind. I will not stop fighting for you. I'll name as many appellate issues as I can, and I'll work to get you the best possible plea deal. Do you understand?"

"Yes."

"Great. Before we go any further, I need you to call your credit card companies, tell them you're about to make a large purchase, ask them to approve the transaction."

I call one card, and my voice shakes as I speak to the kind lady on the other end of the line, "Yes, that's right. Pike Legal. Thank you."

James calls another credit card, approval is granted, and the lawyer is paid.

I am simultaneously grateful for the privilege of having this kind of credit available to us and furious for having to max out two cards because of someone else's bullshit.

The lawyer talks to both James and I for an hour, taking copious amounts of notes, then sends James to the coffee shop across the street. "I need some time with just Alex."

I give my lawyer the answers to the questions he asks.

I met Loretta in 2000.

I was her teacher.

They brought me into their family, sort of like a nanny at the start.

No, I did not ask to move into their house; they offered.

No, I am not the only non-family person they've invited to live at their home; in fact, a grown male friend currently lives with them.

Rose used to call me her godmother; Loretta used to tell people I was "like an aunt, only better."

Ivy only has one sister and they're estranged; Ivy badmouths her to the kids and anyone else who will listen.

Angus is one of four brothers; two have died and he's estranged from the fourth.

Yes, I am a heterosexual woman.

No, nothing imprudent or sexual with Angus. Ew.

No, nothing imprudent or sexual with Ivy. Gross.

And no, absolutely nothing like that with Loretta. That's the most disgusting notion of all.

***

These are only allegations at this point, not actual charges, and there is some confusion over what, exactly, the allegations even are. Some of my friends are convinced this is as far as it'll go, but I'm not so sure, because it quite frankly feels like it shouldn't have gotten this far in the first place. Loretta is 16 years old now and is either lying maliciously or has a broken brain that has tricked her – and subsequently quite a few adults – into believing her stories.

And my goodness, are the stories wild. They are mixed-up jumbles of accurate memories – *yes, they came to visit me in California for spring break* – and falsifications – *no, it wasn't "so hot" in March that I insisted we sleep without pajamas*. This pajama bit is actually so bizarrely untrue that it makes me laugh out loud the first time I hear it. I am notorious with my family and every roommate I've ever had for my extensive pajama collection. I love pajamas. I never sleep without pajamas, not even today when I sleep next to my husband.

I am given a timeline of May 2008 through May 2010 to work with, meaning 16-year-old Loretta claims the allegations took place between her 8th and 10th birthdays. She says she didn't realize it was "abuse" until her sophomore year of high school when a friend told her about his childhood abuse.

It seems like a peculiar timeline to name. "I lived in California until August of 2009," I say to my lawyer, "which means only nine months of those two years – between August and May of 2010 - are what we're actually looking at."

Loretta alleges abuse never happened at her house, always at mine. She says it was always when she was alone, never when Rose was there, too. Except she says it happened once in California, where Rose also was, so we're dealing with contradictions from the start.

This is pretty common, I'm told. Kids are allowed leeway in their re-telling, and it's okay if their dates change, or certain details transfer. That's to be expected, I'm told.

How do you defend against that kind of moving target? It feels overwhelming, but I know I can do it because, again, I'm the one with truth on my side.

***

Eventually, the prosecution provides us their initial pieces of "Discovery," which is the formal exchanging of information between the prosecution and defense about the witnesses and evidence they may present at trial. I am given recordings of the forensic interviews with Loretta and Rose, which are the initial interviews they each provided about a month before my arrest. My lawyer asks me to watch each interview at least twice to note any discrepancies between what the girls say and what I can prove to be otherwise.

Watching these videos will be the first time I've laid eyes on either of the girls in over three years, and I'll finally get to hear what Loretta has to say for herself. I expect the task to be arduous and emotionally wrenching. I tuck myself away in my home office with a box of tissue, a notepad and a pen. I take a few deep breaths, ask for strength from my angels and spirit guides, brace myself for an emotional whirlwind, and press "play."

I am still as Loretta appears on my screen, sitting on a loveseat in a small, bland room with a side table, a square coffee table, and an armchair where the forensic interviewer sits. The interviewer explains that the conversation is being recorded, and that the detective is watching them from another room.

I am surprised at my lack of emotional reaction. First of all, I barely recognize Loretta or her voice. There isn't even a glimpse of the girl I knew. This person on the screen has heavy energy and a scowl on her face. Her hair is bedraggled, and her t-shirt at least two sizes too big. I feel sympathy and alarm – *oh dear one, what happened to you?* – but I watch with a critical eye instead of a crying one, my pen poised to record any and all inconsistencies between her stories and the actual truth.

It doesn't take long. Almost immediately out of the gate, Loretta says we met at a Montessori school, that her Montessori education was the reason she was a delayed reader in first grade. This is false – Loretta never attended a Montessori school. She visited with me at the Montessori schools where I worked, but she herself was never a Montessori student.

This alarms me, but my lawyer doesn't see it as a big deal. "She mixed up schools, so what."

It's not just forgetting the name of a school, though, she's actually staking a claim to a form of education she never received – if she is already getting this easy part about her own life wrong, it's not hard to imagine she's getting other parts wrong, too.

I take pages and pages (and pages) of notes.

"What does she mean when she says her mom helped her figure out timelines?"

"Why does she say she did 'practice interviews' with her therapist?"

"When she says, 'They told me to use as much detail as possible, that it would make it more believable,' who is 'they?' and does this raise a red flag to anyone else?"

Frankly, the interview makes Loretta look like she is in over her head, and after watching Rose's interview, I am feeling incrementally better about the whole situation. Their emotions are raging, but their facts are twisted in ways that I feel relatively confident I can untangle.

When my husband quietly sticks his head through the doorway of my office a couple hours later, he's half-expecting to find a crumpled heap of tears and tissues.

Instead, I look up at him, chipper and smiling.

"Will you make me a bowl of ice cream?" I ask.

***

The night before the story of my arrest "breaks" in the news, Rose searches for my account on Instagram. She didn't follow my account, so she'd taken extra steps to find me and look at the pictures I'd posted. I happen to be active on the app at the time, and my eyes grow wide in amazement when she begins "liking" a handful of my posts. I've been strictly instructed not to reach out to that family in any way, shape, or form, and they've been strictly instructed not to reach out to me. She's not supposed to be here.

I start posting things directly related to the issue at hand – *"the most dangerous liars are those who think they are telling the truth"* and *"a lie has speed, but truth has endurance."*

She takes the bait. One after the other, she likes, likes, likes...

And so, I screenshot, screenshot, screenshot...

September 19, 2016

The detective I spoke to hands the case off to the district attorney's office, whose investigator is similarly lax in his investigating. The district attorney (DA) assigned to my case doesn't seem to mind; she decides to press charges without a completed investigation. What's more, she chooses to go to the media before she lets my lawyer know.

I receive a voice mail.

"Hello, Ms. Kuisis, this is Christine McKnight with channel 4 news. I'm calling to ask if you want to make a statement about the criminal charges being brought against you? You can call me back at your convenience, thanks."

My stomach drops when I listen, and I call my lawyer immediately.

"Why am I finding out from a reporter that I've been charged with criminal felonies? Why does the news reporter know before I do?"

My lawyer is also confused, especially because he'd specifically reached out to the DA to have a conversation about my case. She didn't return his call and later claims she didn't get the message.

There are seven charges brought up against me. Three counts of sexual assault on a child, each with an additional count of "by a person in a position of trust" tacked on, which means my role in Loretta's life was akin to that of a parent in that I was responsible for her general wellbeing anytime she was with me. The seventh count is for the "pattern" that the first three counts would presumably create.

My mug shot appears on all the local television stations and on every online news outlet in our state. I see it float through my Facebook newsfeed because a woman I used to work with shares it alongside cruel commentary about my character. Does she not realize we're Facebook friends and that I'll see this? Or does she just not care? Mutual friends comment on her post, saying things like, "I think we need more information. This doesn't add up."

"Kids don't lie," she shoots back.

But 16-year-olds aren't really kids anymore, not in the sense she's talking about. And 16-year-olds *do* lie. I know this is a fact because I'm living the direct consequence of it.

This is my first indication that I'm not only navigating uncharted territory, but I'm also not even in friendly waters. I un-friend this woman on Facebook immediately. I don't need that kind of negativity in my life. The kind of people who assume automatic guilt based on a 30-second news clip and a mugshot are not my people.

A friend in California sends me a copy of a letter distributed at the request of the prosecution to the entire parent population at the Montessori school in Santa Barbara where I worked. The letter outlines my brief history at the school and lists out the current charges against me. Recipients of the letter are encouraged to contact Denver police if they have similar stories or related information they would like to share. A friend in Denver sends me a copy of a similar letter sent to the parent population at the Denver Montessori school where I worked.

The prosecution is on the hunt, it would seem.

I lock my social media down after a stranger leaves a comment on a random Facebook picture of me smiling at my husband – "*Sicko*" – and it only takes reading the comment section of one article to be reminded why even in the best of times, I never read the comment section. Internet trolls live in the comments, and the combination of assumptions and nasty words is alarming. *"Just look at her ugly face smiling in that mugshot," … "what a pervert," …*

"lock her up for life," ... *"I hope she rots in hell."* All these righteous condemnations of something that never even happened. So much energy, grossly misdirected; so many resources, foolishly misspent; so many people's time, irreplaceably wasted; and so much taxpayer money, irresponsibly flushed down the drain.

Sometimes, kids lie.

I show my lawyer Rose's presence on my Instagram page, as well as the letters being circulated. He finds the media attention odd since I'm not a public figure, and I am sternly reminded to refrain from all social media – "I don't want you posting so much as a flower right now." It is suggested I "lay low and sit tight" for a while, but I don't know what this means or even understand how to do it. I don't want to "sit tight" – I want this problem solved, I want this broken story fixed. I am amped up and poised for action.

I receive an email from my biggest client, terminating our association. They've seen the news. I will be paid through the next 20 days, as per the contract, but my duties are cancelled, effective immediately.

I receive an email from the private school board I'd recently been asked to join; they've also seen the news and are rescinding their invitation.

I receive an email from a relatively new acquaintance, lecturing me on the importance of child molesters owning their actions before launching into a story about how she was abused by her uncle and it screwed her up for life. I do not respond.

I receive a message from a former co-worker, demanding an explanation that will help her make sense of the news stories she has seen, although she "doubts very much" anything I have to say for myself will change her mind about how terrible she has decided I am. I do not respond to her, either.

I receive another message from a different former co-worker, simply saying she is thinking of me, and thought a kind word of support might feel good right now. She is right, and I respond with gratitude.

The media frenzy is the prosecution's attempt to beef up their case – as it is, it's not strong, and something tells me they must know it, or they wouldn't be reaching so far to try and find other stories of me hurting kids in this way. On one level, I am mortified, as I've been raised to value reputation over all else, and this is a direct assault on it. On another level, I can plainly see that there is not one damn thing I can do to stop this avalanche from happening, and there is something oddly freeing about that, too. Let the fires burn, I think. I shall use them to light my path forward.

My lawyer asks me, "Is anything else going to turn up?"

I tell him, "The answer is no, definitely not, but I evidently have no idea how the world works anymore. None of Loretta's stories are true but here we are, so..." I shrug. "We'll see what happens, I guess."

Nothing else turns up.

Per my lawyer's request, I begin making phone calls, reaching out to ask people for letters of character reference and support. Anyone who can speak to my character, my behavior around children (especially these children, and especially Loretta) is called.

"Hi, as you know, I've spent my career in early childhood education, working in a number of capacities including serving as a nanny and babysitter for dozens if not hundreds of children over the years. Now, a young woman I used to know is erroneously claiming that I sexually mishandled her almost 10 years ago. These false allegations have turned into charges of criminal behavior, and I am calling to ask for your help."

In two days, I repeat these sentences almost 75 times. I spend practically all my waking hours on the phone. I talk to people from my childhood, my teenage years, my college years, my early Colorado years, my California years, my recent Colorado years. I speak with former bosses, families I babysat for when I was in high school, former friends from past lives, people I haven't talked to in decades.

Every person I talk to is shocked, and many of them cry during the course of our conversation. It's difficult for people to wrap their minds around. Refrains of *this is preposterous…ludicrous…ridiculous…insane* thread themselves through every conversation I have.

The letters come pouring in. One woman even offers to allow her 5-year-old to testify on my behalf. I collect over 65 letters, so many that even my lawyer is amazed, says he's never seen anything like it. Some people say they will write one but don't, and I automatically dismiss them from my support system. You're either in or you're out.

I also send a text to Saida, my psychic, spirit-channeling friend, for the first time in years.

"*Hi, friend, long time no talk. I have something important I'd like to speak with you about. Will you please call me at your earliest convenience?*"

She texts back a few hours later: "*Hey there…it's been a long time. Glad to hear from you and hope all is well. My schedule is crazy busy. I am literally booked solid. Things lighten up in a few weeks, so I will do my best to give you a call as soon as I can. Hugs and love to you!*"

Well, that won't do. I try again.

"*I wish I was exaggerating when I say I'm dealing with a situation where my life is on the line, but unfortunately, I'm not. So as soon as you can, please do give me a call. Sending love.*"

Within 30 minutes, the phone rings. It's Saida. I explain everything to her, and when we hang up, she sends me another text: "*This is what I initially get: binding prayers need to be done for this young lady, her mother, and her sister. If there is a DA involved, they'll also need a binding. Bindings are a way to block their negative energy from infiltrating yours any more than it already has. Bindings make it so that the energy of an unwelcome spirit or dishonorable intention – in this case, a falsehood designed to hurt and ruin you – is trapped (or bound) away from your soul so you can concentrate on fighting the good fight from a place of love, truth, and integrity, as you have decided to do. Bindings create an invisible but powerful spiritual shield around you that causes any ugliness they spew to bounce right back to them. After all, we reap what we sow. You'll need blessed candles and court prayers for each interaction with Loretta's side. I'll also create a protection prayer bag for you to carry during this time. Let me be clear - you are and will continue to be under spiritual attack…I will explain in detail when we speak next week."*

I receive a package with a set of prayer candles to be used in meditation rituals on the full moon and the new moon, as well as the promised protection prayer bag, a beautiful deep purple silk bag filled with dried roots, leaves, seeds, and flowers that fits in the palm of my hand. This is Saida's gift to me – *"No one can touch that bag but you. It is my contribution to showing you support in believing your innocence. If I did not believe you were innocent, we would be having very different conversations right now."*

Saida asks me to text her my full name, my lawyer's name, the name of the DA, and the full names of Loretta, Ivy, and Rose.

I oblige, and that's when it clicks for Saida exactly who I am talking about. Her text reply comes almost immediately. *"I know these people. I've had sessions with Ivy!"*

I text back. *"I know you do. I know you did."*

Saida is aghast. *"What in the world! This is very bad for her karma!"*

***

On September 30, a text from Saida says: *"I have to share with you that I saw the DA changing or adding another person to help with this case…I saw more than just this lady. In that event, I'll need the names immediately and they'll need bindings, too. With the dark side, sometimes they look for loopholes, and a change in DA would be a loophole, FYI."*

I tell her I will keep her posted, but to my knowledge, it is just the one DA on the case.

The next day, Saida's bindings arrive in the mail. Each binding is a tiny glass jar that Saida has spent hours praying over. In each of the glass jars, there are three nails and a piece of paper with a name written on it. I am instructed to dig four holes in the corners of my backyard into which I should bury the jars, one jar per hole. I am given specific prayers to say over each jar as well as directions on how many times to say them before placing the jar in its hole, covering it up with dirt, and stomping on it three times.

Each morning before I go to court, I'll need to repeat the prayer recitations and ground stomping.

The bindings arrive wrapped profusely in tissue paper and nestled snugly in smaller boxes, yet one of the glass jars has shattered, scattering sharp glass shards throughout the box. The broken jar belongs to Loretta's binding. I text Saida: *"What do I do?"*

Her response: *"That is not good! She was the one that caused a lot of trouble for me during the binding prayers. Her spirit broke out of the binding, that's what she did. I need to redo that and mail it to you first thing Monday. Remind me, is she the one causing the main problem here? There's no way that glass should have broken. Bury the others right away and I will start re-binding her."*

"Yes." I text back, *"Loretta is the one causing the main problem."*

In addition to the binding prayers and burials, Saida sent specific prayer and meditation work for me to do. I receive a brown paper bag full of small blue candles and a candle holder, sacred roots with little dishes for them to live in, and designated dressing oils to slather on the small blue candles before lighting.

Every night before a court date, I am to hold the enclosed root in my left hand while stating my personal intentions out loud (*may the truth prevail, may I experience my rightful freedom, may my heart know peace,*) then recite Psalm 23 aloud 11 times.

The Lord is my shepherd; I shall not want.

He maketh me to lie down in green pastures: he leadeth me beside the still waters.

He restoreth my soul: he leadeth me in the paths of righteousness for his name's sake.

Yea, though I walk through the valley of the shadow of death, I will fear no evil: for thou art with me; thy rod and thy staff they comfort me.

Thou preparest a table before me in the presence of mine enemies: thou anointest my head with oil; my cup runneth over.

Surely goodness and mercy shall follow me all the days of my life: and I will dwell in the house of the Lord forever.

I dress a blessed candle with the provided oil, secure it in the holder, light it with my right hand, and settle in to silently meditate for the full two hours it takes for the dripless candle to burn itself all the way out into nothingness. I am desperate for an outcome in my favor, willing to work towards actively shifting energy for the highest good of all involved, and have experienced Saida's accuracy around my life events already, so I do not even blink at completing her directives. If anything, they make me feel safer and more protected than my country's legal system has so far.

October 2016

My first court date is slated for October 5th, and on the 3rd, I wake up to another text message from Saida: *"I need to speak with you ASAP!"*

When I hear her request, I balk.

"But Saida, there's just no way. I can't go to Loretta's house to get a handful of dirt from their yard. I'm definitely not allowed to do that, and yes, my sister arrives from out of town tomorrow, but they know her so that's not a good idea, either. I can't do it."

But I think for a minute and come up with a solution. I may not be able to go to Loretta's house, but my pal Caroline can. Caroline has her own car, a flexible work schedule, and a gigantic willingness to support me. She's never met Loretta, Ivy, Angus, Rose, or Slater, so there's no chance of being recognized as someone associated with my side. She agrees to the favor without hesitation.

This is how it comes to pass that while Ivy and Angus are in the courtroom watching me complete my first court date, Caroline and her dog are driving an hour south to their house and parking down the street from the address I provided her. As she and her pooch walk past their house, she leans down with a plastic Ziploc bag to scoop imaginary poop off Ivy and Angus's lawn, swiping a handful of grass and dirt in the process. She drives directly to my house afterwards, then I take that bag of dirt straight to the post office, where I overnight it to Saida on the east coast, who prays over it and overnights it right back to me. I'll bury the dirt in my backyard and tell Saida it is done.

"You are in my prayers daily," she'll say, *"May an army of angels and the spirit of god be with you!"*

***

Despite the media attention turning up absolutely nothing, the district attorney acts like this will be an open and shut case. "After all," she smiles at my attorney with a shrug of her shoulder and a bat of her wispy eyelashes, "all I have to prove is opportunity."

When I hear that, my panic levels start to rise, because if that's the case, I am, pardon my language, fucked.

If "opportunity" is all she needs to find, she'll find it. There was plenty of that over the years. It occurs to me then that the DA is not interested in justice, nor is she interested in getting to the bottom of this tangle. The system is not set up for resolution, it is designed for warfare. There will be no conversation, no comparison of memories or even facts. The DA just wants the win and she'll say what she needs to say to get it. It's as if she is getting paid on commission.

Today's court appearance is what's called a docket day, meaning the courtroom will be full of defendants, some out on bail like me, some not as fortunate, brought in through side doors, in handcuffs and striped prison clothes. The presiding judge is going to hear the long list of cases one after another in rapid succession, ruling on each as she goes. For me personally, today is a "pro forma hearing," where we pick a preliminary hearing date and are officially given a copy of the charges. We already have a copy of the charges, so that part is expected to be brief. I am told I will not testify. I am told I will not even speak.

My lawyer will also be asking for "bond modifications," meaning changes to the protective order issued to me at pre-trial when I posted bond. I want the ankle monitor removed, and for an exception to be made to the "no contact with minors under 18" part to allow for Facetime and phone calls with my nieces. As it stands, I am not allowed to engage with them in any way, shape or form.

My sister flies in from Wisconsin to offer her physical and emotional support. I partake in my two-hour meditation the night before, I say my prayers and stomp all over my backyard in the morning while James makes us all breakfast, and then the three of us drive to the courthouse.

We meet my lawyer a block away and walk over together in case there is a media presence. Blessedly, there is not. In the early morning sunlight, we weave our way through the metal detector lines in the marble courthouse lobby and take the elevator to the 5th floor. The courtroom is bustling with people – full pews with folks lining the entire outer perimeter of the room. We find space in the middle of the last row and sit, my sister to my left and my husband to my right.

I am surprised by the volume in the room driven by a constant buzz of side conversations happening while each case on the docket takes its turn being heard by the judge at the front of the room. There is so much happening at once: attorneys greet one another and chat jovially while public defenders randomly call out names from their stack of files in an effort to locate the people they'll be defending in mere moments.

Ivy and Angus enter the room from the back and stand almost directly behind us, hovering on the wall. I glare over my right shoulder in their direction.

"Don't," my husband says, taking my hand, "Don't even look at them."

In my peripheral vision, I see Angus motion to Ivy that they should sit down in the available space next to us.

I dare you, I think. I can tell he's oblivious to our presence, but Ivy notices us, and immediately shuffles off the other way, pushing him with her. They settle about 10 rows ahead of us, to the right.

My lawyer gives me the go-ahead to stand up and wait along the wall on the left side of the room, as it's almost our turn. My knees are knocking and I cannot stop them – I have to lean back against the wall so I don't fall over into a heap on the floor. My stomach is a pit of nerves, I cannot catch my breath, and the edges of my vision keep darkening.

Spirit guides, don't fail me now.

I worry I might faint but then I notice Angus staring at me, trying to intimidate me with what I think he thinks is a menacing glare. It isn't going to work. I straighten my back and lock eyes with him. I fight an impulse to stick out my tongue, to flip him the bird.

I know how disconnected he usually is from what goes on under his roof. Ivy always deferred to Angus when he was around but ran the household a totally different way when he was not. "Ok, but don't tell your dad," used to be one of Ivy's most oft-used phrases. From bedtimes to snack choices to screen time allotments, the girls had one set of rules for when Angus was traveling and a different, stricter set of rules for when he was home. Angus is here for show, and I strongly suspect he doesn't know about what my lawyer is about to share with the court, simply because I know how much Ivy keeps from him. I maintain a steady, steely gaze, and he looks away first.

Love wins.

A few days ago, Ivy sent my lawyer a Linked In request, asking him to be in her professional network. My lawyer called me immediately – "this is the strangest thing, nothing like it has ever happened before," – and showed the DA his screenshot of Ivy's request right before we faced the judge. The DA had no idea.

"Your Honor, before we begin," my lawyer is saying now, "I want to put something on the record that I've just shared with the DA, who wasn't aware before I told her. The accuser's mother has sent me a connection request on Linked In, and since that kind of contact is not really allowed in situations like these, I wanted to bring it to your attention today so it can be addressed."

I can practically feel Angus giving Ivy a dirty look, and it takes all I have not to turn around.

The judge whips her gaze to the DA. "I expect you will make it crystal clear to the entire family what is and is not proper behavior in these sorts of situations, and I shouldn't think I need to remind you that reaching out on any and every social media platform falls directly under what is not proper."

The DA reiterates her ignorance around Ivy's actions and promises the judge she'll go over the required boundaries and expectations with the family... again. The point is made, so we decide to keep Rose's presence on my Instagram page tucked in our back pocket for the time being.

When we ask for the ankle monitor to be taken off, the DA shares that the family is here today because they feel very strongly about it staying on, "for their safety." My lawyer argues it is an unnecessary financial burden ($11 a day!), when all signs point to my always staying in the Denver area, having no reason or even desire to travel the hour to the city where they live.

The judge rules that the monitor stay, but she does something else rather unorthodox, kicking off a long string of what I consider kindnesses extended to me from the judges I stand before. I choose to believe they are signals from the universe to hang in there, but one could argue these unexpected kindnesses might have more to do with my skin color than my private relationship with god. I cannot differentiate between them in the moment because

I am living in survival mode, which does not feel like privilege. Accordingly, each gesture seems benevolent.

Today, there are two gestures of kindnesses and the first is when the judge rather atypically asks the district attorney how she expects me to make money if I'm not allowed to be around children under the age of 18. This catches the DA off guard.

"Er, with all due respect, your Honor, I don't really care. This is a standard restriction of a protection order with charges of this nature."

Guilty until proven innocent.

"Well, I think it's unnecessarily restrictive, taking away an income source and expecting someone to be able to pay for all of this," the judge counters as she vaguely gestures to the courtroom at large. She turns and looks at me.

"How many families do you work with?"

Now I am the one caught off guard. I wasn't expecting this topic of conversation, nor to be asked any direct questions. My mind jumps to action. I babysit regularly, but not as a primary source of income. Still. I think about the broken contracts, the board positions that have been revoked. All that potential income, all those opportunities, vanished.

"Two," I blurt out, immediately wishing I'd chosen a larger number. My lawyer reminds me to speak to only him, not the judge directly.

"Ok, two," she says, "List out their names, and we'll change the protection order to exclude the defendant's nieces and the children from these families."

The DA is flabbergasted. "This is dumb," she says to my lawyer when we confer to the side to list out the names on the new paperwork.

This whole thing is dumb, I think as I thinly smile at her, biting my tongue.

When we're done, I go across the street to check in with my assigned pre-trial officer as I am expected to do after each courtroom appearance.

The second kindness reveals itself when we get home later that morning. Mona, James and I are sitting on the back porch, re-playing the morning, pulling apart the judge's decisions, and studying the new protection order.

Suddenly, I notice something that makes me sit up straighter in my chair.

"Hey, check this out…" I say to my sister and husband as I lay the paper on the table and point.

Initially, there was a restriction on my order prohibiting me from drinking alcohol or using controlled substances, like marijuana, my cocktail of choice. Accordingly, it'd been over a month since I'd so much as had a sip of wine or a puff of green. This isn't a problem for me necessarily, but I find it irritating on principle. I don't understand how the restriction is anything except a systemic power trip, another stripping of my personal choice before any guilt has been proven.

This morning, when we gave the judge the revised paperwork, she completed and signed into effect the back portion where these restrictions were listed.

She had left the alcohol/controlled substance clause untouched. No more restriction.

"Oh, wow," my sister says, "That's interesting. I wonder if she did that on purpose or just didn't see that it was checked on the original."

"Do you want to call your lawyer and double check?" my husband asks.

"Nope." I say cheerfully, "I understand this part perfectly. This order trumps the previous one, and this order clearly has an unchecked box. Who wants a cocktail?"

Kindness collected.

***

During my meditation the night before, my phone had flooded with messages from well-meaning friends:

"I hope you are heard and the truth sets you free."

"Praying for immediate dismissal!"

"I believe in you. I believe you."

"Go give 'em hell,"

and my favorite from my friend Jules,

"You are so strong and brave. I want to be you when I grow up. I want my daughter to be you when she grows up. I love you."

I appreciate their words so much, but I know that unless Loretta decides to come clean, it's not ending here. This court date has simply been a formality, the first in what will be a long, tedious string of them.

Chapter 4

"When a friend says they've got your back, make sure they're not holding a knife." –Unknown

March 2009 - California

I couldn't stop hearing Saida's words.

"Get yourself to Colorado," had taken up prime real estate in my thought rotation since our conversation the month before, especially when Jonathan stood me up on the night of my school's gala. The refrain echoed loudly when he spent an afternoon drinking with friends before our dinner date, effectively ruining our evening. And I heard it repeatedly bouncing through my brain when he spent a school event deep in flirty conversation with a student's mom.

Get yourself to Colorado.

I was buoyed by my upcoming visit with Loretta and Rose, though. Ivy had asked to do a repeat of last year's spring break trip, and it was finally time.

This time Jonathan would be out of town for the majority of the week. It was funny how the prior year, I had been so excited for him to be a part of our visit, and one short year later, I was so excited he wouldn't be. We still needed another adult to be our fourth for the rides at Universal Studios, though, so I asked Grace, my longtime LA-based pal to join us that day.

Aside from that daytrip to Universal Studios, most of our second spring break visit took place in Santa Barbara with just me, Loretta, and Rose. We went horseback riding, painted flower pots, planted a small potted garden by our front door, spent copious amounts of time at multiple beaches, and had prolonged dance parties to Taylor Swift's "Love Story" blasted on repeat.

It was during this visit that precocious seven-year-old Rose had some mighty big questions.

"Alex, what's a tampon? How do they, like, work?"

Which is how Rose, Loretta, and I came to be standing at the bathroom sink, watching what happens when a tampon is taken out of its wrapper and placed under running water from the faucet. We talked about how cotton absorbs liquid to a saturation point, about how tampons are designed to fit in most bodies to stop the flow of blood that happens when the uterine wall sheds each month. All my answers were factual and age-appropriate, just like my university degrees had trained me, just like every other conversation I had with children.

That led to other questions, and that was not unusual – our conversations had always been open and honest with no off-limits subjects; in fact, Ivy routinely handed me the opportunity to answer big questions with a smirk.

I had practiced scripts with both girls for years already around how to keep their bodies healthy and safe: how to say no to a cigarette, how to tell someone you need more space, how to firmly and politely ask Daddy to stop tickling (while simultaneously training Angus to respect their requests), how to ask for help, how to ask for privacy.

That day I reminded them that their questions were welcome and that they could look at the anatomy and human development books on the bookshelf if they wanted. I knew Ivy had some of the exact same books on their bookshelf at home, and I knew Ivy trusted me to answer questions like these. Rose was interested and paged through some books before bed; Loretta was less interested and the subject was therefore dropped.

Jonathan came back from his trip the night before the girls left, and he slept on the couch. He took me and the girls to breakfast the next morning before I drove Loretta and Rose to LAX to sniffle my way through another good-bye.

"Love you lots, tater tots!"

"See you 'round like a donut!"

"Miss you the most, friendly ghost!"

Another photo book was lovingly created on my computer and sent to the girls a few weeks later to commemorate the fun we'd had and the memories we'd made during what we all considered to be another spectacular vacation.

May 2009

The economy was about to tank and there was scuttlebutt around school that positions were being eliminated, combined, and/or absorbed into other departments. I knew this song – last in, first out – and I anxiously awaited the outcome of Monday night's big Board meeting.

"I'm sorry," my boss said to me Tuesday morning in her office. "Your position has been eliminated. The Board wants the Head of School to absorb the Admissions department's responsibilities for the time being."

I was both disappointed and relieved. Here was my way out. There's only so much distraction anti-anxiety medication can provide when you're living a life not meant for you, and I saw this turn of events as a natural way to finally put my exit plan in place.

The next day, my boss called me in again.

"I've thought of a solution. I have a plan to keep you on staff. It involves taking on multiple smaller roles around the school, just until the Board comes to its senses. Your position will likely be re-instated by the winter holidays."

It was tempting, and it felt nice to feel wanted, but...

"I appreciate this, more than you know," I replied. "But I need to decline the offer. I've decided to use this chance to move back to

Colorado. In fact, I literally went home after our meeting yesterday and ended my relationship with Jonathan. It was time – probably past time, to be honest – and this gave me the nudge I needed."

My boss, like so many bosses before her, was sorry to see me go, and she offered a different kind of deal. If I'd stay on at the school until August, until she returned from her long-planned family vacation, I could live in her house while she was on that extended vacation.

I reflected on the previous night's conversation with Jonathan as I considered her offer.

When I'd explained to Jonathan that losing my job meant I'd also decided to move back to Colorado, I thought he'd express the same relief I felt. After all, we'd had plenty of discussions about that very possibility, and he'd even been the one to suggest I broaden my search to include Colorado when my job security first came into question. The idea of splitting up was actually a pretty common conversation at our house.

I assumed I was merely spelling out the writing on the wall. But like with so many other things in our relationship, I had sorely misjudged.

His face became stone, his eyes turned black, and he acted as if he'd been blindsided. His patronizing voice spat words of venom at me, incredulous that I would be so careless with his heart, furious that I'd wasted so much of his time. It was a reaction so incongruent with the reality of our relationship that I initially stood dumbfounded, unclear on how to help him understand. His surprise surprised me. I later learned that it's called "gaslighting," when someone repeatedly twists the reality of a situation so drastically that you start to question your version of events, but I didn't have that language then, so I screamed my frustrations as he angrily stormed around the house, coldly saying that in the grand scheme of things, I was so insignificant to him that in five years, he wouldn't even remember my last name.

I pondered all that as I sat in my boss's office, then I thought about the two months left on my and Jonathan's lease. I'd been hopeful going into last night's conversation that we could maturely handle the relatively brief timeline as a mere inconvenience, but on the other side of our talk, I wasn't so sure.

I accepted her offer.

***

Just like I had in Hawaii, I squeezed the most out of my dwindling time in California. I took myself to pick strawberries in Solvang, I meandered solo through throngs of people celebrating solstice on State Street, and I road tripped to San Francisco for a weekend. There, I met up with a friend from high school, a friend from college, a friend from Hawaii, and Amelia, a brand new friend from the blogging community, with whom I actually stayed that weekend.

It was Amelia's kind invitation in the comment section of my blog to escape the negative vibes at home that prompted my epic San Francisco Girls Weekend. She left me a note of welcome and a key taped to her front door, letting me enter and settle in before she was even home from work.

So our friendship was quite literally built on trust and respect from the very start. Out of the ashes of my relationship with Jonathan was born that friendship with Amelia, a result that made every screaming match at home worth it. As they say, every new beginning comes from some other beginning's end.

I drove back to Santa Barbara two days later feeling refreshed, and was all smiles a few months after that when I began another road trip back to Colorado, back to where my heart felt most at home, back to where I believed, in my bones, I needed to be.

August 2009

I could actively sense the dry Colorado air erasing the ache of the previous few years, lifting the weight of going the wrong direction from my shoulders. I hadn't seen one single heart in nature while I lived in California, but once I was back in Colorado, they started to show up everywhere. Heart clouds in the sky, heart rocks on the trail, heart leaves on my run.

I had an acute awareness of dodging a bullet with Jonathan, and using advice from Saida, I sent him a long, handwritten letter, forgiving us both for trying to make something unworkable work for so long. I did not hear back. I did not expect to.

I was renting a room in my friend Connie's cookie-cutter house in a neighborhood development north of Denver. I lived almost 90 minutes from Loretta, Ivy, Angus, Rose and Slater, but that didn't stop us from acting like we lived around the corner from each other. In fact, the day after I arrived in Colorado, Loretta and Rose came to stay with me for a few days as I unpacked and got settled, then we drove south to their house where I watched all three kids while Ivy and Angus traveled for the weekend. We tried new, colorful vegetables for dinner and went on pajama walks before bed, making grand plans for all the adventures we'd go on now that we were all back together again.

I believed all was well because I wanted to.

A routine began to take shape. Once a week, I drove an hour to work out with a personal trainer I knew and loved from my days at the health club, after which I'd meet Ivy for lunch, her treat. Then I would drive back to Ivy and Angus's house to tidy up until it was time to pick the girls up at school. We'd knock out after-school snacks and homework until it was time to retrieve Slater from daycare down the street. I'd feed the kids dinner, bathe them, and put them all to bed while Ivy and Angus used their evenings as they pleased. I scratched backs and read books and sang to each kiddo as they drifted to sleep.

Sometimes I stayed the night down in their makeshift concrete corner guest room, but most times I made the 90-minute drive back to my place once Ivy and/or Angus got home. I was working on getting my home organizing business up off the ground, and Ivy often paid me to organize various areas of her perpetually disorganized house. It was good practice.

The girls stayed at my house sometimes, too. Usually both of them would visit at the same time, but one night in early February of 2010, Rose was having a birthday slumber party and didn't want Loretta around, nor did Loretta especially want to be there, thank you very much.

"Can Loretta stay with you that night?" Ivy asked me in advance. "Will you take her home after cake and ice cream?"

Of course I said yes, and we made plans for Loretta and me to see a 10:15 p.m. showing of her favorite new movie, Avatar. The movie is three hours long so it was close to 2:00 a.m. when we were finally home and exhaustedly climbing into bed. We drowsily met Ivy, Rose, and Slater for breakfast early the next morning. Then I spent the rest of the lazy, rainy day with my housemates watching the New Orleans Saints beat the Indianapolis Colts in the Super Bowl.

March 2010

My organizing business was picking up. I'd joined the Chamber of Commerce and a few other networking groups and I moved to be closer to downtown Denver. A friend of a friend owned a house with a makeshift apartment in the basement, and she was looking to lease it out. A rent was negotiated and I was given permission to paint the rooms any color I wanted. I chose a cheerful yellow for the hallway kitchen, a dusty green for the living space, and a deep purple for my bedroom.

Just like old times, Loretta, Ivy, Angus, Rose and Slater helped me move into this place, and the girls spent the first weekend in my new home with me.

While I loved my closer proximity to my former downtown stomping grounds, I was less enthused about the screaming matches my friend-of-a-friend and her boyfriend upstairs engaged in almost daily. I turned up the volume on the television to tune out slamming doors and shouted obscenities. I was surprised when they got engaged, and then not surprised when I heard of their divorce years later.

For spring break, I suggested that Ivy and I take Loretta and Rose to Atlanta, Georgia, where my parents lived, with an overnight trip to Savannah, one of my favorite U.S. cities. Ivy was on board but couldn't get the time off work, so she counter-suggested that I take Loretta and Rose by myself, saying she'd cover expenses for our plane tickets and the Savannah overnight. Rose and Loretta and I stayed with my parents the rest of the week, visiting Atlanta attractions like the Coca Cola Museum, the Aquarium, the Jimmy Carter Museum, and per eight-year-old Rose's request, a southern plantation house where I bought the girls bonnets and we ate a lunch of crustless finger sandwiches off delicate mismatched china on the sunporch.

Back in Denver after our trip, I began a part-time nanny job to supplement my organizing income with a family in an affluent section of the city. They soon asked me to occasionally babysit in the evenings, as well as house/dog sit while they went out of town, first for a weekend here and there, and then for their full two-week summer vacation.

July 2010

The first weekend of that two-week house and dog-sitting gig coincided with a previously planned birthday weekend celebration with Rose. Not her actual birthday and not her birthday party, either – that had been in February, the night Loretta and I went to see Avatar.

This was something different. This was the weekend she was cashing in her birthday present. Since I'd moved back to the area (and started organizing their clutter-filled house,) I'd started offering experiences as gifts instead of physical objects. We called them "birthday dates," and each kiddo got to choose from a short list of experience options I would present them on their birthday. The experiences ranged from baseball games to Lego-building sessions, museum visits to concerts in the park, and they often included the option for a sleepover at my house. That past January, Rose had chosen a "summer weekend getaway at Alex's" as her birthday date, and the time had come to deliver.

"Do you mind staying at my house one night and their house one night?" I asked her once I realized the schedule conflict. "You can help walk and feed the dogs and you can take a bath in their jetted basement bathtub if you like, or we can reschedule for later in the summer."

"Let's keep it as is," Rose had enthusiastically replied. "It basically just matters that we're together, it doesn't really matter where."

We are so lucky.

When Loretta heard about the big house and friendly dogs and the way the jetted tub created a mountain of bubbles in Rose's bath, she called her ten-year-old version of bullshit.

"That's not fair!" she protested the following Wednesday night during a backyard barbeque party at her house. It was Angus's 40th birthday.

"I want to see the house and meet the dogs and take a bath, too!" she gently pouted.

"It's okay with me, but dear one," I told her, "you leave for vacation in the morning. It'd have to be this very night. We'd need to leave your dad's birthday party pretty soon here, and I'd need to drop you off at the airport really, really early tomorrow morning to meet your family."

"That works for me," her blue eyes twinkled. "Let's ask Mama."

Ivy didn't mind. "As long as you can meet us at the airport by 7:00 a.m., sure."

Loretta hugged her mom, wished her dad one more happy birthday, and hopped in my car. We walked and fed the dogs, and her jetted bubble bath lived up to the hype. We fell asleep doing Gratitude Alphabets, one of the bedtime practices I'd recently introduced to help foster gratitude and calm wiggly minds before bed.

"A, I'm grateful for the apple pie at Daddy's party; b, I'm grateful for my bubble bath; c, I'm grateful for candy; d, I'm grateful for these dogs; e, I'm grateful for everything; f, I'm grateful for Florida..." as far as we could go before getting too sleepy to think anymore.

I dropped her off early at the airport the next morning, and all felt fair for Loretta and Rose.

***

The need for health care benefits came knocking in my life again, and I actively missed working in a school community anyway, so at the end of the summer, I replaced my part-time nanny job with a meatier part-time position in a downtown Denver Montessori school. I applied to be an assistant teacher, but the Executive Director wanted to create a different position for me in the front office, instead.

"You possess the exact skill set we desperately need," she told me the first time we met. "I feel like you are the answer to my prayers, like you're an angel being sent directly to me."

"Funny," I replied, "Because I feel the same way about you."

I am so lucky.

I continued to build my business through my networking efforts while coordinating events, fundraising, and special events at the school. I made new friends and my social life bumped up a notch. Weeks would go by without seeing Loretta, Ivy, Angus, Rose or Slater. I sent Ivy sporadic emails: "I miss you guys! Let's coordinate calendars and get something scheduled soon!"

December 2010

In September, I'd met a man while volunteering for a week at a Buddhist retreat center in the mountains, and the culmination of our brief-but-intense love affair was a three-week backpacking trip together around Thailand in December.

One lazy, sunny Sunday right before that Thailand trip, I was spending the day at the X Family's house. The kids were watching television, Angus was on a bike ride with friends, and Ivy and I were puttering around the house, organizing and cooking and folding laundry and other random stuff.

Ivy paused by the front door and looked my way. "I'm running to the store. You need anything?"

"No, thanks," I said, sitting down to take a turn at the computer in the dining room that we both signed in and out of regularly. When the screen buzzed to life, I saw my name on it. I could still hear Ivy's car humming in the driveway as I started reading, trying to make sense of what I was seeing.

"She's just so damn annoying. And what's with this Buddhist thing? Why didn't she experiment with it in college like normal people do?"

My eyes burned with sudden, hot tears as my brain registered what this was: an email Ivy had written to her group of high school friends, full of mean words specifically making fun of me.

"I think I was just so desperate for friends when I met her that I lowered my standards A LOT. Now that I'm meeting other people, she just bugs."

I heard Ivy's car drive away. I felt shaky and unclear what I was supposed to do with the information. When Ivy returned from the store, I made an excuse and took myself home without addressing it.

But after talking about it in therapy, I asked Ivy to brunch, where I told her what I read. She didn't deny it because there was no point. She knew she had written it.

She tried to explain.

"When we first became friends, you hated yoga just as much as I did. We made fun of it all the time. Now, you love yoga and do it all the time. Guess what, I still hate yoga. You've been on this constant string of self-exploration and world discovery for years now, ever since you went to grad school and especially since you lived in Hawaii, and I just don't get it. What's with all the spiritual stuff, all this interest in learning about different religions, all these conversations about 'source energy' and 'vibrational matches' and 'shadow work'? You spent a week volunteering at that Buddhist retreat center, and now suddenly you're going to travel across Thailand with some guy you met there? I can't keep up. You keep changing, and I find it a bit hard to swallow. I really don't know how to relate to you anymore. I mean, I'm grateful for the relationship you have with my kids and all, but maybe don't take them to see any more Buddhist shrines in the mountains on the weekend you have them, ok?"

This was where we should have ended the friendship. This is where I should have called it. This is where I should have let go. This is where I should have moved on.

I often look back and wonder how things could have unfolded differently if I'd only understood how clearly her words represented a fixed mindset, which would never be able to match my preferences for growth and expansion, for seeing new places and trying on new ideas. I mean, she wasn't wrong – I had been on a spiritual journey since taking a class in graduate school called, "Understanding the World's Religions," which cracked my recovering-Catholic-and-bitter-about-it mind wide open, allowing me to ascertain and develop my own understanding and relationship to That Which is Greater. Our friendship had begun growing stale, and if I'd only had the maturity at that point to begin distancing myself in light of my discovery, then perhaps the ugly culmination of the legal battle could have been avoided.

But that's not what happened. What happened that day was she apologized and I forgave and forgot.

Sort of.

2011

My beloved grandmother in Arizona fell drastically ill in February and died in April; I dropped everything to visit multiple times in between those two fateful dates. In the spring, I ran a few more half-marathons, one with Ivy and Alice in Salt Lake City, Utah, and two others with different running friends I'd made in different pockets of the country. There was no spring break trip that year.

I still saw the kids, but not nearly as frequently as in recent years. Instead of being the primary caretaker for the long weekends when Ivy and Angus traveled, I became the one-night relief for their neighbors and extended family who had recently moved to town. I still attended their school concerts and donated organizing sessions to their school auction, but more of my weekends were filled by the new friends I'd made at my new job and through my networking groups.

Ivy still sent me links to their family photoshoots and called me after each girl's school conference to give me updates or trouble-shoot concerns, and sometimes, Ivy and Angus dropped all three kids off at my place so they could have date nights in Denver. I loved these evenings, and would have the kids fed, teeth brushed, and waiting in pajamas when Ivy and Angus returned to retrieve them.

In March of 2011, an unexplainable blotchy rash formed on my forearms and slowly started to spread to my upper arms, torso and legs. I visited a handful of doctors over a handful of months, but nobody – not the allergist nor the holistic healer, the dermatologist nor the nutritionist, could figure out the cause. The rash didn't itch or hurt but neither would it disappear. I changed my diet, my laundry detergent, my body lotion, and my soap, and still it lingered.

"Hahaha, it's not contagious," I would self-consciously explain any time I wore short sleeves in public.

It was Ivy who first gave me the idea that my apartment might be making me sick; after all, it wasn't a legal dwelling, just a slapped-together basement that was only as homey as it was because of my presence and paint colors.

I began to search for a new place to live. Per a friend's suggestion, I bought a black mold test from the local hardware store, which gave a positive result. When my friend-of-a-friend landlady mentioned charging me to clean the carpets after I moved out, I literally laughed in her face and showed her the test.

"Sure, let's balance out the cost of cleaning the carpets with the cost of all my doctor appointments these past few months and see who actually owes what to whom. Or we can just call it good."

We called it good.

I saw a gigantic rainbow spanning the sky as I drove away from that house with the last of my stuff. Rainbows have long been my sign that whatever is troubling me will be okay, and within weeks of moving into a sunny, third floor apartment on the other side of town, my skin cleared up. Good riddance.

January 2012

Saida was right. I met the man I would marry in Colorado. He was everything I'd been hoping for and then some. In a nutshell, he was worth the wait.

It happened fast, as "meant to be" things tend to happen. I made my online dating profile active on a Wednesday, the dating app sent my profile to James on Thursday, he reached out to me via email on Friday, and we had what turned into a seven-hour first date on Saturday.

He called the very next day, telling me he didn't believe in playing games. I couldn't stop smiling. He was a breath of fresh air. Our second date happened the following Tuesday: a basketball game followed by drinks and live music. The conversation flowed, our laughter was contagious. James said he wanted to see where we could take this, that he was ready to take down his dating profile. I agreed, mostly.

"Only thing is," I said, "I already have a date with a firefighter set up for next Monday, when I get back into town." I was leaving the next day for a weekend getaway to visit Amelia in San Francisco.

James encouraged me to go on that date. "If this, here, between you and me, is what I think it is, then I'm really not worried about you going on another first date," he said, "And quite frankly, if you have better chemistry with him, then you should, by all means, be with him, instead."

I went on my trip and dished with my San Francisco pals, ultimately deciding to cancel with the firefighter. I emailed him: "I've begun seeing someone and want to see where it leads. Good luck to you!" The firefighter was kind and understood, and about six weeks later, he emailed again "one more time, just to see" if maybe it was a better time for a first date.

"I'm flattered to hear from you, but am actually still dating that same man, so I'll need to decline your invitation indefinitely. Take care!" He was happy for me.

I was happy for me, too. After years and years of heartache, heartbreak, and heart work, I had finally, at age 37, found the one whom my soul loved.

James was straight out of my wildest romantic dreams – hilarious, intelligent, kind, thoughtful, and remarkably skilled in a variety of impressive ways. He could figure out, fix, weld, or wire just about anything, and knew his way around computers, cars, and construction. He played the guitar. He kept a tidy house. He was lovingly attentive to his two dogs, Cleo and Athena. He rode a motorcycle and drove a pick-up truck. He was back in school getting a degree in finance after decades in the restaurant industry. I was delighted with his ability to create masterpieces in the kitchen, not to mention the magic we created together behind closed doors.

Our bond was profoundly beautiful, and seemed to intensify exponentially by the day. We were in awe of one another, and quickly became irreversibly invested in each other's happiness and well-being. I called us "lucky," he called us "deserving." We called each other "the great love of my life."

In March, we decided to live the rest of our lives together, and he commissioned a ring he designed for me.

In April, I broke my lease at the sunny, third floor apartment to move in with him.

In May, we officially got engaged, and I brought him on a family trip to Florida to meet my parents, my sister, and my three-year and 18-month-old nieces, both of whom I asked to be flower girls in our wedding. Everybody loved him.

In June, we hosted a slumber party so Loretta (12), Rose (10), and Slater (5), could meet Annette (11), and Andy (7), James's niece and nephew, as they would all be in our wedding together. The evening was full of spirited fun, but when it was time for bed, Loretta was upset about having to sleep in a sleeping bag on an air mattress in the same room with the other kids – she wanted to cuddle and fall asleep next to me. In fact, all evening long she would push herself in between James and I every chance she got, hugging my waist tightly and looking at him over her shoulder as she said things like, "You know she loved me first."

I flashed back to Loretta meeting my other young friend, Jane, all those years ago: *"My Alex."*

In July, James and I began a tradition of hosting an Independence Day backyard barbecue, inviting a combination of our friends to meet and mingle. Loretta, Ivy, Angus, Rose, and Slater were all there, and I overheard the kids exhibiting collectively possessive attitudes, pulling rank with the other kids at the party. "Well, Alex is sort of like our aunt, so James is sort of becoming our uncle."

A couple weeks after our party, James and I moved into a new house that didn't contain the ghost of his first marriage. Our lease officially began in August, but we were given the keys in mid-July. When Loretta came to have an overnight, she asked me if we could sleep on an air mattress in the basement of the otherwise empty new house instead of sleeping in the old house where James was. For the sake of adventure, and because I had trouble denying her reasonable requests, I said yes, which is how Loretta came to sleep in our new house before even James did.

September 2012

Exactly 38 weeks to the day after we met, James and I married on a high, sunny mountaintop with a backdrop of snow-capped peaks in the distance. Best decision of my life.

Our sisters stood up on either side of us, while Loretta, Rose, and Annette were junior bridesmaids. My nieces Talia and Evangeline stole the show as our darling flower girls, and Andy and Slater executed their ring bearing duties flawlessly. At my request, Ivy had coordinated my best girlfriends to line the aisle I walked down towards my father. Each friend handed me one of their favorite flowers as I passed them, and this became my bouquet, which Ivy wrapped and tied with a long, black, satin ribbon when I finally reached her, while I hugged and exchanged a laugh with my dad, who then walked me the short remainder of the way to where James was waiting with happy tears brimming in his eyes.

Both Loretta and Rose heaved with sobs through the entire ceremony, starting as I walked down the aisle and not stopping until the entire thing was over.

It was noticeable. "I've never been to such an emotional ceremony!" my mom's friends quipped. "Is this a wedding or a funeral?"

As a happy crier myself, I was touched by the show of emotion. I thought it illustrated how close we were.

I'd tried hard to blend James into my friendship with the X Family, and at the reception, I pulled Loretta and Rose to the side. "You know my getting married doesn't change anything, right?" I said to them. "I love you both and I always will."

"We know," they assured me.

But it turned out, I was really wrong.

It would only be a handful of months before the relationship would not only change, it would completely fall apart.

April 2013

Loretta had a track meet one Saturday morning, and I drove the hour south to meet them all there at 7:00 a.m. Loretta broke a personal record that day and as the meet wound down, I took Rose to Target to buy a few frilly spa things the girls would give Ivy for Mother's Day a couple of weeks later. Rose and I drove back to their house where Loretta and Ivy were working in the garden, and then the girls and I snuggled in front of the television for a show or two before I hit the road, driving the hour back home to prepare for dinner guests that night.

Early the very next morning, James and I were getting ready to meet friends for a motorcycle ride in the mountains when I received a text message from Rose's phone: "*I know you've been lying to us. I know you smoke pot.*"

What in the world? I called Ivy's phone. Rose answered it, and she was hysterical.

"How could you *lie* to us, Alex? How could you *hurt* yourself like that? How could you *break the law*?" She was sobbing through her words, and I asked her to take a deep breath. I could hear Loretta murmuring in the background.

"Rosie, where's your mom?" I asked.

"Out getting doughnuts," she answered. "She left her phone at home."

"Ok, then can I talk to Loretta for a minute? I just want to figure out what exactly is going on over there."

Silence.

"She's not here, either," Rose finally said.

Hmm. "Ok, so then you tell me more. What makes you think I smoke pot? Did someone tell you that? How did this subject come up in conversation?"

She was evasive, stumbling over her words. "Well, I don't know, it's just, I mean, that's not really the important part. The point is that you lied to me."

"I didn't lie to you, Rose. I don't lie to you, ever. I may not tell you every detail of my life, but that's not lying. That's being a responsible grown-up. Kids aren't supposed to hold everything from an adult's world. So I keep parts of my private life private, that's all. I do not lie."

She considered this, said she had to go, and hung up.

When I finally got Ivy on the phone a half hour later, she played the confused card. Her favorite card.

"Oh weird, I had no idea they were talking about that. Loretta must have told Rose about the time she found that pot pipe in the pocket of your fuzzy robe when we helped you move into the moldy basement. That's all I can think it would be," Ivy mused.

I was deeply unsatisfied with the conversation because nothing had been answered let alone resolved, but we were already late for our motorcycle ride so I had to leave well enough alone in the moment. I'd been distracted the entire day trying to puzzle through it in my mind.

That April morning would prove to be the beginning of the end for our friendship. The following week, I drove the hour south as previously planned for Loretta's school concert, where Slater happily jumped into my arms in greeting, and Rose chose to sit in my lap, hold my hand, and play with my hair and my earrings for the duration of the performance. When Loretta joined us all after the show, I watched in surprise as Ivy grabbed her by the upper arm and harshly whisper in her ear to go hug me.

I was mortified and devastated. A cardinal rule of keeping kids safe is to never, ever force them to have physical contact with another human being, and here I was, being hugged by a child because her mother was forcing her. It felt awful, and I cried on my drive home.

When Loretta and I texted weeks later, she said it wasn't even about the pot, and she laid into me with confused, 13-year-old emotions. How was she supposed to feel, she said, when her mom, her mom's friend Eileen, and Angus's cousin, Pam, were all hurt by the way I treated them?

My eyebrow shot up. Um, what's that now? This was interesting insight.

I wrote back, "I don't like Eileen, that's true, but it's okay if you do. Pam and I are on good terms as far as I know, and the same goes for your mom. But dear one, if your mom is having a problem with me, she should be talking to me about it, not you. I am sorry you feel caught in the middle of whatever is happening here."

I set down my phone, sat on the edge of my bed, pressed my fingertips against my closed eyes, and thought to myself, "I don't know how to effectively argue with a thirteen-year-old about her mother's issues, nor am I particularly interested in doing so."

I never did get a satisfying explanation about what, exactly, happened that late April day after I left their house. Ivy played dumb, and I didn't feel comfortable grilling the girls. Ivy became a go-between for me and the kids, and the friendship continued to suffer for it.

It was true that we had been drifting apart for a couple of years already at that point, but the relative quickness of their complete absence from my life cut like a knife. With the blink of an eye, there were no more track meets, no more school concerts, no more birthday dates, and no more phone calls. I'd have dreams of spending time with them, and I'd wake up crying, my pillow wet with tears. When I shared my dreams and feelings with Ivy, she'd deflect, saying, "Hopefully we can make that happen soon!"

June 2013

When James and I took a belated ten-day honeymoon, I sent the X Family a postcard from Greece. *"Miss you all! Hope to see you soon!"* When we returned from our trip, I sent text messages to both Loretta and Rose. "Hope you are having a great day! Miss you!" Loretta didn't respond, and Rose sent back "Who is this?"

"It's me, Rosie. Your old pal Alex."

"Oh, sorry! I got a new phone, and my numbers didn't transfer. I miss you! I'd like to see you," she wrote back and my heart soared.

"I miss you too! I'd love to see you too! Talk to your mom about it and let's make it happen."

Radio silence.

When Loretta joined Facebook in late 2013, I sent her a friend request, but she didn't accept. By then, Rose had blocked me from her Instagram account.

"They need more time, just give them more time," Ivy repeated to me as days stretched into the entire rest of 2013, "Both girls still have framed photos of you in their bedrooms. They just need more time. The pot thing really freaked them out, and they aren't sure how to be friends with both you and Eileen, and since Eileen lives closer and all…"

Can't you teach them how? I wondered when she said this. *Isn't it a parent's job to teach their children how to navigate tricky life situations?*

I sent Ivy a birthday card in early November; she sent one back to me in mid-November. Usually each member of the X family individually signed my cards with loving messages; this year it was only Ivy's name that appeared under a generically scribbled "Happy Birthday!"

Months passed. On a random day in mid-2014, Loretta accepted my Facebook friend request, and I was almost embarrassed by how happy it made me. I rushed into the room where James was folding laundry, bubbling over with excitement at the development. He didn't share my enthusiasm. He didn't understand why I wanted the family back in our lives because he didn't understand why I had loved them so much in the first place. "They're sort of shady, babe," he'd say, referencing the low importance they placed on things like truth and living with integrity – the dented cars they continued to drive after collecting insurance money, the way Ivy lied about the kids' ages to pay lower admission prices to fairs, festivals, and movies, and the way they teased and humiliated each other as forms of entertainment. As far as my husband was concerned, we were better off without them. "You can't help who you love!" I'd argue.

Loretta and I rarely interacted directly on the social media platform, but I cherished the glimpse she'd given me into her 14-year-old world. I listened to the songs she posted, I read the books she talked about. When she posted a request in January of 2015 for her friends to share a fun memory they had experienced with her in 2014, I commented, "I don't have any but I sure wish I did!" to which she replied, "Well, maybe we can make some more memories together this year." I beamed the entire rest of the day, my heart content.

Time had done its job! Healing was happening! We were making our way back to each other! Things could only get better from here; I was sure of it.

Chapter 5

"Don't agonize. Organize." -Florynce Kennedy

It is in my nature to organize.

I spent hours of my childhood arranging and re-arranging my bedroom, my books, my dollhouse, my stuffed animals. I designed elaborate imaginary play games down to specific details, and long, choreographed dances for my friends and me to perform on repeat. One time, my dedication to the details led me to glue cotton balls onto my sister's face to make her look more like Santa. I organized holiday caroling with my peers and created countless clubs with my classmates throughout my earliest years.

There was a writing club in elementary school with a lofty goal of producing a newspaper, a rock club where we foraged our Milwaukee neighborhood for interesting and/or beautiful rocks, and a sticker club where we met during lunch recess to ooh and ahh over one another's assortment of puffy, glittery, and scratch-n-sniff treasures, sometimes making trades. Finally, in junior high, at the exact same time the infamous book series was being launched, I established a babysitting club that included a week-long "day camp," which amounted to morning babysitting in the park for a week during the summer.

Being organized is a skill that serves me well in my professional life, too. In my roles at both Montessori schools, I successfully handled complex logistics around multiple events and processes, putting a personal stamp of improvement wherever needed. These experiences led to the creation and expansion of my own organizing business, through which I organized both people's personal belongings as well as non-profit events and fundraisers.

I have seen how creating order only helps matters, and that the initial energetic output required up front to get organized is always returned in spades down the road.

So from the moment this fiasco began back in September of 2016, the value of gathering all the support I could muster was abundantly clear to me. Not only for legal things like collecting support letters, but also for the care and protection of my own sanity, my own heart.

My professional organizing years also taught me how emotionally draining organizing is when you have strong sentimental ties to the subject at hand. In other words, it wouldn't be possible for me to fight this fight and be in charge of rallying the troops. I would need other people to help me.

Upon arriving home from the very first court date in October of 2016, my sister created a private Facebook group "for those of us dedicated to seeing the truth prevail for Alex."

The group was named after two of my personal life paradigms that skyrocketed in importance since the day of the arrest: Truth Matters, Love Wins.

My lawyer advised I exercise caution around trusting people, and while I respected his position, it directly butted up against my very real need to keep the people who wanted the best for me apprised of what the heck was going on over here.

I was not a member of this intimate group at first, partially to appease my lawyer and partially because I didn't want the prosecution being privy to it should they subpoena my computer (which they never did.) But life has taught me to ask for what I need, and what I needed then was my friends, so I asked my sister to post a letter I wrote to them.

"Dear wonderful, beautiful, amazing friends,

First and foremost, thank you for the outpouring of love and support you've shown me. I carry each thought, each vibe, each prayer so close to my heart, and I lean on them over and over again.

I'm told this road will be long. It is hard, but not impossible, to eventually leave this entire thing behind me, but there is much work to do in order for that to happen.

But you know what, that's ok. I have truth on my side, and I am willing to give that truth as long as it needs to show its beautiful face. This is not a time for rushing. As my lawyer keeps reminding me, this is a marathon, not a sprint.

I've run actual marathons before, and I know I'm capable of the kind of discipline and self-care and patience and determination that marathon running demands. I know how to train. And the reward at the end of this marathon is as important as they come. The reward is my freedom to continue living the heck out of this life that I love so deeply.

Many of you have asked what I need, and right now, I need your love.

I need your thoughts.

Please, please keep me in your hearts.

I'm humbly calling you each to continue holding space for James and me each and every day, from wherever you may be.

Please pray.

Please think good things.

Please hold me in light and love.

Please envision perfect outcomes.

Please cross your fingers.

Please send deep breaths and comfort to my sister and parents.

Please include compassion for the district attorney, the alleged victim, and her family — it is only by sending love out that love will return, and I need swarms of it right now. I promise to continue passing it along.

Thank you! Please know I am loving you from here, and that if we were sitting across from one another right now, I'd lean over and give you the tightest squeeze of gratitude – there would probably be tears in my eyes – and I'd whisper, 'You have no idea how much this is helping.'"

The group becomes a hub for shared information and continuous motivation. I peek in through my husband's account now and then, and I give my sister sporadic updates to pass along. I ask for new music suggestions, then use my friends' recommendations to create a Truth Matters, Love Wins playlist that I listen to constantly.

My pragmatic side recognizes the benefit of staying in the right people's uplifting thoughts so as to counterbalance the collective ugly regard in which so many strangers were already holding me. Not only that, but I believe in the power of collective thought to influence, alter, and affect real change, so the way I figured it, the more folks remembering me in their prayers at night, the better.

For the most part my friends responded beautifully, both inside the group and otherwise. I received texts, private messages, emails, cards, and flowers. So many flowers. The week after my arrest made the news, our table was filled edge to edge with all the flowers, and they spilled over to the countertops.

What else could they do? My friends wanted to know. "I don't know how to navigate this, I've never done it before, but I am here for you," Cecily said to me one day at my front door. It was a sentiment echoed by many.

I was so moved by their willingness to stand by my side and take it all as it came, one step at a time. I'd never done this before either.

Cecily hosted a brunch for me and James on her back porch during the early days for our closest local friends to gather together with us to get the scoop. Some friends sent groceries; others insisted on picking up the coffee tab. Some friends stood up for me in local online communities when the story was spreading like wildfire, while still others solicited anonymous, ongoing support for us from their prayer circles, their book clubs, their other social media groups.

There were immediate offers to hold online fundraisers, which I initially declined. Asking for thoughts and prayers was one thing, but money was another. Asking for money felt like more bother than I wanted to be, which was part of a set of beliefs I'd eventually be forced to dismantle. I relented on the fundraising when Cecily offered to frame the ask as simply inviting friends to take turns sponsoring my safety by funding my "protection jewelry," which is what we'd begun calling my ankle monitor.

In typical Alex fashion, I'd already reframed the ankle monitor not as something that was happening *to* me, but as something that was happening *for* me. Wearing the GPS monitor was technically helpful in proving where I actually was, instead of giving Loretta, Ivy, Angus, or Rose any opportunities to claim I'd been somewhere I wasn't.

In her letter to my friends regarding the fundraiser, Cecily wrote:

"Hi friends! Lots of folks have asked how they can help Alex in a tangible way. In talking with her, one burden she has that could use a little lift is the daily cost of her ankle bracelet. We made a little go fund me page. Proceeds go directly to Alex and they help keep her safe. And please keep sending love, glitter, sunshine and support, because those things matter, too!"

***

As the weeks turn into months, I appreciate the love from my friends more and more, but I quickly realize that the life-long emphasis I'd been in the habit of giving other people's opinions needs to be ripped from the top of my internalized priorities. Opinions are unstoppable, and I literally don't have the time or energetic resources to care about them at large any longer.

But knowing and doing are two different things. It's no easy feat to change more than forty years of conditioning and habitual programming overnight, or for that matter, even over the course of dedicated days, weeks, and months. I trip over my own thoughts constantly, trying so hard to not care, don't care, stop caring, and then berating myself for still caring, kind of a lot, actually.

I flash back to scrolling past my mug shot on my Facebook feed, and I try to pick apart why it still makes me so angry, all these months later. In the grand scheme of things, the woman who posted it is completely inconsequential to me – so why am I so hung up on repeatedly drafting scathing, insulting, defensive emails to her? I cannot seem to let it go when all I desperately want is to let it go.

Around and around I go. It's exhausting.

There is a reckoning that comes from that kind of relentless looking inward, and often the disruption of your patterns and habits is the messiest part of the process.

I spend a lot of time feeling vulnerable and exposed.

And now, faced with the biggest obstacle of my life to date, I have to get real about standing in that vulnerable exposure in order to build strength around my historically weak *"I-don't-care-what-you-think-about-me"* force field.

Ironically, I find it helpful to inundate myself with as many good vibrations as possible, to seek out as much sincere love as feasible, and not surprisingly, to organize all the positive support of the people who recognize the impossibility of these accusations.

Collecting letters of character reference at the beginning reinforced this idea. Once I started making calls, telling the story again and again, the outpouring of support created a palpable change in my levels of resolve. I think it's why I ended up calling so many people. I felt the immediate effect of the support anchoring me. An urgency began to form in those first few weeks around finding energetic shelter with those joining me in my unshakeable belief that everything not only *could* be okay, but that it *would* be okay.

It's almost an oxymoron, trying to practice not caring what my haters think by focusing and leaning into what my supporters think, and I do understand that I can't rely solely on others to sustain me, so while I give deep, daily thanks for the way my friends surround me in this time of need, I also take increased responsibility for my own care.

Self-care can mean choosing behaviors to care for yourself that feel good to you and bring you comfort, like hot baths and weekly pedicures, and it can mean acting in an effort to create healthy systems and processes for all aspects of yourself: physical, mental, emotional, and spiritual.

Accordingly, my self-care practice expands to encompass more than just fluffy, yummy spa-like things. I turn inward for some serious soul work. I figure I'm already down in the emotional trenches of my psyche, so I may as well see what I can clean up while I'm here.

I had stopped going to yoga classes in the community in favor of an online yoga membership site, and through it I explore kundalini yoga. I find a local kundalini center where I attend meditation sessions. Forming new friendships at large feels off-limits during this period of my life, but meditating among strangers feels just right.

I become hypervigilant about the security of our home, double- and triple-checking that the gates, windows, and doors are locked each night, that the curtains are tightly drawn against any glimpse from the outside world. At my insistence, we invest in a video doorbell so we can see who is standing outside when it rings. Even so, James becomes the only one who will answer the door. I refuse, even if I am the only one home. Especially if I am the only one home.

I start therapy on a more frequent basis. My therapist, Bea, holds patient, gentle space for me as I slog through metaphorical darkness to sit in the discomfort of the negative stories about myself ingrained into my psyche throughout my life. I pull apart my past, hungry for redemption for the hurts I caused, willing that redemption to alleviate this weight of a hurt I did not do.

Bea asks if I've ever tried Reiki healing. I have not, but I'm willing, so she refers me to a whip-smart practitioner named Katherine.

Reiki is a Japanese method of stress reduction and relaxation that promotes healing on many levels. Based on the idea that human beings all have and share Universal Life Energy, Reiki allows a release and return of residual energy you may carry that belongs to others, while calling home any bits of your precious energy that may have fragmented off along the way.

I love it immediately.

The 90-minute sessions begin with me randomly plucking five or six little glass dropper bottles out from among the dozens filling the little rolling cart. One by one, I place a drop of each oil under my tongue as Katherine reads from any one of her multitude of books and charts to relay the meanings and messages of the oils. Then I hop up on the table, cover my eyes with a sleep mask and my body with a thick blanket, and we move on to the energy movement part, the laying of hands.

After a brief invocation, we locate where my body is energetically stuck – sometimes I know, sometimes Katherine does. More than once, Katherine verbally describes exactly what I am seeing in my mind's eye, things like the color and texture and density of my energy body. More than once, I cry tears of release under my sleep mask.

A few times, Katherine receives visions of my past lives. The first is a life from the late 1600's where I am burned at the stake for being a witch. She guides me through a visualization of being forcefully taken from my home and unjustly locked up behind bars.

Under my sleep mask in a trancelike state on the Reiki table, I watch my witch trial unfold. I see myself react to the boisterous, nasty crowd sneering and jeering, then cheering when I am sentenced to burn. I feel the ropes being tied too tightly around my wrists, then my ankles. I feel the heat of the fire's flames growing, scorching my physical self, melting the shape of my body. I watch my soul leave that body and rise up, brighter than the shell it leaves behind. I watch the lessons of that lifetime find their proper place in my current energy field.

During a different session, Katherine sees a life where Loretta is my daughter. Loretta is sick, and I can care for her, but I cannot save her. In my mind's eye, I watch Loretta die from her illness. I watch her soul leave her body. I forgive her for being angry that I could not intervene, and I forgive myself for the same thing.

It's like therapy on steroids and still it doesn't feel like enough.

A friend connects me to a woman with a gift of channeling a higher spirit on a metaphysical plane, and when I speak to this woman, she tells me my redemption lies in getting closer to god as I understand it. She tells me to sit in meditation and ask for forgiveness of all wrongdoings in all directions of time and space. Of course I do it. I will try just about anything to untangle this karmic mess.

A different friend takes me to meet with a different woman in a room full of crystals.

"The dad," she says, staring at me while waving a feather around my head, "he was in love with you, no?"

"What? Angus? No." I frown, my nose wrinkling at the very idea. "It was definitely not like that. He's from a family of brothers. He'd say I was like the little sister he never knew he wanted. We were absolutely just friends."

She shakes her head. "No. I'm getting a strong sense he had a thing for you. And his wife didn't like it, and that's what your trouble is about, no? A little lover's quarrel?"

I sigh. "No."

I cry in the car afterwards. I want out of this mess so badly but the situation is so delicate and my emotions so fragile that I realize I cannot keeping sharing with anyone willing to listen. I learn to keep my cards a little bit closer to my chest.

***

During these months that turn into years, I spend chunks of very uncomfortable time wrestling with my own thoughts over why other people's opinions of me hold so much weight in my levels of self-esteem anyways.

When did I give away that power?

Did I ever even hold it at all?

I think about how my own childhood abuse set in motion beliefs about the agency I had over my body as well as the disproportionate value I placed on the way it looked to others above all else.

By age five, I'd already learned my body was a form of currency, that other people would pay special attention to me depending on how I used it or how much of it I showed to them. I learned that the appearance of my body mattered the most.

I grew up looking for examples to reinforce this destructive belief. I found one in fourth grade when I needed to wear a bra before any of the other girls in my class, and again in high school when my normal, teenage sexual appetite had boys making bets about how far they could score with me. By the time I went to university, it was practically habit to prioritize the journey my body could take me on over the path my mind and intellect could.

My regrets feel suffocating. I have so many of them. I regret not speaking up when the abuse happened, although I do not blame myself. After all, I was barely out of preschool, and it's not supposed to be a preschooler's responsibility to fight for their body's safety. That's what adults are supposed to be doing.

Even still, I regret the thought patterns of prioritizing other people's comfort over my own that were created and the belief systems around my body being my most valuable contribution to the world that were instilled in the core of my self-definition as a result of being abused.

I regret that my silence regarding my own abuse has been simmering in the background of my life for forty years, shadowing every decision and shaping my behavior in unsavory and sometimes unsafe ways.

I regret how many times over the years when this misguided sense of self resulted in actions, words, and choices that directly hurt other people and believe me, that list is long. I perpetuated a sometimes questionable moral character throughout my childhood and into early adulthood, and I am embarrassed on behalf of that version of myself. Fortunately, my therapist is highly skilled at helping me dismantle the belief that my past dictates my present and reframe it as stepping stones leading me to both emotional and behavioral maturity.

I can clearly see how moving to Colorado after receiving my degree had been a saving grace in that it ultimately set me on a sustainable, positive trajectory of self-discovery and self-improvement. The quest to be kinder, smarter, and healthier has actively been a part of my life ever since.

I evolved into a do-the-emotional-work type, a generational-curse-breaker type, a healer-of-ancestral-wounds type.

I discovered how to read tarot cards to better understand inner conflict and how to communicate with the universe through hearts and rainbows. I seek guidance from dozens of self-help accounts on social media, and I read scores of non-fiction books to expand my worldview. I believe in science, *and* I am into mystics, miracles, and the power of peace and love.

I became a woman who seeks out metaphysical challenges in the name of enlightenment and alignment with the Divine Source of Pure Life Energy. I am what is often referred to as "woo woo," and I own it.

I did not become a woman who goes looking for trouble.

I did not become a woman who hurts children.

My petty, flawed human bullshit has often tangled me up with my peers, but never with authority figures, and definitely never with any children in my care or under my supervision.

Another regret I have is trusting Ivy with my deepest, darkest secret. I'm angry that it's being used against me in this seemingly careless, malevolent manner and that this anger spills out in unexpected directions, like excessively aggressive road rage, as I work to understand what it is and how to handle it constructively.

However, there is gratitude to be found here too, for the sense of relief that arrives after this sudden, irreversible exposure of my childhood trauma.

And I have Ivy to thank for that.

Because while Ivy was not the only confidante I'd told of my childhood abuse, she was the only one who asked me to share my story with her children.

"It just freaks me out," she said to me in early 2010, "because you never told your parents even though you speak so highly of your childhood, and your relationship with them is so strong, and I just think how easy it could be for something to be happening to my girls right under my nose. Will you tell the girls what happened to you? Will you make sure they know they can talk to you in addition to me and Angus?"

Talk about a favor. I'd had to think about it. The circle of people I'd shared this information with at that point was extremely small and still didn't include my parents. And even though I had touched on it in therapy, that didn't mean I was comfortable talking about it at large, and certainly not with children. When Ivy made her request, Loretta was nine, and Rose was eight.

In the end, I agreed to initiate the conversation with the girls, because Loretta and Rose's safety was important to me, too. I chose to broach the subject one afternoon in the car on our way to their house, when I knew I'd have ample time to tell the story and field any questions.

Telling them about my childhood was nothing new – they often requested re-tellings of favorite tales. This time, I mentioned there was a story about something that happened to me as a very young girl that their mom wanted me to share with them, so if they were open to hearing it, I'd like to tell them during this ride back to their house.

They agreed. I kept the storyline simple, telling facts without graphic details.

"One of my babysitters inappropriately touched me when I was very young. She did it more than once, but I never told my parents about it. I wish I would have because telling them would have helped me while I was growing up."

The girls were quiet, absorbing my words. I kept my eyes on the road, my voice casual.

"If anything like that ever happens to either of you, even one time," I reiterated, "it's very important for you to tell a grown up that you trust. That, of course, could be your mom or dad, or your grandma, or your teachers, or me. There are lots of people in your lives who love you and want to keep you safe."

When I asked if they had questions, Rose wanted to know how come I never told my parents.

"That's a great question," I said as I briefly met her eyes in the rearview mirror. "I was a very little girl, younger than you are now, and best I can remember is thinking it was a sort of secret game I got to play with that babysitter, but then as I got older and started to understand what had really happened to me, I think I just got embarrassed. I figured it'd be easier to pretend it never happened and just move on. But it wasn't easier. It actually made some things harder."

Talk about an understatement.

"So," I continued, "I'd like to hear you both say you'll speak up right away if anyone tries to hurt you the way my babysitter hurt me. Can you both promise me that?"

They did. They promised.

And I felt peace around deciding to take my negative experience and use it for good, for helping to keep those girls safe, like an added layer of protection to shield them from anything like this ever happening to them. It felt like I was helping and healing at the same time, right up until I was sitting in that detective's office six years later, being accused of being the babysitter who abused the little girl.

Talk about a backfire.

Except not really. Because it wasn't until after my arrest, when I finally told the truth to my parents, that I realized how very heavy the invisible burden of silence had truly been. My parents were heartbroken for my experience and sorry for not knowing. As the legal battle marched on, they remained unwavering in their support through every twist and turn.

***

The few times I scroll through Ivy's social media – she switches back and forth between an open account and a private one many times over the months – I find emotional posts referring to me as a sociopath and a predator, saying she hopes I get the help I "clearly so desperately" need.

It makes me sad, but not because of her name-calling. I know I'm neither a sociopath nor a predator so it's easy for me to dismiss her rants as the mistakes they are.

The part that makes me sad is the misdirection of her declaration – it is actually her daughter who "clearly so desperately" needs help, but that can't happen until Loretta realizes and can admit she is wrong. Her mental health is further deteriorating with every day that passes, and even with everything that's happened, I still feel bad for her about that.

There was once a time when I would have been a person who could help Loretta navigate this type of tricky life situation, but that ship has sailed.

Through various pieces of submitted Discovery the prosecution provided over the months, I learned that only Rose remembers that the babysitter abuse was my story first. Loretta's memory of our conversation was jogged only by Rose's response when Rose was informed of her sister's allegations.

"Hey," Rose had said, "didn't the same thing happen to Alex as a kid?"

"Oh yeah," Loretta reportedly responded, "I remember something about that now."

Ivy claimed to have no idea I'd ever been abused. She said she first learned of it when Rose asked the question.

But I know better, and I can prove it.

Chapter 6

"Truth will ultimately prevail where there is pains to bring it to light." –George Washington

October 2016 - Colorado

Dear Lawyer,

Quick question about the modifications to the protection order. What is defined as "direct contact" with minors? For example, I have Book Club once a month and some of the women have kids. Am I allowed to go to their homes for the meeting, even if their kids are elsewhere in the house? Additionally, I meet many different friends to walk around the lake near my house on a regular basis. What if I meet a friend and she is pushing her baby in the stroller as we walk?

Thanks,

Alex

Hi Alex,

These are all good questions. Unfortunately, you need to stay away from places where there are kids directly in the home or directly with you. You are only allowed incidental contact, such as walking past a kid at the lake, as opposed to going there to walk with someone who has a kid.

-Lawyer

So my personal world is shrinking and my professional life has imploded into a heap of false rubble around my GPS-monitored feet.

I'd already begun my Health Coach certification program when this debacle landed in my lap, subsequently loosening my grip on my lessons for a few weeks while I tried to make some sense of what appeared to be a new normal for which I was neither bargaining nor prepared. I realize now how important it is to finish my training and collect my certification so I have the credentials and experience to run with it after I can, god willing, put this fiasco behind me.

I start spreading the word of my practice coaching availability in various pockets of the internet that I frequent, a group of friends here, a group of acquaintances there. I get a bite – a local fitness personality I follow on social media, Regina Boxer, is looking for someone like me to join her team. I'm a bit apprehensive due to the fact that this woman has a reputation in the Denver fitness community for being notoriously difficult to deal with, but hey, beggars can't be choosers.

I am forthcoming about my circumstances, and she is soothing and welcoming as she offers to take care of me during this terrible turn of events. She does ask, however, that I do not share my personal situation with anyone else on the team. From a professional point of view, this makes complete sense, but I personally have mixed feelings about the request.

On the one hand, it'd be nice to have a reprieve from my situation in my day-to-day interactions; surprisingly, one of the most emotionally exhausting components of this ordeal is wondering who has seen the news reports, who has read the online articles, who might recognize me from the publicized mugshot.

For example, when our washing machine dies at the beginning of the month, my parents generously offer to buy us a new one, and when we go to Sears to pick it out, the salesperson says, "You look so familiar to me."

My stomach lurches as I raise my eyes, but I see that he is speaking to my husband, not me. I step outside to get some air and steady my racing heart. I'm on the verge of tears the rest of the time we're there.

Our neighbors see the online stories; they offer condolences when we talk over the backyard fence. They decide to not tell their kids. "There's no need to even put the idea in their head." This calms me, makes their belief in me feel evident, and that kind of support makes an astounding difference. Not every interaction with folks "in the know" goes as smoothly.

I'm at Old Navy shopping for new pants that allow for a bulky ankle monitor when I run into the head of the board from which I'd been recently dismissed.

"Hi!" she exclaims in an automatic *I-know-you-from-somewhere-don't-I* kind of way.

I softly smile my "hello," already turning to go as I watch the click of recognition and the flash of judgement land all over her face, an "Oh!" escaping from her lips. I leave without buying anything.

I see another board member at a large, neighborhood gathering of the local Beer Club my husband is a member of. Oh, that's right, we live within blocks of one other. I don't speak to her, and she doesn't speak to me. I spend the rest of the outing wondering who else knows. Are they talking about my situation right now? Am I the proverbial elephant in the room?

I hate it. I hate this feeling of being trapped in an ugly bubble of the media's making so when Regina stipulates I keep my personal situation under wraps at work, carving out eight hours a day where no one has my fiery ball of personal hell in the back of their mind as we speak is appealing. But at the very same time, I recognize how it effectively silences me about the truth of my life during the exact time period when what matters the most is telling the truth about my life. An unusual paradox, to say the least.

However, in this job-offering conversation I am feeling desperate, so I shrug off the embarrassment I feel by promising to keep quiet. It may not sit right, but I can start tomorrow, I'll work from home, and my first paycheck will land in my bank account on Friday. Suddenly, I'll be getting paid to charge my ankle monitor.

The serendipity of the timing is not lost on me, either. I am offered the new position on October 31st, 2016, which is the exact "Pay Until" date on the broken contract from my former client. This will pick up right where I'd been left dangling, and while it'll demand more of my hours than the last gig, I've got nothing but time right now. The increased hours also mean my paychecks will more than double. Hello, silver linings!

I am so lucky.

This opportunity feels like a blessing, and in some ways it is. The company headquarters are situated in a mansion on the beach, and Regina wants to fly me out there right away. Can I come in early December? I explain that my travel is restricted, so there are hoops to jump through first. My lawyer will need to inform the prosecution as well as request permission from the judge at my next court date, which is in a few weeks. She says it's an inconvenience, having to wait, but that she understands. I tell her I will let her know the court's decision as soon as I do.

November 2016

Before we arrive at that court date, the prosecution makes their first plea bargain offer. It takes prison off the table.

A plea bargain is simply a legally binding contract between a criminal defendant and the state that is bringing the charges against the defendant. In the typical plea agreement, a defendant agrees to enter a guilty plea on at least one charge in exchange for one or more of the other charges being dismissed or reduced. A defendant can also elect to enter a no-contest plea, which basically means they are not admitting guilt; they are simply electing to eliminate the expensive, time-consuming process of contesting the accusation.

Here's what I'm offered: in exchange for prison time, I can choose to admit to an underlying assumption of guilt (I'm not given the no-contest option), register on a sex offenders list, go through sex offender rehabilitation therapy, and then go through a probationary period, with a sex felony remaining on my record for the rest of my life.

Objectively speaking, a plea agreement can make sense because trials are risky, juries are unpredictable, and even the best lawyer obviously cannot promise or guarantee a specific result in any given case.

Not only that, but in Colorado specifically, *fewer than five percent* of the charges filed by prosecutors become formal courtroom trials. Prosecutors *depend* on plea bargains to collect "guilty" verdicts.

Colorado isn't alone. According to the Bureau of Justice Statistics for the United States Department of Justice, 90-95% of guilty convictions come from plea bargains each year. Without the use of plea bargains, the criminal court system in all fifty states would quickly become unworkable. Trials take a lot of time and a lot of resources, and they disrupt many people's lives. 90-95% is an overwhelming majority, and it's my understanding that this is often due to the accused being unable or unwilling to afford the required time, money, energy and/or all of the above to adequately defend themselves through the lengthy and confusing process.

I am not guilty of these crimes and cannot stomach the thought of entertaining anything they offer except a dismissal. They may have sucked me up in their current, but I will not get pulled out with their tide. I decline the offer.

My parents, sister, and nieces visit for Thanksgiving, even though it is not typical for us to spend the holiday together. They come in part because of the timing of my court date, which is scheduled for the day before Thanksgiving, and also because we're collectively a little sad and a little nervous about the option being unjustly taken away indefinitely. We feel a need to be in close physical proximity.

They stay in a nearby hotel, but my sister stays at our house the night before court. I meditate for the full two hours it takes the blue candle wax to burn away into nothingness, and I wake up on court day before dawn's first light. I am showered, dressed, and outside by sunrise, praying my prayers and stomping on strategic corners of the backyard.

The Lord is my shepherd; I shall not want.

My sister comes with James and me to the courthouse, which is much quieter today. Neither Ivy, nor Angus, nor the district attorney are there. Instead, a different DA stands in, asking for a continuance of the preliminary hearing on the prosecution's behalf, which is granted.

I am asking for another bond modification today: permission to travel out of state for both my new boss's request as well as a family visit to Wisconsin. I waive my right to a speedy trial today; while I am anxious to get this mess straightened out, I am crystal clear on how important it is to get it right, which means not hurrying. Permission to travel is granted – *kindness, collected* - and another court date is set for the bottom of December.

I go across the street to check in with my assigned pre-trial officer, who predictably asks if I've had any changes to my address or phone number or any interactions of any kind with any police officers. No, no, and no. Every three days, as is expected of me, I call my bondsman, Ricky.

All things considered, it's a wonderful Thanksgiving weekend. My friend Milly offers to take family pictures for us, which we do on a crisp day at the nearby lake. We pass time recounting family stories that have us laughing until we cry, as is our family tradition. We eat like royalty and play board games and watch football, and I recognize that this gift of close proximity happened because of the legal situation, and so I find myself feeling gratitude for Loretta and her family, thanking them for this roundabout way of getting my family together for the holiday.

One afternoon my sister, nieces, and I are enjoying an at-home spa day, complete with DIY face masks, pedicures, deep conditioning hair treatments, and bubble baths for the girls, when nine-year-old Talia asks a question.

"Auntie Alex, why do you have that big black thing attached to your ankle?"

Six-year-old Evangeline looks over to hear my answer, and I choose my words carefully.

"Well, my darling, here's why. Some confused people with ugly in their hearts have told some loud lies about me, and a judge is helping us solve the problem. This monitor is one way the judge is helping me stay safe in the meantime because it keeps track of where I am, so those people can't tell any more lies about where they think I am or what they think I am doing."

Talia stares at the bulky contraption as she digests what I've said, then nods her head. Evangeline has already gone back to her nail polish. We move on.

December 2016

Dear Alex,

To review, at court on Wednesday, we will just be doing a waiver of the preliminary hearing. As we've discussed, a preliminary hearing is when a judge listens to all the collected evidence, including hearsay, and determines if there is enough to warrant a jury trial. We are waiving it in exchange for another plea offer from the prosecution, which I will relay to you as soon as I receive it.

-Lawyer

Dear Lawyer,

I was hoping to revisit the ankle monitor on Wednesday, too? I'm so over it.

-Alex

Dear Alex,

I totally sympathize. We can ask again in this courtroom. But keep in mind we are in front of the same judge for now. Other than some time passing, not much has changed.

Ankle monitors are unfortunately way overused by the courts and it is a habit that is very hard to break them from. The fact the court carved out some exceptions for you to see and care for kids outside of your family is, in and of itself, highly unusual. So I doubt she will go a step further.

Once we waive the Preliminary Hearing and get up to the District Court judge who will hear your case from here on out, we may have a better shot.

But I can still try to ask on Wednesday. With you being compliant on pre-trial and being allowed to travel on the GPS, maybe the court will have a change of heart.

-Lawyer

Dear Lawyer,

Yes, please ask. Thanks!

-Alex

I meditate for two hours the night before, and I double-check all the window and door locks before bed. I pray and stomp around my backyard in the morning. My lawyer emphasized last time that it was unnecessary for my sister to travel out for each and every court date, reminding us "this is a marathon, not a sprint." So this morning it is just me and James who meet him.

We may still be at the same level of court, but we unexpectedly have a different judge on the bench today. When the DA challenges our request for the ankle bracelet removal on behalf of the family like we knew she would, my lawyer takes advantage of the fresh ears.

"Your Honor, the prosecution has dragged my client's name and photo all over the place trying to gather more ammunition, to label her a 'danger to the community,' but it's actually resulted in the opposite effect. My client has experienced an outpouring of support, as evidenced by the letters we've shared with the court thus far.

"It's been four months without one single additional accusation," my lawyer continues, "Four months of an ankle monitor for an accusation that's almost ten years delayed."

This last bit catches the judge's attention. I can tell by his expression that the delayed nature of a single accusation puts a different perspective on the perceived necessity of a monitor. He confirms the timeline of the case with the DA, and then much to my delight, my lawyer's surprise, and the DA's chagrin, the judge rules in my favor. The monitor comes off today.

Kindness, collected.

I am beaming as I offer up an immediate, silent prayer of thanks to the universe followed by another hopeful intention: "May this be but a precursor for freedoms still on their way to me."

I hear my husband's faint "yes!" from behind me in the seated crowd.

It may be a small victory but small victories add up, and because I know my mindset is a crucial component to keeping my spirit strong, I intend to celebrate every single one of them.

Energy flows where attention goes.

I joyfully cross the street to check in with my pre-trial officer, where she unstraps the bulky contraption from my body once and for all. I've been wearing it since my release from jail almost four months ago. At $11 a day, this amounts to a total cost of roughly $1,320. When Cecily's fundraiser ended last month, the total raised was $1,414.

Kindness, collected.

***

As if the cumulative weight of the legal situation isn't heavy enough to lug around on a daily basis, my job quickly becomes a confusing and disappointing way to spend my days, and the rumors turn out to be true - my new boss is a nightmare.

What had once felt like warm and fuzzy divine intervention at the start - *"Even when life shits on you, it can also shine,"* I'd captioned an ocean view on social media during my December trip to the mansion on the beach – quickly reveals itself to be an emotionally unsafe situation full of its own hidden dangers.

Regina is a jarring juxtaposition of an on-screen personality dripping with sweet support mixed with a behind-the-scenes land-mine of verbal daggers, pathological lies, and overt martyrdom. The more I see, the more I question my ability to hold the necessary mental space for the job, but I feel beat down and backed into a professional corner, especially as our legal bills continue to accu-mulate. Other options are nearly impossible to uncover. I am not able to "put myself out there," as my coaching business training program keeps encouraging me to do. This is not the right time to give free talks in the community, attend networking events to spread my name around, or draw any attention of any sort to me at all, so I stomach the micro-managing and tolerate the moving targets of Regina's emotional whims. Working with her is often a lot like diffusing an angry toddler, and I'm skilled at that.

I focus on being grateful that I have a job at all. There are obvious perks to the position, like the flexibility of time off for my court dates, the work travel to the beach where I can also visit with nearby friends and family who are balm to my soul, and of course the paycheck. While I am sincerely appreciative for all these things, I am astounded at their steep exchange rate. It is both shock-ing and acutely uncomfortable when Regina gossips about other team members to me during our calls, how she heaps blame and steals credit, bitching all the while about everyone else's perceived shortcomings. It makes me ill to think about her talking about me like that in other meetings, so I quickly become very guarded with what I share with her, especially about my personal situation.

"How did I end up with the worst job of my life during the worst stretch of my life?" I moan to my husband more than once. The irony of it is almost comical. Almost.

March 2017

On a Wednesday in the middle of the month, I hunker down in a conference room for an eight-hour, emotionally laborious meeting with my lawyer to prepare for my arraignment in court the following Monday, and also to comb through certain aspects of our general defense. An arraignment is when a defendant pleads guilty, not-guilty, or no-contest. The meeting drains my energetic bandwidth and fills my head with scary potentialities. All I want to do is curl up in a ball and cry as I quietly process the weight of this situation.

But I can't. I have a bustling, high-energy, bring-your-A-game work conference to attend in California with Regina. I've been pep talking myself into being excited about it for weeks, but when I wake up before the sun to catch my flight on Thursday morning, I'm fresh out of pep.

It's too much. This is all too much.

The enormity of what I'm up against in the legal system comes crashing down around the sheer dread I'm drowning in from the thought of having to spend concentrated time in Regina's energy vortex. I tip. A full-blown panic attack swoops in and steals my breath, and I crumple in defeat onto the rectangular brown leather ottoman in my living room. My entire body heaves as I gasp and sob and shake with my knees curled into my chest. I hold nothing back, trying to exorcise the pain with guttural howls into the soft early morning sunlight streaming through the gaps in the curtains, as my concerned husband gently, lovingly, rubs my back, his face silent and sad. He is there, which is all I need him to be right now.

When the panic attack subsides, after James has patiently led me through to the calm side of my breath cycle again, I call my sister. I need her no-nonsense guidance and steady voice to help me decompress. It is early, but she answers, and after we hang up she calls back fifteen minutes later. She has booked a last-minute ticket for a lightning-quick trip to Denver so she can be with me in court on Monday. She'll be waiting at my house when I get home on Sunday night. I cry fresh tears of gratitude.

I am so lucky.

The conference in California is a frenzy of energy with thousands of attendees and mercifully I am spared too much alone time with Regina. The weather is warm and sunny, and I manage to sneak in a few bucket-filling, laughing hours with friends who live nearby so the weekend provides more rejuvenation than I was expecting.

Plus, there is peace to be found in the pockets of time I spend by myself in airports and on airplanes, where nobody at all knows me or my story. And all the travel Regina has required of me lately has provided plenty of chances to play Solitaire on my phone, a pleasure I only partake in when I fly. Every time I successfully complete a game, the flashy graphics exclaim, "You win!" and I nod as I silently repeat it like a mantra to myself, every single time, willing it to be true, speaking it into existence.

I win, I win, I win…

True to her word, my sister is waiting for me at the house when I get home on Sunday night, and we sit out on the back porch with James for a nightcap and pep talk conversation.

Meditate. Sleep. Pray. Stomp.

He maketh me to lie down in green pastures; He leadeth me beside the still waters.

The next morning, we are almost through the long, winding, courthouse security line when I see Ivy and Angus walking into the building. This time, Loretta is with them.

We haven't shared space in over three and a half years, and suddenly, here she is, my accuser. I feel the all-too-familiar shards of anxiety settle like stones in my stomach as I watch the X family make their way through the lobby. Because of the layout, our position near the end of the line is mere yards away from their position when they enter the line.

Loretta and I make eye contact. I watch her realize who I am. With a sad smile and disappointed eyes, I give a barely perceptible shake of my head.

Oh dear one, what are you doing?

She looks away.

Angus again tries to stare me down with a menacing look, and I, again, am unflinching with my eye contact. He looks away first. Ivy won't look at me at all.

My lawyer mentions how highly unusual it is for Loretta to be here; there's no need for it, and bringing minors, even 17-year-olds, is frowned upon.

The DA lights up when she sees me, which makes me wonder if she momentarily has forgotten how she knows me. She approaches my lawyer and me and tells us she strongly discouraged Loretta's unorthodox attendance but was told Loretta wants to "see what it is like" to be in a courtroom downtown.

Also: "The family is asking if we can go to trial sooner than later because of Loretta's school schedule. They'd like to wrap things up before August 15, if possible."

My sister's jaw drops open. I know better than to laugh out loud so I bite the inside of my lip instead to fight the impulse. James exhales sharply. My lawyer doesn't even flinch. "No. Loretta's timeline is not even a minor consideration for us. Thanks for relaying the message. The answer is no."

My plea is Not Guilty, because I am not. That they won't let you plead "innocent" feels like just another way the system is slanted, but Not Guilty will have to do for now.

I hold my head high, my shoulders back. I smile. This one feels good.

I go across the street to check in with my pre-trial officer; every three days, I call my bondsman.

April 2017

The DA extends another offer, and once again, my lawyer suggests I take it.

Hi Alex,

Please allow me to re-emphasize that the F4 non-sex child abuse offer that the DA made is an excellent and highly unusual offer to receive in a case such as this.

You are looking at 8-to-24 years to life in prison if convicted on the pattern count, and 20-life probation if convicted on the other counts. If you took the F4 plea, you could argue for and might get just probation. Even if you got prison, the max prison you would do is 6 years, instead of 8-24 to life.

If you take the F4 offer, you'll still have to agree to an underlying factual basis of sexual contact, which would in turn trigger sex offender treatment and registration but you would not have a sex offense on your record.

I know that a plea and sex offender treatment/registration of any kind are things you have not been willing to accept so far. But it is my responsibility to explore all offers, and to stress to you that this is a very good offer. Even if it ends up being the final offer, it is one you must strongly consider taking. That said, you are the one who ultimately must make this decision and I will support and fight for you whatever direction you decide to take.

Let me know,

Lawyer

Dear Lawyer,

No, thanks. No offers. I decline.

Thanks, Alex

***

In therapy, I am asked, "Do you realize you're not breathing? You sit still as a statue for extended periods of time then you take giant gasps for air. You do it over and over again."

I am six months into this experience and still in such a state of trauma that I cannot catch my breath.

June 2, 2017

Meditate. Check the locks. Sleep. Pray. Stomp.

He restoreth my soul; He leadeth me in the paths of righteousness for his name's sake.

Today in court is a Motions Hearing, where we'll argue with the prosecution about what can and cannot be allowed into evidence at trial, which is set to begin in November.

Jury selection is assigned to the 14th, and trial will begin on November 15th, which happens to be my birthday. I decide to take this as another good sign. The way I'm choosing to see it, there is no better birthday present than letting the truth set you free.

Loretta, Ivy, and Angus are also in the courtroom today. Angus taps away at his laptop the entire time, distracted.

My friends Alice and Cecily sit in our row with me and James. I'd reached out for a physical show of support for this appearance because I am requesting yet another bond modification: if people are well aware of my situation, why can't they choose for their own families whether or not to allow me around their children? The prosecution offers a flimsy argument around needing to protect "the safety of the community."

But the judge isn't having it. "Why does this alleged victim's family get to have a say in what happens with somebody else's family?" he asks. "The defendant has not been convicted of anything. That doesn't make sense. I am very uncomfortable with forbidding people who have basically nothing to do with this case from doing what they will with their own children. I'll modify the bond in favor of Ms. Kuisis."

Kindness collected.

I go across the street to check in with my pre-trial officer, and every three days, I call my bondsman, Ricky.

Ricky has gotten chatty over the months. Conversations that started out with two-line dialogues have morphed into 5-10 minute back and forths where Ricky shares his opinions about my case – he thinks it's preposterous – and tells me details of other cases he's bonded. He always asks the latest that my lawyer has to say. I placate him the best I can without actually sharing any real detail. I rejoice every time I get sent to voicemail.

October 2017

One night early in the month, Cecily and I ditch out of our book club retreat a night early to hunker down at my house to create what I call my Box of Proof: a file box filled with folders that chronologically parallel Loretta's allegation timespan, May of 2008 to May of 2010, one folder assigned to each week.

I'd first gotten the idea for the Box of Proof shortly after we learned the confusing allegations. I wanted to overlay what Loretta was claiming with what I'd actually been doing. Since I am an enthusiastic lifelong recorder of personal history, I immediately had confidence in how much information the completed project had the potential to convey.

When I say "enthusiastic lifelong recorder of personal history," what I mean is I am an avid photographer, a regular journal keeper, and a faithful ticket-stub collector. Like with organizing, these have been parts of my livelihood since childhood.

Additionally, there was that public blog about my personal life from 2004-2014, and although they'd been since pulled off the internet, I have dated online copies of the thousands of entries I wrote documenting that decade.

What's more, Ivy and I shared countless Instant Messenger (IM) conversations over those years, which I soon learn are all accessible to me simply by searching for her name in my Gmail search bar.

Since my arrest, I'd spent multiple hours poring over those conversations, those blog entries, those photographs, those ticket stubs, and those journals. Cecily and I were dedicating a whole evening to organizing everything while completing a corresponding spreadsheet for easy reference of which kind of supporting evidence existed for each weekend.

My lawyer initially seems puzzled by my project. He warns there's no way a judge will ever let us spell out 104 weeks' worth of file folder contents, but I am not fazed. This is a tangible way to use my personal strengths to be active in my own defense. I just know I can line up these resources I have available to me in a concise if not complex way that will support the truth of my innocence, and so I proceed.

"Trust me," I tell him.

When I later share my progress, the value of what I am producing takes shape for him, and he encourages me to keep going, even beyond the named time period if I can.

And I can. I track through to the end of 2010, and then to the end of 2011, even after I'd moved out of the moldy basement apartment and into that sunny 3rd floor apartment across town, a place Loretta doesn't mention in any of her accusations.

According to Loretta, misdoings only occurred in places where I lived or where I brought her, never in her home, and only when she was alone with me, never while her sister was there, too. This automatically narrows the field of plausible opportunity, since the kids never stayed at my house on school nights (you may recall that I lived anywhere from sixty minutes to 1,100 miles away during her alleged timeframe), and Loretta's solo sleepovers over the years were actually rather few and far between.

In my Box of Proof, each dated folder contains some combination of those indications of where I was, what I was doing, and with whom I was doing it on any given weekend: a blog post, a journal entry, photographs, ticket stubs, and/or instant messenger conversations with Ivy.

Weekend by weekend, I relive places and faces of the past.

Folder by folder, I collect nuggets of my whereabouts that shape a narrative of my innocence.

I literally dance around my home the first time I realize how fully I can complete this puzzle. To say my spirits are buoyed by this is an understatement. It's still a complicated story, but if we break it down one allegation at a time...

Loretta is saying abuse happened "for sure" in 2008 in a house where I was housesitting, with a bathtub that made bubbles as high as the ceiling. She's talking about my part-time nanny family, the ones I can prove I didn't meet until 2010. I still lived in Santa Barbara in 2008, with an extended stay at my sister's in Wisconsin that summer. I did not housesit in Colorado in 2008.

Loretta says there was "definitely" a hot tub at that housesitting location, but there was not. She says Ivy and Rose dropped her off there, that we all did a pajama walk together before Ivy and Rose left. I can show that the night she stayed over there was the night of Angus's 40th birthday party, and that I dropped Loretta off to Ivy at the airport the next morning. Rose saw the house because she had also stayed there with me a few nights prior. Ivy had never been there at all.

Loretta is saying abuse happened in the moldy basement apartment, maybe even twice. She's not sure, she says, it could have been twice. But all my weekends are accounted for; I literally have the receipts to prove it. There was not even one night Loretta stayed over by herself, let alone two. Sure, she'd *visited* that moldy basement plenty of times, and she did sleep over a couple nights with Rose and even once with Ivy and Slater, too, but by herself?

Nope. Not even one single time!

And finally, Loretta is saying that abuse happened at the home I moved to upon my 2009 Colorado return, the cookie-cutter home in the suburbs. At this house she did stay with me by herself one single time. It was the night Ivy asked me to take Loretta after Rose's birthday party in 2010, the night Loretta and I saw the 10:00 p.m. showing of the three-hour "Avatar" movie, the night we got home close to 2:00 a.m., then met Ivy, Rose, and Slater for breakfast the next morning.

It's the only one of her claims that falls in the realm of possible. And since the rest of her stories are provable falsehoods, will a jury see the reasonable doubt around the plausibility of this one?

I sure hope so.

There is one more story Loretta has about spring break 2009, the second year she and Rose came to visit me in Santa Barbara, the year we talked about tampons, which the prosecution is using as a grooming angle. It's not an actual charge, this California allegation, because Colorado courts can only make charges on allegations reported to have happened in Colorado, not California. But the prosecution will be telling the California story anyway in an effort to sway the jury in their direction, so we still need to defend against it.

Perhaps not surprisingly, the California tale is also confusing. Loretta claims it was so hot we slept without pajamas and that Rose slept by herself in a different bedroom. But historical weather data shows the nighttime lows in the mid-40's – low-50's range the week they visited, and Rose herself confirmed in her forensic interview that we all three slept in the same place on all nights of the vacation.

Into the box it all goes.

***

With the evidence from my own mini-investigation falling into place, I turn my attention to the psychology of a trial. I need to prepare both my troops and my thoughts.

Enter Amelia. Wonderful, thoughtful, amazing Amelia.

Amelia had cried with me when I first told her what was unfolding, and then basically sprung to action in the next breath.

She created "Love in Action," a smaller, still private subset of the "Truth Matters. Love Wins" group, designed to corral friends both local and long-distance who were ready and willing to activate their support.

Additionally, she crowd-sourced thousands of lawyers in various groups she is a part of, collecting both helpful intel and seasoned perspective, welcome advice and creative ideas. Between her consultations and the internet articles I read ad nauseam, we honed in on a few tangible ways to build on the positive momentum my friends have created with their solidarity and support.

For example, does it matter what I wear during trial?

Yes, the collective answer immediately comes.

"Watch almost any movie with a trial in it, you'll notice the good guys are always in white, while the bad guys all wear black."

I already own one white blazer, and I scour sale racks to procure two more. I spend entire evenings trying on various configurations of outfits, sending pictures to Amelia for feedback. We spread the word to anyone planning on coming to court – we're all wearing pastels this week, gang!

October 13, 2017

Meditate. Check the locks. Sleep. Pray. Stomp.

Yea, though I walk through the valley of the shadow of death, I will fear no evil; for thou art with me.

Breathe.

Trial is being postponed.

I am furious when it is first decided. So many people from my side have cashed in vacation time from work, arranged hotel stays, and secured airfare. But the last thing the legal system concerns itself with is the convenience of those affected. Plus, the move is actually my side's doing.

Months ago, way back in February, my lawyer asked me to reach out to Jonathan, to see if he'd be willing to testify on my behalf. I had hesitated.

"Do I have to? I'd really rather not. Things between us didn't end well. In fact, he might not even remember my last name."

"Well, you don't have to do anything," my lawyer had responded. "But it is definitely in your best interest to turn over every stone here, don't you think?"

Of course he's right. It would seem this situation is just one opportunity after another to get over myself. I am up for the challenge, but I negotiate with my lawyer anyway.

"If I can track Jonathan down and give him a basic introduction to what's going on here, will you be the point person going forward?"

My lawyer agrees.

I still have a few social media connections leftover from the Jonathan days, and I reach out to one of them. "I know it's been a while, and that this is coming out of left field, but I need to get in touch with Jonathan, and am wondering if you have his current contact information?"

After my contact reaches out to him for permission as a courtesy, Jonathan's number is shared with me. So he hasn't forgotten who I am.

I call him from my car after the meeting with my lawyer. I feel a twinge of residual nerves trying to surface as I punch in the numbers, but I dismiss it immediately. I've come too far and surmounted too much, especially in the recent past, to slide back into antiquated mindsets of bygone eras.

Jonathan answers on the third ring, and we exchange brief pleasantries before I fill him in on my reason for calling.

"Oh wow," he says, "That's messed up. You're, like, the exact last person in the world who would do something like that."

I ask if he remembers the girls. He does. I ask if he remembers witnessing our interactions. He does. I ask if he'll help. He will.

"I'm so sorry this is happening to you," he says. "It's not right, and I will for sure help get you out of this mess in any way I can."

Kindness collected.

I am grateful and relieved. I thank him and tell him my lawyer will be in touch.

Eventually, it comes to light that Jonathan is scheduled to be out of the country conducting international business during the November trial dates, and because my lawyer feels Jonathan is an integral part of our defense, we conclude that we need a new trial date. My initial anger has settled into a steadfast attitude of "whatever it takes."

Today we're in court to set that new trial date.

When the date is assigned, I can't help but smile. Instead of beginning on my birthday in November, trial will begin in April, on my beloved late grandmother's birthday. Another good sign, especially when I remember that today is the birthday that my maternal grandfather and paternal grandmother shared when they were both alive. My ancestors keep showing up in big ways. I am not alone.

I go across the street to check in with my pre-trial officer, and every three days, I call my bondsman.

January 2018

The district attorney assigned to my case has accepted a position in a new division, and my case is re-assigned to two new district attorneys.

That's right, two. Just like Saida suggested might happen sixteen months ago.

I reach out to Saida to confirm her vision and to ask for more glass jar bindings to bury in my backyard. I decide to bind the judge, too, now that I know he'll be presiding over the rest of my case.

Three more holes are dug in the backyard. Three more glass jars buried. Three more stomping grounds anointed.

Saida also sends me extremely specific instructions for additional meditations she directs me to do – what color ink to use, which hand to use to light the candle, where to sprinkle the enclosed powder, how many times to say which prayer, and when.

Example One, **The Root Prayer**
- *Say the Lord's Prayer three times.*
- *Anoint the three enclosed roots with court oil then place them back in the bag.*
- *Hold the root bag in your left hand while reciting Psalm 35 nine times.*

Example Two, **The Jar Bindings**
- *Recite The Lord's Prayer three times.*
- *Recite Psalm 80 three times.*
- *Use red ink to write down the names of those involved on each individual paper. For example, attorneys, judges, jury members.*
- *Hold the Root bag in your right hand. Say each name three times then add their name to the jar.*
- *Once all done, recite Psalm 80 three more times and shake the jar six times.*
- *Place the jar under the sink or in the corner of a dark closet.*
- *Each morning before going to court, say Psalm 80 three times and shake the jar six times.*
- *Write Psalm 120 on the enclosed large piece of paper. Write the judge's name on the same paper. Fold the paper 4 times and carry the paper in your pocket the next day in court.*

I follow every directive to the letter, despite the seemingly random nature of the details. I may not understand why Saida is asking for these specific actions to be taken, but our history has taught me I can trust her. The downloads and messages she gets from the spirit world are, like me, only interested in serving the highest good of all involved. So on the nights before court, I faithfully retreat to my office for two full hours. I spend the first 40 minutes chanting the assigned prayers and recitations over the burning blue candle, followed by moving meditation in the form of an online yoga class focused on empowerment – "twist away worry, twist away doubt." I finish with guided meditations focused on courage and confidence, watching the flame grow smaller and smaller until it extinguishes itself in the holder.

I emerge from each session with a gaggle of encouraging text messages from friends scattered around the country. I am being held in some deep, loving thoughts.

I am humbled beyond words at each and every show of support. My heart practically shatters with gratitude each time somebody else shares their intentions to stand by me, either physically or energetically. I don't take any of it, not one single gesture, for granted.

I am so lucky.

I am also so ready. This trial has been 18 months in the making, and as they say, the only way out is through.

March 2018

The Prosecution makes another offer. My lawyer, who has taken on a partner who will also be defending my case, calls me into the office.

"This one is extra important," he says. "Can James come with you?"

James is out of town on business, so I go alone. Both of my lawyers are there and we sit in the conference room, all three of us along the same side of the long table, all three of us facing the white board wall.

On the wall, there are three sections:

- a list of possible outcomes of going to trial,
- the basic points of the offers I've already declined, and
- the outline of what the new offer is.

In the new offer, the DAs are asking me to plead guilty to a Class 5 felony, which is "Attempted Sex Assault on a Child." The sentence would be a 4-year deferred judgment and sentence, meaning that after 4 years, and successful completion of the terms, the felony sex assault would be totally dismissed. We cannot seal it, which my lawyer touts as optimal, but I would no longer have a felony conviction or a sex offense conviction.

This time they agree to no jail, but I still would need to complete sex offender treatment as a condition of the deferment, and I would also need to register as a sex offender. After completing the deferred sentence in 4 years, I could immediately petition to de-register at that time.

Additionally, they want me to plead to a misdemeanor of non-sex child abuse with 5 years of probation running concurrent to the 4-year deferred plea. This would remain a permanent conviction, but it is a non-sex misdemeanor that would not require registration.

My lawyers are jazzed about this. Beyond jazzed. They want me to take it so badly. They say they've never seen anything like it. They both do their very best to convince me, dangling images of a happy future with James in front of me, asking me if I'm willing to risk losing him forever by going to prison.

I am annoyed. I disrupted my whole day for this. Haven't I already expressed my disinterest in accepting a deal, again and again and again? I tell them to decline the offer.

They say I have until close of business to decide, and they won't accept my answer of "no" until I go home and talk it over with my husband.

So I go home and talk to James. He responds, "I always trust you to make the right choice for you, so it's totally up to you, baby."

Then I call my sister, who says, "Of course we'll still fight for you if this all goes south, and yes, you can write a book from prison if that's what ends up happening here." Then I call my mom: "Honey, make the decision that allows you to look yourself in the eye for the rest of your life."

I play devil's advocate with myself, despite the immediate resistance I have to the heaviness of the mental exercise. I ask myself, why would a jury believe me?

What I am contending with is a young woman telling multiple stories about suffering abuse by my hand multiple times. The prosecution is slanting information to build an angle that I groomed her, that I manipulated and used her family for years, that I crossed inappropriate boundaries with my conversations and topics of discussion, that my childhood abuse only means I have a predisposition to abuse others.

I think about the discourse of the recent Me Too movement, rightly demanding that women who allege assault or abuse be listened to and believed. Will a jury realize that while believing is an important first step, allegations must also be investigated and verified before we can vilify? I think about the warranted public outrage around the recent USA Gymnastics scandal, where the sexual abuse and subsequent emotional turmoil of hundreds of minors by their team doctor's hand, covered up for decades, was finally brought to light. Will a jury be susceptible to transferring fury from that story onto this one, despite the many differences between them? There is no way to know for sure.

I start to feel legitimately sick to my stomach.

Am I writing my own prison sentence here?

I take a deep breath. I stand in front of bathroom mirror and I look myself in the eye. I take another deep breath. Then I write the email.

Dear Lawyer,

Thank you for taking focused time this morning to go over all my viable options at this point in the case. I appreciate that. I've given it all a lot of thought this afternoon, conferred with my inner circle, and I am still not interested in taking the plea.

See you soon,

Alex

My lawyer writes back.

Dear Alex,

I wanted to make sure you had the outline of our conversation this morning in writing before making any big decisions. Again, here are (1) possible trial outcomes (2) initial F4 plea offer points and (3) the new F5 deferred plea offer.

As you know, I have strongly encouraged you to accept the new offer of a deferred judgment. It is an excellent outcome that puts your life, your future and your freedom in your hands. It greatly minimizes your risk and allows you to avoid putting your fate – including an extremely long, potentially lifetime prison sentence – in the hands of jurors, the court, and the trial process.

We'll of course fight like hell if we go to trial, but there are too many variables at trial to guarantee the best trial outcome. In comparison, this amazing plea offer is a set result with a definitive, relatively short time span compared to your entire life.

The DAs have agreed to give you to 9:00am tomorrow morning to decide."

What part of "no" am I not making clear?

I am so frustrated, but I'm also chuckling a bit at this point. It almost feels like he's messing with me by not accepting my answer that I've now given him three times, but that's not really his style. Either way, my mind is made up, but I wait until the morning to respond.

Good morning, Lawyer,

After hours of deliberation, discussion, and soul-searching, **I am still not interested in taking the offer.**

I remain confident that our case is strong enough to prove a reasonable doubt during the trial, and that we have the tools, witnesses, evidence, and experts to help us do it.

Additionally, as I've previously expressed, this essentially boils down to the fact that I cannot live with myself if I volunteer for felony and misdemeanor charges, sex offender registration lists, and years of related therapy programs for something I not only have never done but also would never elect to do. Living in the aftermath of that kind of lie would crush my spirit and negatively affect me on a fundamental level.

As we've discussed, *I* was abused as a young child. As we've also discussed, I myself have never abused a child. Loretta is using my very own childhood story against me, so for me to agree to a plea deal that would label me as an abuser is, in a twisted way, akin to my accepting a punishment for being abused all those years ago. Nothing feels right or just or "amazing" about that.

Accordingly, and since there's *also* a chance a jury will find me Not Guilty of all charges (which means I can get back to living my life on my terms in just a few weeks' time, how exciting is that?!) I respectfully, again, decline the plea offer.

Thanks,

Alex

This time the message lands. He hears me, he understands, and they are ready to fight.

Hold onto your hats. We're going to trial.

Chapter 7

"It ain't what they call you, it's what you answer to."
–W.C. Fields

Monday, April 2, 2018 - Colorado

Amelia posts in "Love in Action."
"Good morning!

The big week is here - the week love wins, truth wins, and Alex begins to put this situation behind her and move forward. She is incredibly thankful for all the love and support this group has offered.

For those attending trial this week, here are the details.

Trial will begin at 8:30 am on Wednesday. It should end by 5:00pm each day, and is scheduled to last through next Monday. The prosecution will set forth its case after opening arguments Wednesday and part of Thursday. Alex's witnesses are scheduled to speak Thursday and Friday. Closing arguments are slated for Monday.

The trial will be held at the Courthouse on West Colfax Avenue in Denver.

Trial will be in room 5H.

Alex and her team are sitting on the left hand side. Please sit on that side! It's like a wedding that way, sit behind the person you are there for.

Please bring an ID with you. Please do not bring a camera - you won't be allowed to take it in. Please plan plenty of time to park downtown, or take the light rail which drops off very close by.

People can quietly come and go as they please from the court-room. There will be breaks throughout the day. Please don't leave in the middle of an important witness if you can help it.

We want the jury to feel that those who support Alex are support-ive of the system and not disrespectful or disruptive, and they can read into anything we do.

Please try very hard not to show anger while you are there. We are aiming for compassion and shedding light on the truth. We are all angry but the important thing here is setting a tone for the jurors' perception of our friend.

Please remember to wear light-colored clothing. Aim for some-thing friendly-looking but not too casual or too conservative. No dark suits. Research has found that defendants who wear light colors are seen in a more positive light so Alex will be wearing spring colors or white and white jackets. No need to come all in white but let's stay away from black and navy.

If you attend trial and don't mind sharing your thoughts and observations here each day, that would be so helpful. Or, send them to me and I will post a daily summary along with a mantra for us to focus on for the next day. I won't be there physically but if you have any questions text me and I can likely get them answered for you.

I don't know many of you but I love what you all have done for our friend. Let's get her through this week and next.

Xo,

Amelia"

***

In our research, we'd learned it would help to fill our side of the courtroom with as many people as possible on as many days as possible. To that end, Amelia put a spreadsheet schedule in place, lining people up for morning, afternoon, or full-day shifts.

I'd told out-of-state friends not to worry about attending, hoping the declaration would relieve them of feeling any obligation to travel or guilt about not wanting or being able to come.

"Plan a trip for when we celebrate our victory, instead," I say. People come anyway.

Carys, who was there at the beginning and has been an active curator of love in the groups, says it wouldn't feel right not to be there at the end.

Another faraway friend, Jules, changes her plans last minute and hops on a plane to Denver, bringing me to tears with her message, "I can't not be there. I'm on my way."

My parents, my sister, my aunt, my cousin. Some drive, some fly, but they all arrive with brave faces and big hearts to rally around me. My aunt and cousin have to go shopping when they arrive and learn of our light, bright clothing strategy; they hail from Los Angeles, and all they packed was black.

Some local friends take vacation days from work and/or clear their schedules. I receive streams of beautiful cards in the mail, of supportive texts on the regular, and love-bomb packages filled with assortments of treasures to enhance my priority of taking gentle, loving care of myself.

I am so lucky.

***

I have high hopes for not only the outcome of the trial but also the opportunity it provides to possibly fill in some of the missing details of all the bewildering stories coming from Loretta and her family, especially. Perhaps after hearing what they have to say on stand, I can begin to pinpoint where exactly everything went so horribly sideways, because the fragments of what their collective interviews have so far provided are confusingly incomplete.

For example, when Loretta was initially interviewed, the forensic interviewer asked her to include any sensory details she could remember about her allegations. When this alleged abuse was happening, what could she see, what could she hear, what could she smell?

"Oh, I don't have a sense of smell," Loretta had quickly interjected.

I'd known that about Ivy, that Ivy had no real sense of smell, but not Loretta. Is it hereditary? A thing you grow into? Maybe. Or is this another example of Loretta taking someone else's detail and making it her own?

In any case, Loretta laid claim – twice – to having no sense of smell.

But later, Loretta recounted a story about an emotional kerfuffle that took place during a family vacation centered around things she could smell, which then triggered memories of her alleged abuse.

Loretta's boyfriend at the time was also along on this family vacation, and by all accounts they'd spent a long day on the water in the southern sun. There was an emotional disturbance that happened at the end of that long day, but exactly what happened depends on who you ask.

Loretta and her boyfriend were in a room, either lying next to one another in a bed or sitting next to one another on the couch, depending on who you ask. The boyfriend offered to rub something – either lotion, Noxema, or aloe vera, depending on who you ask – on Loretta's sunburned back, the scent of which created a strong, unfavorable reaction from Loretta. As a result, Loretta locked herself in a bathroom for 20 minutes or many hours, depending on who you ask.

Once locked in said bathroom, Loretta called a different friend back in Colorado, Ricardo, to tell him she was triggered by the smell. Ricardo would later tell investigators it was the scent of cologne that triggered Loretta's outburst, because it was the same smell that was present when she was molested.

All of this from a girl who reported having no sense of smell.

In addition to that curiosity, there are also missing parts to how, exactly, these stories came to light, and how, exactly, Ivy factors into it.

What the prosecution has shared so far is that Ivy became concerned about Loretta when a break-up with an older boy at school led Loretta to stop showering, eating, or studying.

Ivy told investigators she began to periodically log in to Loretta's social media accounts to snoop around and keep an eye on things. One night, the story goes, Ivy woke up in the wee hours to use the bathroom and decided to take a quick peek at the direct message conversations in Loretta's Facebook. Ivy says she found a conversation between Loretta and her friend, Duncan, in which Duncan was encouraging Loretta to cheer up about life in general, and Loretta responded with a laundry list of ways her life had been hard, including a claim that she'd been abused by one of her mom's friends. She did not name the friend.

Ivy said she was shocked when she read that, thought of two possible people it might have been, and then... went back to bed.

The next morning, Ivy looked for the conversation again, but she could not find it. She assumed it had been deleted.

Ivy chose to confront Loretta about it after school that day, and when Loretta did not want to talk to her about it, Ivy drove Loretta directly to talk to another family friend, instead.

Ivy took Loretta to this family friend – not a therapist, not a counselor, not a teacher – a handful of times, until Ivy said she could hear Loretta and the family friend hollering at one another through the closed door. Only then did Ivy decide to take Loretta to a licensed therapist. According to the therapist's notes, it took six weeks for Loretta to provide a first name (mine) and another four weeks for the family to call back with my last name. The new therapist, as a mandatory reporter, then took this information to the police.

When the police finally talked to Ivy and Angus – together in the same room and a full year after my arrest – Ivy told the police she still did not know what Loretta's actual allegations were, just that Alex seemed to be the one responsible for hurting her.

Loretta's interviews are sprinkled with a multitude of red flags we are hoping to address, as well. In her initial recorded conversation with the forensic interviewer in the summer of 2016, Loretta mentions she was feeling much calmer than she did during her "practice interview" with the therapist. Practice interviews are a big no-no in situations like these because the whole point is to hear the child's own, original account, so Loretta's choice of words is a red flag for both my lawyer and me. Loretta then mentions disassociating through most of the interview, like she does "most of the time" in her life. Disassociation is another word for *dissociate*, which means disconnecting from the reality around you and getting mentally stuck in the freeze command of the sympathetic nervous system's *fight, flee, or freeze* responses to perceived danger. It is a defense mechanism used to help the mind cope with excessive stress, such as during a traumatic event. Most people experience it at some point during their life, but experiencing excessive amounts too often can lead to a dissociative disorder, historically known as "multiple personality disorder." To say she spends most of her life dissociating is a slightly alarming statement for Loretta to make, but she is not asked any follow up questions about it.

And there's even more. Loretta reports she was told to include as many details as she could to make her story seem more believable. This turn of phrase – "I was told to include..." – raises another red flag. Told by whom?

She mentions how Ivy helped her put together timelines and layouts of houses. A parent directly interfering with the way a child is telling the story of alleged abuse? My lawyer is incredulous; I think his head might explode with red flags.

Her whole story is disjointed: unanswered question after unanswered question.

How does someone with no sense of smell know how things smell?

How can a scent trigger a memory if scents are not part of your everyday life?

Who is this unnamed family friend Ivy took Loretta to see?

What did the family friend talk about with Loretta during those meetings?

What is this practice interview of which Loretta speaks?

Who, exactly, told her to use details to make things "seem more believable?"

Why was her mother helping her put a story together before the interview?

Why were there no follow-up questions to Loretta's claims of dissociation during the interview?

Why did it take investigators over a year to have a conversation with Loretta's parents?

Why did Ivy go back to bed after discovering her daughter had allegedly been abused?

What happened to the Facebook conversation Ivy saw? Did Loretta delete it or did Ivy imagine it?

I'm chomping at the bit to hear the prosecution tell this story start to finish, especially now that I have physical evidence showing where I was and what I was doing for years on end, and can dismantle the overwhelming majority of her accusations with my trusty Box of Proof.

***

Last week, my lawyer organized a few of his own things to prepare me for the mental stamina needed to thrive during the long and tedious trial proceedings. He arranged a mock cross-examination with a female lawyer from down the hall, and I endured ninety minutes of both my lawyers and her drilling me with deep, personal, borderline rude questions. They role-played purposely misunderstanding me, twisting my words in terrible ways, using crass language to provoke and antagonize me. I cried at the end of the session, angry, frustrated, and insulted. Is that what I could expect from the prosecution? I'm furious that my parents will be unnecessarily subject to watching their daughter be accused of such ugly things in such dehumanizing ways. I started sobbing at the conference table when my lawyer asked what was going through my mind to stir up the kind of emotion. He wanted to use it to our advantage.

"This is the real, raw kind of reaction we want the jury to see from you, Alex," my lawyer had explained. "The prosecution is going to give a lot of attention to how difficult this has been for Loretta, but they are not going to so much as mention how difficult it has been for you, too. Anything you can do to show the jury your level of distress around all this without actually calling yourself a victim is great."

I can't cry on demand any more than I can stop crying on demand, so I'm not sure what to make of the request. I'd told him I will do my best but I can't make any promises, which is exactly what he keeps telling me about going to trial. He'll do his best, but there are no guarantees.

Tuesday, April 3, 2018

Day one – jury selection.

This is the hardest day.

My lawyers had mentioned during last week's prep sessions that the day Loretta testified might be the toughest for me, but no. For me, it's jury selection day that proves to be the worst.

I meditated last night, turning in early, and I wake up well before my 6:00 a.m. alarm. James rises with me and makes breakfast while I shower, get dressed, pray, and stomp all around the backyard.

I will fear no evil; for thou art with me.

In my bag I pack my lunch, snacks, and a small silk bag filled with a variety of stones and crystals carefully selected for their qualities of protection, truth-telling, and clarity. Some of these stones I already happened to own, some were sent to me from Saida, some came from other friends, and some were gifts from my husband, who bought himself a matching set to keep in his pocket for the duration of the trial. By nature, my husband is not a "keep crystals in his pocket" type of man, and I am moved to tears by the act of solidarity.

Into my bag I also tuck my yellow legal pad, the one I've been taking notes on during all my lawyer meetings. My plan is to take copious amounts of notes each day in court as things unfold and journal my recollections each night when I get home, and that is exactly what I do.

Additionally, per Amelia's request, there is a rich running commentary all week long in the "Love in Action" group, summaries from my friends who attend each day in the courtroom with me, highlighting the basics of each witness and overall tone of the proceedings to faraway pals. So it is not only my memory I rely on to recount these days; it is also my courtroom notes, evening journal entries, and detailed posts from other people who were there.

Thank goodness for those people, by the way. Because witnesses in a trial are not allowed in the courtroom until after they testify, neither my husband, sister, nor mother would be present that day – or all week, it would turn out. Fortunately, the presence of my father, my aunt, my cousin, my in-laws, and my friends mitigated my initial angst at having to arrive alone.

I drive by myself to court the first morning of the trial, and every morning thereafter. An "I Am" guided affirmation meditation for courage and inner power plays over my car's speakers, the same affirmations I repeat each night to conclude my evening meditation session. Both the recording and my commute are twenty minutes long so it feels like an easy, if not auspicious, listening choice.

"I am blessed with many things to be grateful for...I am strong and balanced...I am unstoppable...I am deciding now that this day is my opportunity to turn things around for the better..."

The parking garage is a zoo. There are more people milling about than any other day I've been here during the past year and a half. As we all stand around waiting for our turn to pay the parking machine, I notice jury summons in many peoples' hands. One lady has lavender hair and smiles at me. A different lady asks me for directions, shows me her paper, and asks me which building she needs.

I'm not holding a paper, which implies I know where I'm going, I suppose. I look like a lawyer. I give her directions to where she needs to be.

When I get to the courthouse, through the security line, and up to the 5th floor, I am happy to find the bathroom empty.

I look myself in the eye. *Hello, sweetheart.*

I take a few deep, measured breaths. *You are so brave, so strong, so fierce.*

I pull out my phone and take a mirror selfie. I caption it on Instagram: *"There is no force more powerful than a woman determined to rise."*

My tone is set.

One final deep stare into my own eyes – *truth matters, love wins, and you have both on your side* – then I hold my head high as I walk the full length of the sunlit hallway, pull the heavy, wooden double doors at the very end open, and enter the courtroom.

My lawyer has instructed me specifically not to bring Starbucks with me; I don't want to evoke any potential resentment from any potential jurors. What if, my lawyer said, someone gets annoyed because they have to spend their day sitting here without Starbucks but there I am, sipping away on mine?

I find my spot at our table on the left and set my pink travel coffee mug down before I hang my white winter coat over the back of my chair, revealing my carefully chosen outfit: a white dress patterned with light blue flowers and a white blazer. I watch as both DAs waltz into the room carrying the biggest, tallest Starbucks drinks available, dressed head to toe in black.

***

There is a pool of eighty-five people all in the courtroom at once and we will painstakingly whittle it down to a panel of thirteen. I stand now and face all eighty-five of them, as do my lawyers next to me, and the two replacement DAs on the other side of the courtroom. They are both young women relatively fresh out of law school, a blond with big eyes and a saccharine smile, and a brunette with a pointy nose and a sour scowl. Their combined years of practice don't come close to touching my lawyer's experience, and I have to wonder why they were assigned jointly to this case. Perhaps neither is equipped to handle it individually, or perhaps it's not quite as "open and shut" as the original district attorney seemed to think it was.

I take note of a few people I'd seen in the parking garage this morning. I see the lady with lavender hair. I see her see me.

The judge welcomes and thanks everyone, then the DAs introduce themselves, after which my lawyers introduce themselves, pleasantly surprising me with their language, "… I am *honored* to be representing Ms. Kuisis."

I do not speak.

I barely move.

I keep my face as neutral as possible under the weighted stare of 170 eyes on me as the judge reads the seven felony accusations out loud, word for word, in all their confusing glory.

"**Count one:** Between and including approximately May 6, 2008, and May 6, 2010, Alexandra Kuisis unlawfully, feloniously, and knowingly subjected Loretta X, not her spouse, to sexual contact, and the victim was less than 15 years of age and the defendant was at least four years older than the victim. **This is what will be known as the incident at Connie's house.**

Count two: Between and including approximately May 6, 2008, and May 6, 2010, Alexandra Kuisis unlawfully, feloniously, and knowingly subjected Loretta X, not her spouse, to sexual contact, and the victim was less than 15 years of age and the defendant was at least four years older than the victim. **This is what will be known as the bath incident.**

Count three: Between and including approximately May 6, 2008, and May 6, 2010, Alexandra Kuisis unlawfully, feloniously, and knowingly subjected Loretta X, not her spouse, to sexual contact, and the victim was less than 15 years of age and the defendant was in a position of trust with respect to the victim. **This is what will also be known as the bed incident at Connie's house.**

Count four: Between and including approximately May 6, 2008, and May 6, 2010, Alexandra Kuisis unlawfully, feloniously, and knowingly subjected Loretta X, not her spouse, to sexual contact, and the victim was less than 15 years of age and the defendant was at least four years older than the victim. **This is what will be known as the bed incident at the couple's house.**

Count five: Between and including approximately May 6, 2008, and May 6, 2010, Alexandra Kuisis unlawfully, feloniously, and knowingly subjected Loretta X, not her spouse, to sexual contact, and the victim was less than 15 years of age and the defendant was in a position of trust with respect to the victim. **This is also the bath incident.**

Count six: Between and including approximately May 6, 2008, and May 6, 2010, Alexandra Kuisis unlawfully, feloniously, and knowingly subjected Loretta X, not her spouse, to sexual contact, and the victim was less than 15 years of age and the defendant was in a position of trust with respect to the victim. **This is what will also be known as the bed incident at the couple's house.**

Count seven: Between and including approximately May 6, 2008, and May 6, 2010, Alexandra Kuisis unlawfully, feloniously, and knowingly subjected Loretta X, not her spouse, to **a pattern of abuse** of sexual contact, and the victim was less than 15 years of age and the defendant was at least four years older than the victim."

For months in therapy, I'd been putting a concentrated effort into dismantling my attachment to other people's opinions of me, but in that moment any progress that's been made eludes me, and my anxiety comes ferociously roaring back with a vengeance, temporarily sucking the breath from my lungs. My vision goes dark for the briefest of moments, and it is only by the grace of god that I manage to stay upright.

These people are literally here to judge me.

The judge continues reading his standard trial introduction verbiage. "To these charges the defendant has pled not guilty. The charges against the defendant are not evidence of anything. By pleading not guilty to this information, the defendant says that she did not commit these crimes.

"The defendant is presumed to be innocent. The prosecution therefore has the burden of proving the charges beyond a reasonable doubt. The jury who is selected will decide whether the prosecution has proven beyond a reasonable doubt that the defendant has done the things that are contained in the information. The information is a mere accusation against the defendant, and it is not, in and of itself, any evidence of guilt of the defendant, and no juror should permit himself or herself to be influenced to any extent, however slight, against the defendant because of or on account of the filing of the information."

I wish he'd opened with all that, but better late than never.

The potential jurors are asked to complete a two-sided questionnaire, and when they finish, the court clerk photocopies all eighty-five questionnaires six times each – twice for the prosecution, twice for the defense, once for the judge and once for the clerk. When the photocopying is done, both sides need to read through the eighty-five questionnaires for red flags or obvious dismissals.

It takes a significant chunk of time, but it's worth it because the answers we receive shrink the pool considerably. A fair number are dismissed directly while most of the rest are brought back to the judge's chambers, one by one, to hold individual interviews with the judge, the two D.A.s, both my lawyers, and me.

Once again, I am the only one who does not speak.

Some people have indicated on their questionnaire that they have personal childhood experiences of being abused, and these individuals take their turns answering the judge's questions around their perceived ability to remain impartial on such sensitive subject matter if they were selected for the jury. Some people are teachers, and they are asked the same things. One man is brought back to explain why he wrote "because she is guilty" as a reason he should be dismissed. "Well, she looks guilty to me. From the minute I first looked at her to right now looking at her, and I will still think she is guilty no matter what anyone says during trial." That man is trying to get out of jury duty, and it works. The judge excuses him.

After the individual interviews are finally over, we re-emerge to the courtroom and with the dozens of potential jurors still remaining, we begin the process of filling the seats of the juror box with a carefully-argued configuration. All four lawyers alternate asking questions and presenting scenarios for the potential jurors to consider.

At one point, a woman sitting in the juror's box asks for the microphone and bluntly states, "These are people's lives we are being asked to hold in our hands. There is a respect for both sides that is demanded of the people who end up being on this jury. This is serious and needs to be seen as such. I just want to remind everyone of that."

The group questioning takes so much time that we are not done by the time the day is through. We'll need to finish tomorrow morning.

We haven't even really begun, and we are already behind schedule.

I go home and tell my husband and my sister all about the day on the back porch as we eat dinner, then I retire for my meditation and yoga session, and then I finally put my exhausted self to bed, and I sleep.

Wednesday, April 4, 2018

Day two. Happy birthday in heaven, Grandma.
I pray, I stomp.
For thou art with me.

I drive myself to court early, listening to my meditation. *"I am courageous…I am strong…I am guided by the universe…I am open and allowing for positive things to unfold…I am protected by my higher self…"*

It takes all morning, but a jury is finally chosen. It includes the lady with the lavender hair. It includes the lady who asked for the microphone yesterday.

On my yellow legal pad, I write the jury's initials in the order they are sitting, a heart in-between each letter: N♥J♥G♥K♥A♥B♥E♥R♥M♥D♥J♥A♥S. Underneath, an intention: *may they use logic to cut through confusion, see the inconsistencies, and recognize the reasonable doubt plastered all over this case.*

And so it shall be.

We begin the afternoon with opening arguments. The prosecution wants to paint me as a child molester savvy enough to groom an entire family for years, whereas the defense is pointing out how important verification is with any allegation, especially allegations of this nature, and especially *delayed* allegations of this nature, because, as we'll show, memory is inherently faulty, and Loretta's stories are riddled with factual inaccuracies. Believe the child, yes, then verify their story.

After opening arguments, the prosecution begins. In total, they call eleven people to the stand, some personal witnesses, some professional, and they begin with Angus, Rose, and Ivy.

Angus is mostly forgettable, except for his comment about what a blow to his ego this whole situation has been, and Rose is mainly emotional. She looks scared when she gets sworn in, and I feel heartstrings tugging. I want to soothe her, to tell her not to be afraid, that she has it in her to be brave and do hard things. But then she starts talking and that instinct is squelched. She is all attitude and drama but what stays with me the most from Rose's testimony is when she shares that she could tell that something was going on in her family before she was told of Loretta's allegations. She thought it was that her parents were getting a divorce. This paints such a clear picture of their home life to me, and it makes me sad for them but it also makes sense. That whole family is hurting, and hurt people look for ways to hurt other people.

Rose reiterates that we always slept three to a bed when we had sleepovers, and that she remembers the day I told the girls about my childhood abuse. She remembers that it was my story first.

Ivy is nervous when she testifies, fidgeting with the hair tie around her wrist, a blank look on her face. She characterizes our friendship as very positive, and describes my relationship with the girls as very loving and close. She talks about how much I love to take pictures, how much I love to document things, and how lucky she was to have someone like me love her kids.

The DA asks Ivy if she had any concerns about Loretta's behavior after the girls visited me in Santa Barbara in 2008.

Ivy answers, "No."

Any concerns after the 2009 visit?

No.

Had Ivy specifically asked me to talk to the girls about sex? About menstrual cycles?

"No, not specifically," she says, "but if my girls had asked her questions like that, I would have felt comfortable with Alex responding honestly and openly. She was a close friend, like a part of our family, and a teacher. She adored the children, and I trusted her."

They ask if I'd ever told Ivy about my own childhood abuse, and she says, "No."

They ask if she has since learned about it, and she says, "Yes."

"But you did not ask Alex to talk to Loretta or Rose about it?"

Ivy leans into the microphone to reiterate. "No."

I watch Ivy carefully. I wonder if she believes she is telling the truth.

Memory research shows that memories can be changed by the things we are told, even by things we tell ourselves. I think about the work of Dr. Elizabeth Loftus, a name I'd recently become familiar with after my favorite uncle, a clinical psychologist, suggested I watch her Ted Talk. By the time those seventeen minutes were over, I knew I was onto something.

Dr. Loftus is a distinguished professor and cognitive psychologist who studies human memory, and a multitude of her scientific experiments reveal how facts, ideas, suggestions and other post-event information can modify our memories to make us think things happened when they didn't, or make us think we were someplace when we weren't.

Because the legal field is so reliant on memories in general, it has been the focus of a significant application of her memory research, and Dr. Loftus has testified or consulted as an expert witness in many high-profile cases, including those of OJ Simpson, Michael Jackson, Oliver North, and Martha Stewart, with good reason.

Among Dr. Loftus's credentials are a Ph.D. from Stanford, seven honorary Ph.D.s from universities around the world, and author credits for approximately 25 books and 500 articles. Her work has been funded by, among others, grants from the National Science Foundation, the National Institute of Mental Health, and the U.S. Department of Transportation, and she has been sought out for consultation with agencies such as the Secret Service, the Central Intelligence Agency, the Department of Justice, and the Internal Revenue Service. She's kind of a big deal in the field of memory.

As I listen to Ivy deny her knowledge of my childhood abuse, I think about what Dr. Loftus refers to as an "honest liar" – someone who remembers things that didn't happen or happened differently from their recollection, to the point of believing their erroneous memory as truth.

I am fascinated to watch a version of it in action.

I have to admit I'm smiling on the inside right now in sweet anticipation of proving Ivy wrong. I am looking forward to showing the jury in real time how easy it can be to get facts mixed-up with fabrications when you rely on memory alone, and how dangerous it can be to throw these kinds of allegations around like stones when your memory is a glass house.

But that will come during cross-examination. Right now, the DA is asking Ivy about how our friendship ended, and my ears perk up from her answers.

Most of what Ivy is saying tracks with my recollection of how it all unfolded, too.

We were all at Loretta's track meet together that Saturday morning in April of 2013, after which I'd taken Rose to Target and then come back to their house for a bit. Ivy explains how after I left, her conversations with the girls led to the next morning's flurry of phone calls, including the call where Ivy told me that Loretta spooked Rose by telling her I'd smoked pot.

But now, here in this courtroom five years later, Ivy is singing a different tune. Today, she is explaining to the jury that she was the one who told Rose about the marijuana.

"I didn't think it would end the friendship," Ivy says. "The scent of weed wafted across our backyard from the neighbor's house that day after Alex left, and Rose got so judgmental about it so quickly that I thought I'd give her some perspective, and so I told her, 'You know, Alex smokes pot.' And Rose just absolutely freaked out, wanted to call and confront Alex immediately. I made her sleep on it, thinking she would calm down, but then the next morning when I left to get donuts, all hell broke loose."

This time, I know Ivy is telling the truth. This makes so much more sense than what she'd fed me five years ago. This is the missing piece of that puzzle.

It hadn't been Loretta who told Rose; it'd been Ivy. And then Ivy had thrown Loretta under the bus to me instead of owning up to her actions. Why would Ivy do that? As I try this idea on in my thoughts, I think of the way our friendship morphed into a series of sharp edges over the years.

There'd always been a bit of competitive edge to our dynamic, a dash of mean girl to keep things spicy. I teased her for being a debutant when she was younger; she made fun of me for being the president of my sorority in college. I think of her tendency to copy my purchasing habits, my decorating style, my organization skills, my party ideas. James and I had a "Make Your Own Trail Mix" bar at our wedding, and I recall how, when I went to a party at the X house two weeks later, Ivy had the exact same trail mix bar set up in their backyard. I think of how I wore cowboy boots during my wedding reception and how Ivy then bought cowboy boots to wear at her party. I think about the gorgeous, fancy camera James bought me for our first Christmas and how Ivy bought the exact same camera for Loretta a few weeks later, just for kicks. I think of how often over the years other friends had to remind me, "imitation is a form of flattery," when really it just felt like I was being scrutinized all the damn time. I think about having to dodge Ivy's passive-aggressive verbal digs, how I repeatedly felt a need to be the decisive firecracker to her apathetic wallflower. I think of the time she claimed envy at how deeply I seemed to feel my feelings, and she expressed remorse that she was so comparatively vanilla. I think of how I started medication to help me manage my emotional high highs and low lows, and she, confusingly, asked her doctor for medication, too. I think of her telling me she was disappointed to find out that my sister was pregnant with her second girl because Ivy wanted *her* two girls to be the only two girls in my life. I think about Ivy's friend Eileen, the way she would pointedly ignore me when I was with Ivy, the way Ivy thought it was funny. "Oh, you know Eileen, she's just like that."

Had it been Ivy who sabotaged our friendship, all along?

I think about her habit of reminding me with a laugh which of our mutual acquaintances didn't like me and why not. I think about the email to her high school friends that I had stumbled upon, the one making fun of who I was and the things I was interested in.

It actually tracks.

As I suspected, watching my lawyer cross-examine her is deeply satisfying. Ivy confirms our past practice of frequently communicating via Instant Messenger, then re-confirms she did not know about my childhood experience of abuse during our friendship. My lawyer then hands her the print out of the exact Instant Messenger conversation where she specifically asks me to talk about my childhood abuse with her children.

She studies the piece of paper, describes what she is reading to the jury when prompted, and acknowledges the conversation's apparent authenticity. She says she clearly must have known about my abuse, but she doesn't remember knowing.

The memory can play tricks, you see.

Believe, then verify.

If Ivy is an honest liar, which is what my intuition is telling me, she just was made to look a fool.

And if she is an actual liar, she just got caught on stand.

Either way, she squirms in her seat and fidgets with her hair tie, and I know she feels the weight of my stare. She doesn't so much as glance in my direction.

Thursday, April 5, 2018

Meditate. Sleep. Pray. Stomp.

The Lord is my shepherd; I shall not want.

Drive into the city. Let the meditation wash over me.

"I am healing deeply…my potential to succeed is infinite…"

I park in the structure, walk to the courthouse. I go through security, get into the elevator, ride it to the fifth floor. I walk down the hallway and find my place at our table. I set my coffee down and slip my white coat onto the back of my chair. I pull out my silk bag of rocks and hold it in my left hand.

On a fresh sheet of my legal pad, I write today's date and the jury's initials: N♥J♥G♥K♥A♥B♥E♥R♥M♥D♥J♥A♥S. I add my intention: *all love all clarity all truth all good things best possible outcome.* I add the initials of the judge, the district attorneys, my lawyers: W♥T♥F♥B♥T♥D. I pray for perseverance, justice, and victory.

Just like yesterday, I am anchored by the strong showing of support filing into the rows behind me. Just like yesterday, it is only Ivy's mom who sits on the other side of the aisle. I'd wondered if Ivy, Angus, or Rose would join her in the courtroom today for Loretta's testimony, but they do not.

When Loretta testifies, she reiterates her stories practically verbatim, leaving us with more questions than answers. For example, she tries to explain the confusion around her sense of smell by saying that over the past couple of years, she can sometimes smell certain things when she visits family in the south. She doesn't know why it happens; she thinks it might have something to do with humidity levels.

To me, the sticky thing about Loretta's testimony is that for every single story she tells, someone else has a different version of it. Her mother, her sister, her former boyfriend, her former high school pals – they each provide such different accounts of how any given situation unfolded. We are inundated with examples of how the memory plays tricks on people before our very eyes. And once the memory is tricked, it can become nearly impossible to remember anything accurately. In fact, it becomes easier to believe that the tricked memory is the real one.

According to Dr. Loftus, "False memories, once created — either through misinformation or through these suggestive processes — can be experienced with a great deal of emotion, a great deal of confidence and a lot of detail, even though they're false." The deeper Loretta found herself in this mess, the easier it would have become to commit to the lie than admit to the truth. To save herself from feeling the gravity of what she's done, she would have no choice but to believe it. She's turned it into truth in her mind because to psychologically survive, she's had to.

Loretta answers all the questions asked during her relatively short time on the stand, and she also volunteers a few thoughts. "Look, I never wanted it to come to all this. I know Alex loved me, and I loved her, too. It's not like I don't remember all the good stuff. I remember. There was lots of good stuff."

I quietly cry as I watch her up on the stand, tears sliding down my face, splashing all over my white jacket. I can't help it. My heart is breaking for this broken girl I loved so dearly.

After Loretta testifies, the forensic interviewer and the licensed therapist who did the mandatory reporting recount and defend the standardized nature of their interactions with Loretta, and finally Detective Sherbert, the one who arrested me that night in 2016, is called to the stand. The mere sight of him entering the courtroom makes my blood start to boil.

Our eyes meet. Mine narrow. He couldn't care less.

Fortunately, his detective work is clearly and quickly shown to be lazy by his testimony. Over and over, my lawyer asks if the detective completed various steps of protocol in this particular investigation; over and over, the detective answers, "No."

Did he speak to Loretta's parents in a timely fashion?

No.

Did he drive to the houses Loretta named to double check locations and floor plans to see if her descriptions were accurate?

No.

Did he follow up with Loretta's claim of doing a "practice interview" with her therapist?

No.

Did he follow-up with questions about Loretta's self-admitted dissociation during her forensic interview?

No.

Why not?

"I just didn't. I handed the case over to the district attorney's office."

He goes on to say that the extent of his full investigation into the matter was the single conversation he had with me in his office on September 1, 2016. He says that based on my affirmative answers to his questions that day such as *Did you live at these addresses?* and *Did Loretta ever visit these houses?*, he felt there was no need to do more investigating. For as infuriating as his answers are, I am grateful that he at least has the decency to admit it on stand.

My lawyer shakes hands with the detective at the end of the day, and they exchange a few pleasantries as the courtroom empties. My future hanging in the balance is just another day at the office for these guys.

That night, I reflect on the day and write in my journal.

Oh, Loretta. What happened to you, dear one? You've obviously been traumatized by something or someone, and it broke my heart to watch you on that stand today. I hardly recognize you anymore, which is such a shame – you were such a bubbly, light child, and now your energy is dark and heavy, fragmented and strange. I am sorry someone hurt you and I'm sorry you aren't getting the help you need. I'm sorry I was the only safe place you could think of to project the impact of your trauma, and I'm sorry I have to fight back, but I obviously have no choice. I can't give up my life for your lies, my dear. You're going to have to shoulder this mess you've made without me. I pray you find eventual healing.

I share the gist of my sentiments with my lawyer the next day.

"Yeah, you're not going to say one word of any of that up on stand. Not one single word."

Friday, April 6, 2018

I meditate, I sleep, I pray, I stomp.

I will fear no evil, for thou art with me; thy rod and thy staff, they comfort me.

I drive into the city for day four. *"I am curious about all the solutions I haven't even thought of yet."*

I find my way to the courtroom. I pull out my notepad, date a fresh page. N♥J♥G♥K♥A♥B♥E♥R♥M♥D♥J♥A♥S. Then the judge, district attorneys and my lawyers: W♥T♥F♥B♥D♥T. I add the initials of the witnesses slated to testify on my behalf today: E♥J♥G. I take a few deep, measured breaths and jot down what comes to me: *Truth matters. Love wins. Perfect divine timing is on our side. Highest good for all involved. Breathe.*

Obviously, this trial will not be ending today as originally indicated. The prosecution is disorganized and so unprepared that I wouldn't have believed it if I hadn't seen it play out again and again with my own eyes. On multiple occasions, one of the district attorneys begins a speech by referencing established case law, then pauses mid-sentence, studies her paperwork with a scrunched forehead, finally stammering something along the lines of, "Uh, Your Honor, if you'll just excuse me a moment, I seem to be reading from the wrong case."

Cue a mad scramble to find the proper piece of paper.

Rinse and repeat.

I'd think it was funny if it wasn't such a colossal waste of my time, of all of our time, my money, and taxpayer money.

Today, the prosecution still has six witnesses left to call: four high school students, the district attorney's investigator, and one expert witness who doesn't know the particulars of this case and will be speaking to the generalities of abused child behavior.

Then it will finally be our turn, and my three out-of-state witnesses, all of whom are prepared to fly back to their respective homes first thing in the morning, are ready: Jonathan, Grace (my friend who spent a day with Loretta, Rose, and me during the second California spring break), and my first expert witness.

But if the prosecution continues at the rate they've been going, my witnesses might not get their turn today. This would be detrimental to my case, as well as my pocketbook. I've paid for all three witnesses to fly here, sleep here, and eat here. If they leave tomorrow without testifying, it's all for naught.

My jaw is stress-clenched most of the morning as the high school students take their sweet time telling different versions of stories that only reiterate how faulty memory can be when there is no proof or evidence to corroborate a story.

Believe, then verify.

One witness, the boyfriend Loretta brought along on her family vacation, shares that that trip happened in June of 2016. According to him, he was giving Loretta a back rub with some Olay lotion after a long day out on the water when she became exceedingly tense, claiming it reminded her of the past. According to him, Loretta ran and locked herself in the bathroom to take a shower, and was in there for at least 45 minutes, maybe longer, but he didn't know for sure because he fell asleep before Loretta re-emerged.

The next witness to testify is Ricardo, the young man who says he and Loretta were texting back and forth for hours the night she locked herself in that bathroom; Ricardo was in Colorado at the time. He gives a different account of that night than Loretta's ex-boyfriend. According to Ricardo, Loretta was upset in the bathroom that night because her boyfriend was wearing cologne that reminded her of the time when she was molested. He also shares that the trip was definitely either winter break 2015 or spring break 2016.

Under my lawyer's cross-examination, Ricardo confirms yes, it was cologne that triggered Loretta that night, not Noxema like Loretta had said or Olay lotion like the boyfriend had said, and yes, the trip happened during either winter or spring break, not summer break like the boyfriend had said. Ricardo said he remembered because he and Loretta were no longer friends by the time that summer rolled around.

The memory plays tricks.

To round out the morning, we listen to the investigator from the district attorney's office mimic the detective's testimony from yesterday.

"No, I did not follow up with any of the initial phone calls I made. No, I did not visit the alleged named locations. No, I do not recognize that booklet you're showing me, the one that spells out my department's protocols, policies, and procedures. No, I did not consult this booklet when doing this investigation, as is best practice."

Essentially: no, I did not do my job. I did not investigate.

We are given an extended lunch recess, and I begrudge every minute that ticks away on the clock during the ninety minutes. I understand the importance of giving the jury a substantial mid-day break to refuel and recharge, especially on a Friday afternoon, but I am steamed because the jury's wellbeing isn't the reason for the extension. The reason is that the prosecution's final witness – a licensed clinical social worker who does this kind of testifying in court a lot – is running late. We are literally sitting around waiting for her while my afternoon window for witnesses shrinks by the second.

Once she finally arrives and takes the stand, she talks about how all kids respond differently to trauma, allowing a wide variety of behaviors to become possible. For example, some kids may close off after telling, some may feel an unburdening and want to keep telling. Basically, it can look like A, B, C, or X, Y, Z. When someone befriends and loves a child, they may be grooming them to abuse them, or they may just be befriending and loving a child.

Cross-examination does a good job of clarifying that her point is just that any number of things can cause a behavior, so when a young woman stops showering, changing her clothes, and eating nutritional food, any number of things could be the trigger.

"That's correct," she confirms.

My favorite moment comes from a jury question for this expert witness. The juror wants to know, as an explanation for a child's erratic behavior, *"Could it be possible for a child to make something up and then get caught up in the lie and just not know how to get out of it?"*

The answer is yes, it is possible.

"Not probable," the expert hastens to add, which of course someone from the prosecution would stipulate, but the question has been asked. The question is out there. If even one juror is wondering about that, it feels like a good sign. I'll only go to prison for the rest of my life if all twelve jurors agree I am guilty of all seven charges.

The prosecution finally rests in the late afternoon. I am fuming at the timing; calling three witnesses is out of the question at this point. We barely have time to call one.

The judge calls a short recess, and I storm out of the courtroom on the verge of tears. I see Jonathan and Grace waiting together in the hall, and I raise a "just a minute" finger to them as I breeze past to the bathroom, where I look myself in the mirror as my bubbling anger and frustration simmers down a few degrees. When I join them again, I thank them profusely for being here and give them the quick rundown of why they haven't been called to the stand as they'd been expecting.

A quick hallway strategy session with my lawyer determines we won't have Grace testify after all, and while Jonathan's testimony is considered important, the best use of our limited Friday afternoon time is to actually put my very expensive expert witness up on stand first, in hopes that the information she shares leaves the jury with some nice, juicy food for thought to chew on throughout the weekend.

I apologize to Jonathan for wasting his time, and then in the most gracious act of our entire relationship, he offers to come back next week to testify. I am floored by the gesture.

"It's not a problem," he insists.

Spending these hallway hours with Grace has given him a chance to hear about the group effort he'd unknowingly become a part of, and he's pleased to participate in some Truth Matters, Love Wins solidarity. He offers to fly home tomorrow morning as scheduled, and then back on Monday night for a Tuesday morning turn on the stand. My verge-of-tears status turns into real tears of gratitude and humility, and every transgression of our shared history is forgiven, the slate wiped clean.

I am so lucky.

The new plan is activated. Jonathan leaves, Grace comes into the room to sit on my side in support, and court is called back into session.

Grace isn't the only one who joins us in the courtroom at this stage in the game. Word of this trial has spread through the District Attorney's office, and despite it being the tail end of Friday afternoon, the last row of the courtroom is humming with deputy district attorneys, including the one originally assigned to the case. Everyone wants to see my expert witness on stand, and I don't blame them, because I have hired Dr. Elizabeth Loftus.

Chapter 8

"I am not afraid. I was born to do this." –Joan of Arc

As anticipated, Dr. Loftus takes the stand and blows everyone away when she shares her impressive credentials and caliber of work. Although diminutive in stature with a loose, shoulder-length shag haircut and glasses, her confidence and self-assuredness make her seem seven feet tall. This is a woman who commands a room. The judge had allowed her to join my lawyers and me at our courtroom table during the prosecution's final expert witness, and Dr. Loftus and I passed notes back and forth during the testimony – her observations and questions, my answers and commentary. I like her energy a lot; she is kind but no-nonsense, and possibly smarter than this entire room put together. Seeing her finally take the stand after months of preparing for it feels like a pressure valve being released somewhere inside me.

Dr. Loftus explains to the jury how her extensive research over the decades of her esteemed career clearly indicates that memories can be manipulated, falsified, changed, even planted... and then believed anyway. She references one of her better-known studies in which participants were told they'd experienced a semi-traumatic event as a young child, something akin to nearly drowning in a swimming pool or getting lost for hours in a busy shopping mall, and even though these suggestions were falsehoods, the more the participants thought about it, the more likely they were to "discover" memories of the planted traumas. That is to say, their brain created memories based on someone else's story. Her testimony is smart, fascinating, and persuasive.

The jury is impressed, hanging on her every word. The whole courtroom is. Jurors are watching her intently, some furiously scribbling notes. You could hear a pin drop in the space between the questions and Dr. Loftus's answers.

Alas, also as we anticipated, we run out of proverbial daylight before the DAs can finish their cross-examination, and now they are crying foul.

The court places an ultimatum on the table: either I redeliver Dr. Loftus back to the courtroom on Monday to finish her cross-examination, or everything she has said today will be officially stricken from the record. We are instructed to work details out amongst ourselves over the weekend and be ready with a solution when we reconvene on Monday.

I am gob smacked by how unfair this feels to me. Had their final witness been on time this afternoon, this likely would have been a non-issue. Had they been even a smidge more organized this week, it definitely wouldn't have been an issue. Now I'll be getting the short end of the stick unless I can allocate another massive chunk of change to extend Dr. Loftus's services for the prosecution's benefit. To be truthful, I couldn't even afford it the first time – it is only through an exceedingly generous financial gift from my aunt that Dr. Loftus is here at all.

My lawyers ask me to join them, Dr. Loftus, and Jonathan for a dinner meeting that night to discuss options, but it's been a long week, and as grateful as I am to Jonathan for his kind flexibility, I don't want to have dinner with him, and as fascinating a dinner companion as I'm sure Dr. Loftus is, I'm fresh out of the type of social niceties required for polite dinner conversation. I'm already scheduled to spend a chunk of Sunday with my legal team, and I have out-of-town family and friends I love dearly coming over for a pizza party at our place tonight. I just want to change into comfortable clothes, drink a glass of wine, eat some pizza, and laugh with my people. I decline the invitation, although I am still billed for the dinner.

Monday, April 9th

I meditate. I sleep. I pray. I stomp.

Thou preparest a table before me in the presence of mine enemies; thou anointest my head with oil; my cup runneth over.

Today, court is starting at 1:00 p.m., but I have an 8:30 a.m. meeting with my legal team, and as I listen to my meditation during the morning drive downtown – *"I am open and allowing for positive things to unfold"* – I think about how surprisingly relaxing the weekend was.

Our Friday night gathering turned out to be a rather cheerful affair, all things considered, with buzzing energy around our group analysis of what had transpired during the course of the week. My Sunday meeting with my legal team got pushed to Monday morning, so both Saturday and Sunday turned into quiet, at-home days for just James and me and the dogs. We puttered in the garden, lounged in the sunshine, and ate delicious meals. All in all, a perfect pause for this intense of a process.

"I always find surprisingly good solutions to everything... my ability to conquer my challenges is limitless...."

At their Friday night dinner, my lawyers and Dr. Loftus had agreed to try tele-conferencing over the weekend to offer it as a substitution for Dr. Loftus's physical presence. Everything was smooth when they tested it yesterday, but this morning the DAs refuse our work-around, saying it isn't a fair or reliable option, and, unfortunately, the judge agrees with them.

Dr. Loftus's testimony is stricken from the record.

For as fired up as I was about this on Friday afternoon, I honestly don't mind too much at this point – the jury marinated in Dr. Loftus's words all weekend long, and no matter what a court tells them to do, they won't be able to erase her compelling research and influential testimony from their memories completely.

But boy oh boy, is the prosecution mad that we didn't deliver Dr. Loftus to them. They spent six weeks preparing for their Loftus cross, they say, and now the multiple binders they put together are useless. Their time is wasted.

I can empathize with feeling frustrated because your time is being wasted; it is a feeling I am intimately acquainted with these days, and it sucks. Empathy typically evokes compassion in me, but not this time; knowing they are frustrated gives me a solid dose of Schadenfreude, which is the experience of feeling pleasure and satisfaction at someone else's misfortune. I make eye contact with each of them, and I smile sweetly.

The jury is instructed not to wonder why the Dr. Loftus testimony has been struck, and my side continues calling from our witness list. Today, I feel not only uplifted from my weekend but also comforted by the dozen or so friends and family filling the rows behind our table: I am supported, I am loved, I am believed.

I am so lucky.

The other side of the room is again empty except for Ivy's mom sitting way in the back, a listening device pressed to her ear.

The jury hears brief testimony from my mother first, which gives them the chance to imagine me as somebody's daughter, and my husband next, which reminds them I am somebody's wife. Because of her chronic health conditions, my mom uses her motorized scooter to reach the front of the courtroom but declines the invitation from the judge to testify from it. After her laborious climb onto the stand, she answers questions about vacations taken and holidays spent with Loretta, Ivy, Angus, Rose and Slater over the years.

"They were like family," she says. "I know my daughter considered them to be."

I can't help but smile *and* cry when James speaks of our beautiful life together, our happy home, our beloved dogs, our mountain motorcycle rides, and our shared passion for turning our house into a home one DIY project at a time. He never cared for anyone in the X family, he found them all to be strangely attached to me, and he says so.

Both James and my mom recall anecdotes about the oddly possessive side of Loretta, from when I began dating James all the way through to our actual wedding.

My Alex.

*She loved **me** first.*

*She's known **me** longer.*

And then it is finally my turn to testify.

I had expected the opportunity to speak openly and freely when I took the stand. To tell my truth, the whole truth, and nothing but the truth, so help me. I'd fantasized about marching up there with my Box of Proof and using my teacher skills to take the entire courtroom through it all, week by week, folder by folder, until every last one of us is crystal clear on a few key points, like the high improbability (and in most cases, sheer impossibility) of these charges.

Although my time on the stand lasts through the rest of Monday afternoon and resumes again on Tuesday morning, neither day of testifying produces the kind of verbal release I'd been anticipating.

Instead, being on stand is essentially more of the same prescriptive, curated process that the past 18 months have been. I am but a pawn in the game that these lawyers and this judge are playing, a game of who can argue their points most convincingly. There seems to be less interest in getting to the root of the accusation and why it is or isn't true, and more focus on bickering about what can and cannot be submitted into evidence (like Loretta's forensic interview video), what can and cannot be asked of certain people (this is why the DAs keep trying to discredit my expert witnesses, so they can't be asked certain questions while testifying), and how much context the jury will or will not get (for example, around why the testimony from Dr. Loftus has been stricken).

My Box of Proof sits on our table, visible to both the prosecution, who knows exactly what it is, and the jury, who doesn't.

It occurs to me that maybe the only thing being accomplished so far is massively confusing the jury. They were encouraged to take notes at the beginning, and I'm praying at least a couple of them are, because even laid out fully on paper, this case is complex.

I am truthful on stand, as clear and resolute as I can be. My voice starts soft, but once I hit my stride, my personality starts to come through. I answer a direct question by emphatically declaring that of course I wear pajamas every time I go to sleep, what if there is a fire in the middle of the night? I'm not necessarily trying to be cute, but the jury laughs at my answer, as does the audience.

My lawyer is dependably fantastic and strategically brilliant. My friends later point out how, despite what appear on the surface to be a few hiccups throughout my questioning, such as pictures being shown that are not supposed to be shown and being asked certain questions more than once, they might not actually be hiccups at all. Every "oops" picture shown represents me being an excellent caregiver to a number of young children, and every repeated question is either about my accomplishments (*"Wait, where did you go to graduate school again?"*) or exceedingly important information we need to cement into the jury's collective brain (*"Wait, not sure if I already asked this, but did you ever touch Loretta in a sexual manner at that house?"*)

All of the meaningful details are pointed out more than once. (*For the record, University of Colorado – Boulder, and no.*)

I keep my composure even when the DA tries to trip me up with her line of questioning about the birthday dates I took Loretta, Rose, and Slater on. I won't let her. I use extra caution by clarifying my understanding of the prosecutor's questions, after she insinuates through her word choice that the fun experiences I offered to the kids – amusement parks, baseball games, concerts in the park – were "special" things that neither Ivy nor Angus would do with them. I can't let the implication go without clarifying the nuance. This is a habit of mine, a leftover tic of all the arguing I had done with Jonathan.

"Well, I did fun things with the kids, yes, but nothing their own parents wouldn't or didn't also do with them."

"That's not the point of what I'm saying."

"Ok, but that's what you asked me."

"Fine, let me rephrase – did you invite Loretta and Rose to do fun things with you?"

"Yes, I did."

I hear her mutter under her breath, "Was that so hard?"

She studies her papers for a moment, glances at the other DA who gives her a half shrug and a shake of her head, then leans into the microphone: "No further questions."

It feels like she'd been trying to go somewhere with her questions but stopped short before arrival; as if she belatedly realized her plan of attack was no good, and rather than changing course, she just abandoned ship. There is no wow moment, like when we'd handed Ivy the copy of that instant messenger conversation. Their cross-examination just fizzles.

After I am excused from the stand, my lawyers call back-to-back mothers of young children I'd been a nanny to during different stretches of time. My heart bursts with gratitude as the first sits polished and poised on the stand, gracefully and confidently recounting the type of trustworthy Mary-Poppins-esque nanny I was to her family back in those early Colorado days when I faithfully provided consistent weekly childcare and occasional weekend overnight care for her three children and their robust group of neighborhood friends.

I am equally grateful for the second mother who takes the stand, the woman I'd worked for in 2010. It was her home for which I'd been housesitting and her dogs for whom I'd been dog-sitting in July of 2010, when first Rose and then Loretta took turns sleeping over to help with the dogs and take bubble baths in the amazing jetted tub – the house where the "bath incident" allegedly took place. She'd been a bit surprised to hear from me at first. It'd been almost seven years since we'd last spoken when I found her on

Facebook and asked for a phone call, yet she had immediately jumped on board to help me any way she could. On the stand, she confirms the 2010 timeline my side has already introduced, verifying that she did not yet know me in 2008, the year Loretta picked to place this story. This is a critical distinction for the jury to understand, that the timing is nowhere near right, and she does a brilliant job of getting it across clearly and definitively. She also confirms there was no hot tub at the house, something Loretta had said was "definitely" there.

Next, it is time for Jonathan to testify, and just like I figured he would, he kills it. He is charming, low-key, and cool with his long dreadlocks and sharp suit. The jury appears to love him; I see lots of smiling and laughing during his engaging testimony. The prosecution asks him, among other things, about the layout of the home we shared together, and what average temperatures are historically like in Santa Barbara during the March – April timeframe. I know exactly why they do this.

They ask about the layout because Loretta said she and Rose stayed in different rooms during the 2009 spring break trip, that I had alternated which girl I slept next to each night. Rose has already given contradicting testimony to her sister's story, correctly recalling that we always co-slept three to a bed. Now Jonathan confirms that the other two bedrooms in our home contained only one twin bed apiece, increasing the improbability of Loretta's claim, which was that one child slept solo in the queen bed every other night while I slept in a twin bed with the other child.

And the average early spring temperature questioning is to determine the probability of Loretta's claims that she was encouraged to take off her pajamas and sleep nude since it was "just so hot." Jonathan confirms that temperatures at night at the end of March are never, ever considered "hot," let alone "so hot." Another detail, contradicted.

After Jonathan finishes mid-morning, I excitedly realize there is a small chance the trial could end today. We have only one more expert witness to call to the stand, a retired Denver police chief with over thirty years of experience in running investigations who agrees the investigation in my case was executed pretty poorly.

After my side rests, the prosecution will be electing to exercise their option of taking another turn by calling my friend and former roommate, Alice, to the stand. Alice had been on my original list of witnesses but, like Grace, was ultimately cut for timing reasons, along with my sister and two other friends familiar with both my professional history as well as my friendship with Loretta, Ivy, Angus, Rose, and Slater. There is slight intrigue circulating amongst us around why the prosecution wants to chat with Alice. Before the trial began, the prosecution telephoned everybody on my witness list asking for conversations, and only my mother and Alice had complied. I'd seen the summaries of both those conversations when they'd come through as discovery weeks ago, and nothing of concern happened during them. To me this feels like the prosecution simply grasping at straws, while wasting even more of everybody's time.

In any case, after these last two witnesses are called to the stand, it will be time for jury instructions, closing arguments, and jury deliberations. The end is in sight.

My final expert witness, Mr. Jackson Pace, confidently speaks to what a botched investigation this was from every angle. He reiterates that the longer an investigation is delayed – think about how Ivy and Angus were interviewed a *full year* after my arrest – the harder it makes it to get things right. He points out that speaking to Ivy and Angus in a prompt manner would have been very important for a number of reasons, especially since Ivy is reportedly the one who made the Facebook messenger discovery that led to the official outcry with the police. Knowing the context of that discovery is key.

For example, what exactly did the parent(s) see? What did they know? How did they know it? What were their discussions? Who else did they tell? Why did they tell anybody else at all? What were their initial thoughts? What did they do next?

And there's more than just the incident in question, he says. As an investigator, you need to also be curious about behaviors in general and the intersection of the two. How does the child act in normal settings? What's the environment of the household generally like? How do these parents get along with their kids? What are the family dynamics?

I think about Rose's assumption that her parents were getting divorced.

These are the kinds of questions, Mr. Pace suggests, that any good investigator will ask of parents in a timely fashion when their child is making this type of accusation, but none of it happened here.

The jury watches him closely, interested in what he is saying. I know this because I am watching them, a habit I have picked up over the course of the trial. A refrain piece of advice from Amelia's lawyer buddies was for me to attempt to make eye contact with as many of the jurors as possible, as often as possible, and for as long as possible. I have managed to achieve this to varying levels with each of them; a few sympathetic smiles have been bestowed upon me. Yesterday, a juror even approached me in the ladies' room, placing her hand gently on my forearm and looking at me with sympathetic eyes as she said, "I'm praying for you every night."

I had no choice but to tell my lawyer about it; the same juror approached a friend of mine in the ladies' room last week, asking if my friend was my sister. "We're trying to figure out who everybody is," the juror had explained with a smile.

"No," my pal had smiled back, "but her sister and lots of other family *are* here. I'm a friend of Alex's, like so many of us that you're seeing, here to support her because we love her light and believe her story." While it admittedly feels good having this nugget of promising inside information – The jury is discussing us! They've noticed our numbers! – I reiterated to my friend to shut conversations like that down immediately. Interactions between the jurors and anybody else in a courtroom are strictly prohibited, and too many violations can throw this whole case out the window, forcing us to start the entire process over again from the start. I've come too far for that.

Accordingly, my lawyer told the judge about the praying juror, and now as the judge calls for a lunch recess before Jackson Pace is cross-examined, she is asked to hang back when the jury is dismissed. When told why, she explains she is praying for *everyone* involved in the case, not just me, and no, she has not yet made up her mind about my guilt or innocence, as the judge has repeatedly instructed jury members not to do until both sides have rested. She vows to stop chatting with folks outside the jury.

We break for a normal-length lunch, then Jackson Pace climbs back up on stand for his cross, where they predictably try to discredit him like they've tried to discredit everybody, but the attempts are in vain.

My favorite moment comes at the end of the cross-examination when the DA asks Mr. Pace, "Sir, who are you responsible to?"

"My boss, the community, the department, the victims, and the defendants to make sure I get the investigation right," he answers.

"So you have a responsibility to the victim?"

"Yes, I do."

"And how much are you getting paid to be here today, Mr. Pace?"

"Nothing."

It isn't the answer she's expecting, but it is the truth. Mr. Pace hasn't charged me one penny to testify on my behalf, and the DA sits down in a huff without another word. After a moment of confused silence, the judge has to ask if she is finished.

She is, so the defense rests, and the prosecution calls a very nervous Alice to the stand for a very anticlimactic rebuttal. They only ask a few questions about date ranges that Alice, it turns out, doesn't remember one way or another, so the point of putting her on stand remains unclear. After one single clarifying question from my lawyer to give the jury a fighting chance of seeing that her testimony is just noise, Alice is dismissed.

Now both sides have rested. Ears perk up in the jury box when the judge mentions the possibility of finishing today before issuing an afternoon recess. He instructs the jury (and the rest of us by proxy) to be back in the courtroom at 3:00 p.m. for jury instructions and closing arguments.

Jury instructions are just what they sound like: instructions given by the judge to the jury. The judge reads a long list of directives to the jurors regarding each of the charges, including what they can consider, what they can't consider, and what they need to ultimately decide for that particular charge. My lawyers (with my input) and the DAs drafted our agreed-upon jury instructions beforehand.

In closing arguments, each side summarizes their case before the jury goes to deliberate and decide. The DAs have asked for an hour for their closing, but the judge limits each side to forty-five minutes apiece.

I start doing the math in my head, adding up minutes against what's left on the clock, and I don't think the judge is right. I don't see how we could wrap this all up in the next two hours.

And it turns out, after giving it a bit more thought during our recess, the judge realizes it, too. "Folks, I was overzealous when I said we might finish today. Due to the severity and complexity of this case, I do not think rushing anything along is a good idea. With the time we have left, we just won't be able to get through all the jury instructions, copy all of the paperwork, explain everything, give each side forty-five minutes for their closing, and do jury deliberations. It's too much for two hours, so we're going to end our day here instead, and come back in the morning to do all of that with fresh energy."

Don't get me wrong, I am undoubtedly ready to put this fiasco behind me, and the jury is visibly disappointed by this turn of events, so my guess is they are ready, too. However, I am grateful nonetheless for the judge's decision. I feel it is far better to slow down and get this right, to take more time to be careful and deliberate rather than trying to rush things along after a long day of an already long trial.

Wednesday, April 11th

I meditate, I sleep, I pray, I stomp.

My cup runneth over.

I drive into the city, the recorded meditation my only company.

"I am flexible to changes happening in my life…change is a sign of life, and I choose life."

My white jacket is hung on the back of my chair. My silk bag of crystals sits on the table next to my pink travel mug of coffee that I had filled in the café downstairs. "Keep fighting the good fight!" the barista tells me when I thank him that morning. He thinks I'm a lawyer. I do not correct him.

I pull out my notepad, my pen. N♥J♥G♥K♥A♥B♥E♥R♥M♥D♥J♥A♥S. *All good things for all involved…truth, clarity, justice.*

I have come this far. I can do this. I can and I will, one breath at a time.

The "Love in Action" group has been a flurry of activity and running commentary for the duration of this trial, and today it's absolutely buzzing.

Helen (Maryland): Those of you attending today - first of all, THANK YOU. If you could keep us posted about the big transitions - especially when the jury leaves to deliberate, I would be so grateful. I am hoping to stop everything to pray and meditate at that moment.

Maeve (Texas): Yes, I humbly request the same. Please and thank you. And thank you all so much for being there.

Allison (Washington D.C.): Yes, please. Me as well. Thank you thank you!

Charlotte (New York): Me, four!

Tina (Illinois): Me, five!

Milly (Colorado): On a family vacation and I cannot put down my phone. Refresh, refresh, refresh...

Update: Wednesday, 9:13 a.m.

Amelia (California): DA starting their closing now. Only Loretta and Rose are there in the courtroom, not their parents, and the girls aren't even sitting by one another.

Charlotte (New York): That is so strange to me.

Carys (Wisconsin): What? Please tell me I'm not the only one who thinks that's ridiculous and quite telling...

Amelia (California): It's odd to me, too.

Melanie (Minnesota): How can you let your child go through this alone?

Helen (Maryland): I simply cannot understand this.

Carys (Wisconsin): I wonder if the DA suggested this may make Loretta look or seem more vulnerable on the day they are depending on the jury's sympathy.

Jules (Wisconsin): I assumed it was a strategy too - but if I was the parent, no way. I'd want to hear every single word said. I'd want to look the person in the face.

Amelia (California): Alex's sister, Mona, just texted me - the grandma is there, too, but not sitting with either of the girls.

Jules (Wisconsin): What?!

Eleanor (Colorado): What?! They actually have two minor girls sitting by themselves in a courtroom? And the one family member present isn't even sitting near them? That makes no sense at all.

Caroline (Colorado): Wow. Just, wow.

Jill (Wisconsin): I can't comprehend this.

Charlotte (New York): I am so confused by this family's actions; I can't even find the right words.

Corrine (California): What a strange situation, to have such a visible lack of support.

Grace (Rhode Island): Well, at least Alex doesn't have that problem!

Cecily (Colorado): I love that the judge can't pronounce Alex's first OR last name. Alexandria Quickiss is having a rough day. Alex Kuisis is a total rockstar. I like to think of it as the judge blocking energy that's not meant for Alex, anyway.

Alice (Colorado): Omg, I thought the exact same thing! Clearly they have the wrong person.

Mona (in courtroom): I do appreciate the judge's dedication to the mispronunciation.

Update: Wednesday, 10:48 a.m.

Amelia (California): Defense is doing its closing arguments now.

Eleanor (Colorado): Her attorney has such a great delivery and friendly tone. I would imagine the jury will listen intently to him.

Melanie (Minnesota): May they be short and concise.

Ainsley (Colorado): May they stress Reasonable Doubt and therefore Not Guilty.

Corrine (California): May the jury listen with their ears, hearts and heads. May they hear and know the truth.

Mona (in courtroom): Alex's lawyer did a great job. The closing revolved around finding reasonable doubt and recognizing credibility issues, as well as the countless ways the investigation was not completed properly. He talked about how the witnesses tell varying versions of similar events, which shows us how questionable relying on memory alone is. Believe then verify! He reminded the jury of the presumption of Alex's innocence, and asked them to hold the Government to their burden of proof. Then he outlined the multitude of reasons he believes the Government failed to do exactly that.

Update: Wednesday, 11:37 a.m.

Amelia (California): The case has gone to the jury... send good thoughts, friends!

Melanie (Minnesota): Let's all focus love and clarity and wisdom to the jurors. Focus on them. May all of the love we feel for Alex and her family and friends, may all of the love and light we have experienced because of Alex, just blind them now. Let them know, without doubt, the truth. Let them know that Alex is innocent and come back with a verdict of innocent tonight.

Zoe (Wisconsin): Both my husband and I work in the court/jail system, and in our experiences, jury deliberations can be short or very long. The jury will have questions regarding the case, and things they want clarification on and such. The lawyers and Alex will be brought back into the courtroom to hear those, and typically, the public can go in for those, too. Often they just want clarification on something that was said or they want to see a particular piece of evidence.

Once they are done deliberating, the attorneys will be called to return. Typically, attorneys are told to not be more than 5 minutes from the courthouse. If her supporters aren't going to be with her while waiting but want to be there for the verdict, make sure they stay close to the courthouse and have someone from her team call them when the verdict comes in.

***

We sit outside the courthouse. Temperatures are mild for mid-April; no jackets are necessary.

A smattering of friends waits with us. Caroline, Cecily, Alice, my therapist, Bea, and a few others all mill about in the quiet, bearing witness while lifting one another up with occasional bouts of laughter and sisterhood feelings of solidarity. Mona, my parents, my aunt, and my beloved cousin, Lana, are also there, adding to the spirit of keeping things light and positive. My in-laws, too, ostensibly to support me, but really to support James, and I am thankful for their focus of providing him comfort like families should.

There is hopeful anticipation singed with an undercurrent of nervous worry permeating the air. Some of us read books, some of us crack jokes, some of us stare at our phones, some, like my dad, doze in the sunlight, while some, like me, can't sit still at all.

I am equal parts mind-numbingly terrified and deeply at peace in my soul. I have done all I can do, and now the biggest challenge is remembering to breathe deeply.

James and I hold hands as we take a short walk to a nearby coffee shop. My sweet husband gently wraps his strong arms around me as we wait for our drinks, and I sink into the familiarity of his loving, protective embrace. We do not say much at all. We have said so much already over the past eighteen months.

When we return, Bea asks to walk around the courtyard with me, and we engage in a mini-therapy session right there on the lawn. Per her suggestion, I slip my shoes off and stand in the cool, green grass in my nylon-clad feet, drawing power up from Mother Earth. We call on my spirit guides – Archangel Michael, the Yeti, the goddess Athena – to protect and sustain me. We send love to the jurors, visualizing waves of truth and clarity filling the room in which they debate my future. She holds both of my hands, and we breathe.

Inhale love and confidence, exhale fear and doubt.

Update: Wednesday, 4:21 p.m.

Amelia (California): Some on the jury are a hard guilty. Some are not comfortable with using testimony only, they want to see the video of Loretta's forensic interview.

Carys (Wisconsin): Excuse me? How is "hard guilty" even a possibility? How many is "some?" Two? Three? Eleven? I'm fuckin' flipping out here.

Amelia (California): We don't know.

Melanie (Minnesota): I am sick and stunned and speechless how anyone could possibly believe Alex is anything but innocent.

Grace (Rhode Island): Me, too

Jill (Wisconsin): I am fucking sick right now.

Victoria (Wisconsin): No, no, no, no, no. They have to follow the "reasonable doubt" rule. They have to feel the truth in their bones. Please, let them feel the truth!

Allison (Washington D.C.): I just… no words.

Jill (Wisconsin): I honestly 100% believed this would be open and shut.

Victoria (Wisconsin): Me, too.

Jules (Wisconsin): 100% agree.

Caroline (Colorado): Me, too.

Charlotte (New York): Me, too. Reading this feels like a sucker punch to the gut.

Kendall (New York): I'm stunned. No words.

Zoe (Wisconsin): Un-fucking-real.

Ainsley (Colorado): A declarative statement is not evidence. As a teacher of argument, I am astounded. There is no evidence! There is a law student on the jury. Hoping she brings common sense to the discussion.

Millie (Colorado): I had to read this update twice. How is this possible?!

Carys (Wisconsin): I'm a firm believer that their final decision will be made not only on what they heard from the lawyers, Alex, Loretta, etc., but will also be influenced by things they won't even know they're taking into consideration. Things like we all wore bright colors instead of dark (signifying hope over fear,) not to mention the sheer number of us, and how our spots were replaced with other supporters in our stead when we couldn't be there. They may not even be able to explain why they feel a certain way 100% but the fact they feel a certain way will certainly make a positive difference for our Alex.

Amelia (California): That's exactly why we've put so much effort into supporting her!

Helen (Maryland): I want closure for Alex. I want her to hear the words "not guilty."

Jules (Wisconsin): Wait. How is a hard guilty even possible?! They have no case. What happens if they cannot resolve this?

Amelia (California): It's declared a mistrial. And if the DAs decide to retry the case, we start all the way over.

Update: Wednesday, 4:55 p.m.

Amelia (California): The instruction from the judge to the jury is that they have all the evidence they are going to get to make their decision – they will not be allowed to see Loretta's forensic interview. Since they had not yet decided on a verdict, the judge has dismissed them, and we will come back tomorrow.

Victoria (Wisconsin): Deep, deep breaths, everybody. All it takes is one person on that jury to know the truth and to start convincing others. They shouldn't need convincing but we live in a culture where it's bad form to doubt alleged "victims." We all know the truth. We all know that Alex is 100% innocent of these charges. Let's focus our energy on clarity for the jury and reminders to their souls of the "reasonable doubt" factor. Please lord, let truth prevail!

Amelia (California): I truly believe in the power of good people coming together to create the change they want to see in the world. Supporting Alex with all of you for the past 18 months has been the only part of this that didn't feel terrible. Thank you all for responding and donating and posting and commenting and loving. This time tomorrow I'm hoping the jury has done their work and that we are all celebrating in this space - the beginning of the end of this nightmare. Love to everyone around the world and especially in Denver!

Maeve (Texas): I have been so grateful for this space over the course of this whole thing. Often it is the only outlet I have and it is absolutely my only source of information. Thank you thank you thank you everyone. Holding all hope and love in my heart. Until tomorrow...

Thursday, April 12th

Zoe (Wisconsin): Good morning! May the light of today's sun burn the night's fog into oblivion and bring a renewed strength to this day. Truth fundamentally has to matter. Love always wins. Strength, love, courage, and clarity being sent via this morning's gorgeous crescent moon to some very important people I may never meet and those on the jury whom I will never know.

Jill (Wisconsin): It is a beautiful, sunny day here and I woke up believing with all my heart that today is the day truth wins. Focusing all my energy today on amplifying the voices of those jurors who have heard the truth and feel it in their souls.

Charlotte (New York): Same here!

Allison (Washington D.C.): Yes!

Annie (Colorado): 100% agree!

Maeve (Texas): Yes, yes, yes. Keeping hope alive! Sending all my positivity!

Aggie (Wisconsin): So. Much. Yes. So. Much. Love.

Amelia (California): YES. Let's end this today. All hearts on deck! Thanks to everyone who changed their social media profile pics last night to be pictures of you and Alex – so fun to see so many different photos of our girl! Anyone in court today in addition to Mona and the rest of her family?

Annie (Colorado): I'll be there!

Alice (Colorado): Me, too!

Lynn (Colorado): Me, three!

Ramona (Colorado): Already on my way! See you all there!

***

I meditate. I sleep. I wake up bone tired, the kind of exhausted that comes from a place having nothing to do with getting more rest.

I pray – oh, how I pray – and I stomp around my backyard.

Though I walk through the valley of the shadow of death, I will fear no evil.

For the eighth weekday in a row, I drive downtown.

"I am motivated and inspired to make choices for my highest good and the highest good of everyone involved…"

I meet James and Mona in the parking garage and we find our way through security, up the elevators, to the courtroom. I begin my rituals. Jacket on the chair, notepad, pen, and crystals on the table. I date a fresh page: *Day 8 of the Neverending Trial.* I jot down the series of jury initials, easily, from memory now: N♥J♥G♥K♥A♥B♥E♥R♥M♥D♥J♥A♥S. I take a deep breath and write this morning's intention: *clarity…conclusion… Best Possible Outcome…yes, I can…yes, I will, thank you Universe… thank you again.*

Good mornings are said and proceedings begin. The jury retreats immediately to its room and, the rest of us are excused to begin our waiting.

At 9:20 a.m., we are called back to the courtroom because the jury has a question. We rise as the judge walks in, then sit right back down as he predictably waves his hand at us, mumbling his familiar, "Take a seat, take a seat." The jury files into the jury box, finds their seats, then the foreperson – the woman with the lavender hair, it turns out – hands the clerk a folded piece of paper for the judge.

The jury again wants to know if they can watch Loretta's ninety-minute forensic interview, and if not, why not?

After a conference at the bench with my lawyers and the DAs, an answer is issued: No, you can't see it, and you're not to wonder about why not. The jury retreats to the deliberating room, and we are reminded not to go far as we are excused from the courtroom.

An hour and a half passes. At 10:56 a.m., the jury has another question. We reconvene in the courtroom as quickly as possible.

This time their question is of a more logistical nature. They wonder how long they need to keep talking if they have decided on some counts but are not getting anywhere on the other counts.

The judge volleys back two questions in return:

1) *Has any progress been made towards an agreement?*

2) *What is the likelihood of reaching an agreement on any of the others?*

I am not privy to the answers they provide on their slip of paper, but the judge is, and he encourages them to remain in deliberations. We are again excused from the courtroom, and another hour passes.

At 11:50 a.m., we receive another alert to return to the courtroom. This time it's not for a question, though. This time it's for the answer.

I clutch my bag of crystals in my left hand and stress scribble in my notepad with my right as we wait for the jury. *"Holy shit…this is easily the most scared I have ever been in my entire life. I barely feel my body. This is for the highest good of all involved. Spirit Guides, don't fail me now. Yes, I can. Yes, I will. Please. Please. Here we go…"*

At 12:07 p.m., I write in my notepad again. *"The jury emerged to announce their verdict, then realized something hadn't been signed that was supposed to be signed, so they all stood back up and shuffled back out. Then, a few minutes later they sent word out that they actually want to deliberate just a little bit more, so they'll let us know when they are really, truly finished. I mean, you can't make this stuff up."*

Update: 12:33 p.m.

Amelia (California): JURY IS IN!

They found Alex NOT GUILTY on two of the charges and had a mistrial on the other five! For the remaining five counts, only one juror thought guilty, while the other eleven jurors believed she was innocent.

The not guilty charges were the two counts associated with what they called "the bath incident." The mistrial counts come from the accusations at Connie's house and the couple's house. What this means is the DA could choose to retry the remaining counts, but with a jury so heavily leaning towards the defendant, it seems unlikely.

Millie (Colorado): Only one thought guilty! That's enough for me to breathe. Victory!

Lynn (Colorado): Crying uncontrollably. So crazy happy!

Corrine (California): Oh thank you, Universe.

Ramona (Colorado): It is a relief but bittersweet because I did want to see not guilty across the board.

Jules (Wisconsin): 11-1?! That's both incredible and so upsetting. One person.

Trey (Georgia): One stubborn holdout who was apparently listening to different testimony than the other eleven, or not paying attention at all. 11-1 against the other five charges pretty much clinches those charges won't be retried.

Zoe (Wisconsin): A retrial would be purely out of spite, especially with numbers like that. It'd be a ludicrous waste of the court's time, let alone taxpayer money.

Jules (Wisconsin): In my opinion, no way they'll retry this case – they retry when it is clear and they can win. It isn't and they can't so my guess (my hope) is they won't.

Ainsley (Colorado): Only if the DA is profoundly hellbent on mucking up her career stats will they retry. They can't win. They scored a huge break with striking Dr. Loftus's testimony and they still couldn't get one single guilty verdict. This is so done – Alex gets her life back. It's a huge day for her.

Corrine (California): One reason I feel this won't be retried is because clearly there are evidentiary issues. The accuser and her parents would have to want her to testify again, and Loretta may not want to go through all that to keep her lies afloat. Unless, of course, it's all a ploy for attention?

Serena (California): Thanks for posting all the updates and clarifications, Amelia! I've been so worried (and now so relieved) for Alex, James, and their families.

Amelia (California): Of course! I'd do anything for her except let's never do this again!

***

A few days later, my husband posts in the group.

James (Colorado): Just wanted to express my gratitude to everyone here. It has meant the absolute world to us, and clearly made a difference! We are not out of the woods just yet, but remain hopeful that there will not be a second trial. The meeting to find out is soon. Please keep us in your thoughts and we will be sure to update when we know!

The love pours in through the comments; the emotional support my friends continue to offer is how we stay afloat through each wave we are asked to surf.

"Thank you, James! Still sending so many positive thoughts your way!"

"Hoping for some closure once and for all!"

"Thank you for loving our girl! All our good thoughts continuing in your direction!"

"All our very best to you! Hug each other from me, ok?"

"Thank you for being the best partner Alex could have had throughout this."

"Continuing to blast you all with vibes for no retrial! #stopthebullshit"

"Remember: the prosecution convinced only one person on the jury of some of the charges. Everyone else knew it was BS. Common sense says they won't retry."

"Good luck, for sure. Thinking about you both and sending all good stuff your way. Please let us know how it goes."

April 23, 2018

I meditate, I sleep.

I pray, I stomp.

The Lord is my shepherd; I shall not want.

James and I drive into the city to learn that the DAs have decided to re-try the five remaining counts. We are stunned and speechless as another trial in the same courtroom with the same judge is set for October 2018.

Chapter 9

"Courage is the price life exacts for granting peace." –
Amelia Earhart

My intention is set before we even leave the courtroom that day –
the second trial will not come to fruition – and the very next order
of business is re-hiring my lawyer.

When he tells me his fees have gone up since I first hired him
back in September of 2016, I think about how often and adamantly
he encouraged me to take offers, and I wonder if I've been more
work than he bargained for, although if that's the case, I like to
think he's enjoyed the challenge. I'll be honest, I expect him to
offer me a discount of some sort. You know, a "buy one trial get
the second one half off" kind of thing, but no such offer is forthcoming. I pay the higher fee because at this point, what else am I
going to do, shop for a new lawyer? I am not.

I post in the group to keep my friends in the loop.

"Hi everyone,

I miss you. Please know I am continually humbled by and
constantly grateful for your generous and thoughtful shows of support.

I see hearts everywhere, daily.

The DAs have indeed decided to retry the mis-tried counts from
the first trial, so another trial has been set for October. You may
recall we've had quite a birthday theme going with so many of these
court dates, and this one is no different. It's slated to begin on my
niece's birthday, which feels like – you guessed it – a good sign that
we will ultimately prevail. Prevailing just seems to be taking longer
than anticipated, I guess.

I remain hopeful, as one must, and have set an intention, as one does, for this wretched situation to go away once and for all before a second trial comes to fruition. I've manifested wilder things before, so we'll see how this all unfolds, won't we?

Right now I feel energetically drained and emotionally depleted. I'm looking forward to a quiet-ish summer at home with James and the dogs, spending time in the garden, walking around the lake, and writing. I plan on writing a lot.

I love you, I miss you, I appreciate you, and I hope you are having a beautiful spring.

Keep the faith, friends!"

***

One thing I definitely can't do right now is quit my job, which I'd been hoping against hope would be the case.

When I return to work after my two-week "vacation," multiple team members share with me that our boss has been spreading the word, as well as links to news articles, about my personal situation with less-than-charitable commentary. I'm angry and hurt and sad – how dare she! – but not shocked. It's very on brand for Regina's chew-'em-up-and-spit-'em-out style of leadership.

I shift to the bare minimum to satisfy my job description during my work hours, which I finagle to minimize as much direct contact with Regina as I can. I choose to pour my precious energy and sacred talents into my court case and my studies instead. Since completing my health coach certification back in May of 2017, I've been chipping away at an additional life coaching certification. I have big plans, and none of them involve Regina.

***

At first, while the first trial is still so fresh in my mind, all I want to do is strategize for the second trial. I review my Box of Proof start to finish, determined to make it more of a focal point this time.

I tell my lawyer to extend an offer to the X family: I will give them a significant amount of money to get Loretta real therapy for whatever it is that actually happened to her, and they will leave me the hell alone forevermore, and we can all just move on with our lives. If they were trying to create a hardship for me, they can rest assured that they have succeeded. My lawyer says they likely won't accept that because as far as he can tell, they don't want money. Like Ivy's Instagram captions, every offer letter the prosecution has sent so far has mentioned their desire to get me "help."

"Well," I say, "please let them know it would 'help' if they could acknowledge that putting everyone through the time and expense of repeating this circus of lies is in absolutely *nobody*'s best interest, least of all their very own daughter, who is clearly hurting from a very broken place deep inside, and that their failure to address it because they are so wrapped up in these falsehoods borders on neglect. How about you let them know I said all that when you make my offer?"

***

It's a long six months. I try to puzzle out a deeper meaning, figure out a higher message, get a bird's eye view of why this extension of containment is necessary. The best I can guess is that somebody involved in this situation needs to learn something they have not learned yet. The obvious would be me or Loretta, but it could be anyone touched by this, really.

I clearly can't speak for Loretta's levels of self-awareness, but I am willing to continue doing my part to untangle the knot of bitter energy that could be keeping us stuck in these unfortunate circumstances. I swan dive right back into the murky inner work of upending stagnant beliefs around my worthiness in the world, warts and all, and shedding stale relationship dynamics by doing better as soon as I know better, wise advice I have not always followed. I practice letting go of seemingly expired friendships without so much as a grudge or a regret. I have to practice for many months before it feels even the slightest bit comfortable.

That there is still so much work to be done both exhausts and invigorates me.

My spiritual life expands exponentially, and my meditation practice intensifies. Saida tells me she does not see a second trial. Of course I want to believe her (and she was right about two DAs) because her vision matches my intention. It becomes harder and harder to do, though, as I watch the prosecution's discovery come in bit by bit as they try to clean up their investigation beginning mere days after the conclusion of the first trial and continuing throughout the spring and summer.

They are not giving up.

April 19, 2018

Discovery Update: The investigator who works for the district attorney's office speaks to someone at the Denver Police Department about obtaining Facebook messages that have been deleted. He learns of one way that the messages could be located – in the archived threads tab in the Facebook messenger application. With consent from Loretta granted for the purpose of seeing if the messages in question could be recovered, he searches for the message Ivy claimed to have seen, the exchange between Loretta and her buddy, Duncan, where she first says she'd been hurt by one of her mom's (nameless) friends.

The investigator reports that through trying this method, he is unable to locate any archived thread messages between them, so further investigation still needs to be done.

May 7, 2018

Discovery Update: The DA's investigator submits discovery of five pictures from Google Earth of the house Jonathan and I shared in

Santa Barbara, and twenty-five pictures from a real estate website of the house known as "Connie's house."

May 24, 2018

Discovery Update: The DA's investigator sends a search warrant to Facebook for that elusive message exchange between Loretta and Duncan.

June 2, 2018

Today is a hard day for me emotionally. From the moment I wake, my attitude clashes with the buckets of morning light pouring into the room. I feel so dark and violent inside that the sunshine almost feels like a mockery of my frame of mind.

I experience intense bouts of anger towards the X family surging through my veins as I go through my morning routine. I sob in the shower, my hot tears dissolving instantly into the hot water. My anger relentlessly clouds my mood.

Tears find me again during my yoga practice; hip releases are notorious for this. I take advantage of being alone in my backyard instead of in the middle of a crowded studio class by sobbing my way through pigeon pose, lifting the edge of my shirt to swipe at my runny nose.

Let go, let go, let go...

Some of my tears feel therapeutic, while others feel like pure rage erupting from my eyes.

On paper, their case is so weak. Why hasn't this ended yet? What kind of drama and destruction addicts am I dealing with here? Nothing in life comes without lessons, so what do I need to still learn from this? What am I missing? What needs to be seen? I am willing to show up, I am here. I'm willing to do the work, I'm listening. But I'm also tired. I think this is what being at the end of my rope feels like. I am emotionally scraping at the bottom of the barrel.

I put away dry dishes in a sad daze and distractedly fold a load of laundry. I fantasize about throwing flaming bags of dog shit onto Ivy and Angus's front porch, catapulting a rock through every window in their house. I think back to the friend of mine, who, when this had all started, told me he'd seriously considered going to the X's house in the middle of the night and slashing the brakes in all of their cars, that's how furious he was at them. I let my thoughts take me there, playing out the whole tragic scene in my mind's eye. My imagination really gets going, and I begin dreaming up a variety of grim scenarios, all of which end very badly for them.

My mindset alarms me a bit. I am furious, and I don't have a lot of experience feeling, let alone successfully managing, these levels of rage, so round and round I go, feeling irate, then ashamed for wanting them to hurt like they've made me hurt.

I don't know how to snap out of it.

It feels easier to sink into the seductive logic of suicidal thoughts, a pull I am familiar with from bouts of past episodes of depression. I am mesmerized by the seemingly uncomplicated, soothing allure of permanent rest, as I am so bone tired and excruciatingly disenchanted with the idea of doing this bullshit over again that total termination begins to feel like a compelling option. The promise of more living as a reward for staying alive doesn't entice me, it only multiplies my feelings of exhaustion.

June 14, 2018

Discovery Update: Facebook responds to the search warrant.

The message Ivy reported seeing in the middle of the night does not exist.

It does not exist.

Our list of questions for the second trial grows. Did Ivy dream it or make it up entirely?

June 19, 2018

Discovery Update: The DA's investigator speaks to the mother of the family I worked for in Santa Barbara. She says her kids liked me, and she trusted me even if she considered me lazy. It's an interview of no consequence.

July 4, 2018

James and I host our 7th annual Independence Day pot luck party. It starts at noon, and this year we serve hot dogs, brats, and sausages, as well as a tasting station of the more exotic fare our local butcher shop offers, like kangaroo, wild boar, and rattlesnake. Our friends and their families filter in throughout the afternoon, bringing salads and side dishes and sweets.

The gift of gathering in our backyard oasis in the name of theoretical freedom and independence is not lost on me, and I am grateful to be wearing sunglasses because they hide the perpetual happy tears rimming my eyes.

A guest casually asks how trial prep is going, and I am relieved when my husband shuts it down immediately, a friendly smile on his face. "Not today, buddy," James says cheerfully as he claps our pal on the shoulder. "Today is for talking about everything but that."

And so we do. Our social circle is such that, while the majority of our party guests like each other a lot and are perhaps connected on social media, they only see one another at parties at our house, which makes for plenty of jovial catching up when we do all come together. Today is no exception.

We sit around the tables under the shade umbrellas, exchanging stories and ripping on the president. When the final guest leaves ten hours after the party began, I am joyfully exhausted, and I cry in earnest as I change out of my party dress and into my pajamas.

I am so lucky.

The party serves as a poignant reminder of how people truly thrive when they are surrounded by kindness and encouraged to be great. It's such a stark contrast to the daily work environment I have to endure with Regina, and I feel a yearning in my heart, a palpable desire in my bones, to be someday surrounded by professional people who lift me up, excite me, and challenge me in positive and stimulating ways, making me stronger, happier, and more confident in all my best qualities. I know I am worthy of it because we all are.

July 14, 2018

My sister calls me in an excited tizzy. She'd started an Instagram account when the legal debacle began for the sole purpose of posting memes about our Truth Matters, Love Wins motto. Her feed represents the soul of our side's overall attitude, and we've been wondering all along if anyone from the X family is watching. Now we know they are – Ivy just "liked" one of Mona's posts.

I ask Mona to take a screenshot and send it my way so I can forward it to my lawyer, who stashes such things in a second trial file specifically dedicated to all the ways the X family violates the "no contact" rule, the same rule used to reprimand the praying juror during the first trial. It's not a difficult rule to understand. You are not to reach out in any way, shape, or form (i.e. social media) to anyone on the opposing side, and especially not anyone who is/ has been on the witness list.

Catching the X family in these smaller violations always feels like a catch 22. On one hand, it is satisfying to have tangible indications of them refusing to comply with the judge's orders because it shows the lack of integrity with which they operate in general, but on the other hand, just like with the praying juror situation during the trial, too many of these violations could create harsh consequences, like having to begin these two years of red tape all over again.

We started the file back in 2016 when Ivy sent my lawyer the LinkedIn request and Rose liked the series of my Instagram posts the night before my arrest made the news. We were still adding to it a mere week before the first trial began, after Loretta liked one of my sister's Instagram posts, a meme about how damaging lies can be.

July 27, 2018

I don't feel physically great today. It's like the third day in a row. My head hurts, my body aches, and my energy is nil. Consequently, we nixed our plans to crest a few mountaintops on the motorcycle, and here I soak instead, in bubbles and salts and bath bombs galore, an essential oil diffuser dispelling its nurturing aromas throughout this tiny bathroom.

I started physical therapy this summer to correct a misalignment in my shoulder, and it has been fascinating to witness the nucleus of discomfort ping pong around my entire upper carriage, like a domino effect of realignment, each muscle group taking its turn learning new re-patterning skills through diligently executed daily exercise combinations.

It's not entirely surprising that the process is stirring up some deep, murky emotional patterns as well, and the combination is literally making me sick to my stomach. The body stores emotion, so when we start to move or use or hold our bodies differently, those emotional loops that were so snugly ensconced in the shadows can find themselves yanked into sudden broad daylight, feeling raw and exposed and desperately needing attention before they freak out and start wreaking havoc on everything.

So just like I'm doing the work to correct my physical self, I'm taking a long, hard look at what's coming up for me emotionally these days, too, and looking for healthy ways to deal with it. Factor in all the political looney toons activity in the world in general, and the time feels ripe for laying low, looking inward, and shedding as many layers of stagnation as possible.

And napping. Oh my goodness, the time also feels ripe for lots of napping. I am so drained, even though it feels like all I do is sleep.

August 8, 2018

Discovery Update: The DA's investigator reaches out to the X's "family friend therapist" mentioned during the first trial. Her name is Fiona, and she is both a self-described "spiritual therapist" and a Universal Life Minister, which is a designation anybody is welcome to achieve online in literally 90 seconds. Fiona says she only met with Loretta one time, and when Loretta told her the story about the alleged abuse, Fiona brought Ivy into the room immediately. Ivy's rendition was that Loretta had multiple sessions with Fiona, one of which included a screaming match behind closed doors.

Two different versions… how completely unsurprising.

Unfortunately, Fiona has no record of any of this one way or the other, as she says she's never taken so much as a page of notes in her 45 years of ministering to people. She cannot help.

And so it goes.

August 11, 2018

Ivy is watching the Instagram stories on my professional health coach page on a daily basis, as is Angus's cousin, Pam. I have the feeling they don't know I know, but I've known for a handful of weeks already, because Instagram provides lists of accounts that have watched each story. I've been taking screenshots and sending them to my lawyer all the while.

In my stories, I mostly talk about the importance of self-care practices like mindful breathing, drinking enough water, and daily movement, but once I learn they are watching, I begin tailoring my messages to include my opinions about the truth, the importance of telling it, and how frustrating it can be to deal with people who won't.

August 14, 2018

I get a call from my lawyer. The prosecution has made another offer.

He emails me the details.

Hi Alex,

As I anticipated and as we spoke about on the phone, they weren't interested in accepting the offer you'd posed earlier this summer. However, they have another offer for you.

The new offer is: a four-year Deferred Judgment (DJ) to an (F4) Negligent Child Abuse + completion of Colorado's Sexual Offender Intensive Supervision Program.

The three big benefits of this plea over the prior offer are: it is deferred without any probation, the case would be dismissed completely after four years with no permanent conviction, and the offense you are pleading to is a "non-sex" child abuse (versus an "attempted sexual assault on a child.")

The downside is you would still have to admit to underlying factual basis of sexual contact and do sex offender therapy, which I know you have been very clear you will not do.

But I am obligated to seek and relay all offers. In addition, given the risk of trial even with the prior partial mistrial/acquittal, I submit to you that this is an excellent offer. It now enables you to fully control and remove future risk and have no permanent conviction whatsoever, plus move to de-register in four years.

Let me know.

Thanks,
Lawyer
I write him back immediately.
Dear Lawyer,
Offer declined.
Thanks,
Alex

August 17, 2018

We're back in the courtroom today for the first time since April. I, of course, meditated last night, slept sound as a rock, stomped around my backyard, and prayed with the morning sun.

The Lord is my shepherd; I shall not want.

Today we are here because the prosecution wants to amend their complaint. They want to take the timeline of the allegations from the original 2008-2010 period that Loretta first named and extend it to a wider 2008-2014 window. They want to do this because back in April, Loretta said on stand that she wasn't exactly sure when the alleged abuse stopped – it could have been when she was ten, but maybe she was twelve or thirteen? Maybe even fourteen?

Their request does not worry me in the slightest. It's easy for me to prove that our friendship ended in 2013, right around her 13th birthday, so if she was getting hurt when she was twelve, thirteen, fourteen years old, that would mean a couple of important-to-note things: 1) she's talking about time periods where I lived in different locations than the ones she's named, and 2) she's talking about time periods when I was no longer in any kind of regular daily contact with anyone in the X family.

So as I see it, extending the timeline is not a big deal. It shows me they are blindly throwing darts at a wall, hoping something somewhere might stick.

Even so, my lawyer still argues with the judge that the timeline shouldn't change – that the second trial is only supposed to re-try what was already in motion, not start anything over. I know he does this to have the argument on the record, should we need reasons to appeal a decision down the road. He's been doing it all along, and I am grateful for his savvy.

As somewhat expected, the judge disagrees with him. "This trial is kind of a new day," the judge says by way of explanation. "They can make amendments to their charges if they want to."

In that case, my lawyer points out, shouldn't we be pressing "reset" on all relevant components, such as my right to a preliminary hearing?

"My client waived her right to a preliminary hearing back in December of 2016 based on the original timeline of the original complaint. If we are saying the complaint gets to be different now, shouldn't my client also have the chance to make different choices based on it?"

"Interesting," the judge says from his bench, "I do hear what you are saying. Anybody have any relevant case law handy for us to review around this point?"

"No," the prosecution says, "but it exists and I know what it says – that Ms. Kuisis is actually *not* entitled to a preliminary hearing at this point."

"Get me that case law," the judge tells her before centering himself in his seat to re-address all of us, "but until then, we'll plan on re-visiting this in September when we meet about whether or not the forensic interview video can be allowed in as evidence."

Another court date is set for next month, and we are dismissed.

I go across the street to check in at pre-trial, and I call Ricky, my bondsman, to check in, just like I've been doing for almost two solid years.

From day one, the expectation was that I call him every three days, and even after months upon months (upon months) of compliance, Ricky still balked at my occasional requests to lower the frequency.

"You're definitely the highest-maintenance part of this whole ordeal," I told him once, much to his bemusement. "Even my pre-trial officer only requires I call and leave a message once a month, and when I go to check in at pre-trial after each of my court dates, they don't even make me wait to meet with my officer face-to-face anymore. I just check in at the front desk. But here I am, still trying to remember to call you every third day, for literally years now. There are a lot of moving parts in my life and your 'every three days' butts heads against any kind of weekly routine I try to establish. Can I at least go to a Monday, Wednesday, Friday schedule?"

"Too bad and no way." he'd said, "Those are my rules, and the rules are the rules. I don't change the rules for anyone. You need to call me every three days. I don't care about your routines or schedules. That's the way it is, and that's final."

However, they say everyone has a price and earlier this summer I'd stumbled upon Ricky's. When he learned I write things professionally during one of our calls, Ricky asked me to write an online review for him. I recognized an opportunity.

"I'll write you a review if you let me call you less often."

He paused, and then started to laugh.

"Ok, fine. Whatever. You win. You've got yourself a deal. Post the review online, and call me once a week."

It may all be a game, but I've been figuring out how to play.

August 20, 2018

Saida reaches out to tell me she's had a vision of multiple judges hearing my case. This gives me pause and a slightly sick feeling in the pit of my stomach. I hope it's not an indication of needing to appeal an unfavorable outcome of the second trial, but I can't make much sense of it otherwise, so I file it away in my thoughts for later before I invite any panic into my mind. One day at a time, I remind myself. Just put one foot in front of the other and keep breathing.

August 27, 2018

Discovery Update: The DA's investigator speaks to the owner of the moldy basement and then to her ex-husband, both of whom have plenty of mean-spirited opinions to share. They label my Buddhist beliefs as "different, creepy, and odd," and my propensity for natural remedies (to try and cure myself of the black mold rash that I got from living in their house) as "strange, homeopathic, and hippy dippy."

Name-calling aside, neither of them has anything relevant to add and as I read through the notes from both conversations that the prosecution has provided to my lawyer, I feel such relief that these drama llamas are out of my life.

Good riddance, I think, and not for the first time.

September 6, 2018

An email comes from my lawyer; he's heard from the judge. Based on the case law submitted by the prosecution, our request for a preliminary hearing on the amended counts has been denied.

September 10, 2018

My lawyer calls to talk strategy for this week's upcoming court date. We'll be arguing motions around allowing Loretta's forensic interview video into the second trial as evidence. We're saying "no," the prosecution is saying "yes." Additionally, despite the judge's ruling on the preliminary hearing, my lawyer plans on re-visiting the argument to make a few more points on the record. "Should we need to appeal the decision," he reminds me, as if I need reminding.

He also mentions his intention to play a rather unorthodox card if need be, and I am intrigued. Should the judge rule against us in one of our key motions around a child hearsay argument, we're going to respond by filing what my lawyer calls a "Rule 21," effectively halting our case's proceedings for a direct appeal to the Colorado Supreme Court.

If the higher court deigns this particular point in my case worth hearing, and my lawyer seems to think they might, then all seven members of the court – *multiple judges* – would rule on this particular point before sending it back down to the district level where we've been all along to continue with the rest of the trial.

Everything depends on how our current judge rules when we see him later this week.

September 12, 2018

I meditate. I sleep.

I pray. I stomp.

For thou art with me; thy rod and thy staff, they comfort me.

A friend texts that today happens to be the birthday of Ganesha, a Hindu god known to be the remover of obstacles. I'll take it.

I am the first person to arrive in the courtroom, and the lights all spring to action when I pull open the second set of double wooden doors. I have trained myself to stand in confidence, faith, and love when I walk into this room, and today feels no different. A fresh wave of determination washes over me. I smile to myself and snap a few pictures of the empty room. I want to remember this feeling later.

I solicit good thoughts and spare prayers from my Love in Action group, wearing their quick responses like hugs.

People slowly trickle in after me, but not many. Mine is the only case being discussed here today, so this gigantic room is populated by less than a dozen of us. Both DAs are here, and they've asked Loretta's forensic interviewer, who testified at the first trial, to be here today since we'll be discussing her role in the video. She and two of her associates sit in the benches on the prosecution's side. My lawyer is here, a court reporter I recognize from the trial, as well as Kim, the friendly and bright court clerk. And, of course, the judge.

I like this judge, I do. He looks like he is falling asleep 80% of the time and can't remember how to pronounce my name for the life of him, but I trust him, and I have from the very beginning. He is stern but fundamentally kind, and has been a respected judge for a very long time. There is a rumor he is retiring at the end of the year, which, if true, will likely make my case the last trial of his career.

This afternoon we are here to argue the motions around Loretta's forensic interview video. Well, I personally am just going to sit here practicing my poker face, but my lawyer will undoubtedly do a stellar job arguing on my behalf.

As promised, he immediately re-visits the preliminary hearing decision, pointing out that in the case submitted by the prosecution as supporting case law, a preliminary hearing had actually been granted, so, basically, what gives?

And as for the forensic interview, he also cleverly argues, because of the way the original district attorney charged this case – some charges allow for the showing of the video, but some charges do not – the only real solution is to actually have *two* more trials, dividing the counts accordingly.

Two more trials! The very thought makes my head spin, even though I know we're essentially introducing the idea for its dramatic effect. I feel almost exhilarated by the sheer audacity of what we're proposing and a bit delighted as I watch the implications of the suggestion slowly register on the prosecutors' faces. The brunette purses her lips together tightly as her nostrils flare, while the blonde is a deer in headlights, staring at the judge. Two trials are a bit more than they bargained for. They've spent the summer bending over backwards trying to patch together enough justification for even one more trial, and here they are being unexpectedly smacked in the face with the prospect of needing to muster up enough probability to do it twice. Whatever bolster of confidence they got from boldly declaring their decision to retry the remaining counts last April appears to be evaporating, especially against the rising tide of creativity and brilliance from which my lawyer is delivering his arguments. It is a true pleasure to watch him work today. He's fired up and on a roll. His experience, intelligence, and wisdom are no match for even the combined best efforts of these district attorneys. He's at the top of his game, and I know he's got more where this all came from.

The judge says he'll need to think about it some more. The DA asks to address some of the points my lawyer just mentioned in his two-more-trials argument, but the judge tells her no, that we need to move onto our original reason for meeting today, which is to learn how the prosecution plans to cleanly and completely redact any/all language alluding to the first trial's two acquitted charges from the forensic video, an assignment issued to them from the judge at our last meeting. If they can't do it, then the video can't be used.

The DAs are rattled. The brunette glumly sits in her seat, silently reading from a binder, while the blonde frantically rifles through papers on their table. She can feel me studying her and shoots me a dirty look. Her attention surprises me, and I instinctively raise both my eyebrows and smirk. She looks away, irritated. I busy myself with taking notes.

She can't find the interview transcript she is trying to reference to make her point, and the judge is visibly irritated as he issues a reprimand. "You all are so hot to get in here and explain how to redact the acquitted charges, so where are these explanations?"

The DA's hands are shaking. Her voice is shaking. She is on the verge of losing her composure right here in front of us all, and I think she might cry. I am only slightly concerned at how entertained I am by this.

"Your Honor," she begins, "we weren't aware or on notice of what the Defense Lawyer was going to address today."

"No, no, no," the judge interrupts her. "That shouldn't matter. That's a different issue. You knew we were talking about the forensic video today, so where's the rest of your forensic interview argument?"

Her voice is barely a whisper. "I don't seem to have it all here, Your Honor."

The judge stares at her for a moment before announcing that he's going to take some time to think about everything we discussed today. He says we'll hear from him "sooner than later" as he dismisses us and retreats to his chambers.

My lawyer walks over to the prosecution's table. "So, about fixing that transcript issu-" but the DAs won't let him finish his sentence. They won't even look him in the eye. The blonde holds up her hand in front of my lawyer's face and says, "No! Everything in writing," before turning on her heel and marching out of the courtroom, the brunette right behind her.

I smile at my lawyer. This actually feels fun, a welcome change from my usual emotions of frustrated, terrified, and aggravated. After a debriefing, I go across the street to check in with pre-trial, and I am still chuckling about it on my drive home. I'm in a great mood all day.

October 9, 2018

I am not everyone's cup of tea and that's cool, because not everyone is mine, either. Nevertheless, I do have an overwhelming desire for people to know the truth of this particular situation, the *impossibility* of the stories being told here, before they draw conclusions where I am the villain.

I spend a fair amount of time reflecting on how no one in the X family bothered to sit in the courtroom on either of the days I testified, as if they have no need to hear my side of the story, as if they aren't even willing to consider that Loretta got something wrong, as if there's no way that this could be a mix-up gone horribly awry. They simply want their version to be true, and that's the end of the discussion for them. They are cutting off their nose to spite their face, and I am the collateral damage.

So it turns out not everyone is interested in hearing what I have to say before making me the villain, and that's confusing for a justice-driven person like myself. If only they *understood*, if only they'd *listen*, if only they *knew*...

Alas, I remind myself I can only walk my line, tell my truth, and rest assured that karma is keeping very close tabs on what's going on around here. What doesn't align with the truth has no choice but to fall away eventually.

I do perspective work almost daily. I practice re-framing "Why is this happening to me?" into "What is this teaching me?" as if my life depends on it because in some ways, it feels like it does. I flip narratives of "this is happening *to* me" into "this is happening *for* me," and "I *have* to..." into "I *get* to..."

I sit longer with uncomfortable emotions, becoming more adept at gleaning nuggets of wisdom from them. I am always looking for the lessons, hyper-aware of remaining open to expansion, elevation, education. Often times, I've learned, it's when life feels the most out of control that the biggest opportunities for enlightenment are lurking around the corner.

Plus, I'm tired of dealing with all these ridiculous people. I'm tired of the X family and their lies. I'm tired of the District Attorneys and the blatant shortcoming of their inexperience. I'm tired of working for Regina and having to endure her cruelty disguised as kindness. I'm weary from the way that these prolonged negative interactions only exacerbate the relentless weight of my own familiar shade, the hauntings of my own minor transgressions, and a perpetual line-up of my own choices standing front and center behind the glass wall of my memory, taking every chance they can to keep me small by replaying past humiliations and shame.

I have to mindfully remember I am capable of extending forgiveness to others and allowed to forgive myself for being human. After all, feeling a range of emotion is a basic tenet of the human experience. Even so, I forget this easily, and the shame is so clever that I repeatedly find myself spiraling down it before I even realize it's arrived.

Oh yeah, forgiveness is the thing I'm doing now. Every time an uncomfortable memory taunts me, I practice sitting with the feeling and a focus to forgive.

I forgive Grade School Me for being bossy and attention-seeking. I forgive High School Me for that shoplifting phase. I forgive College Me for drinking and smoking and being promiscuous. I forgive Young Adult Me for gossiping with hurtful intentions. I forgive All Past Ages of Me for repeatedly insulting my own intelligence when it came to choosing romantic partners. I forgive Current Me for doing the bare minimum at work as a passive aggressive middle finger to my emotionally abusive boss.

I recognize that I can continue to evolve no matter what is happening in my life, and the ultimate privilege is elevating my life by elevating the quality of my decisions. Choices of my past are not indicators of my present character. At most, they were stages necessary for the cultivation of this version of me who strives to be mindful, compassionate, and kind.

I am a soul having a human manifestation, here for enlightenment and experience, and all of my circumstances are prime settings for both if I can just stay present long enough to let them be.

October 12, 2018

It has been exactly a month since our last court date, when the judge said he would get us his decision "sooner than later." Trial is set to begin in just over two weeks, and we still haven't heard a peep. I am exasperated and confused. How are we supposed to prepare?

Why is he being so lackadaisical about this? I send my lawyer a text
– a meme with the phrase "Hello, I'd like a large dose of attention,
please." He promises he'll let me know as soon as he does.

October 17, 2018

I receive a call mid-morning.

"Are you working today?" my lawyer wants to know.

I confirm that I am.

"Ok, can you make time to meet? Say, at my office in about an
hour? I have a development on the case that I need to discuss with
you in person. Bring James if you can."

I sigh.

The last time my lawyer suddenly called me in to discuss
something important was about that offer he strongly suggested
I take, and I gave him an earful for it. No offers, I've repeatedly
told him, and no ambushing my schedule for dramatic displays
of pressure.

Right now I just say sure, I'll meet him at his office in about
an hour, but I mention that James has a full day of calls so he won't
be joining me.

James and I agonize briefly over what we think the meeting
is about as I change my clothes, brush my teeth, and gather my
lawyer-meeting things: laptop, notepad, a couple snacks, a full
water bottle. I assume the ruling on the video has come in. I figure
it is not in our favor, and we need to talk about the ramifications,
like the unwelcome possibility my lawyer has already mentioned of
pushing the next trial all the way to the spring, or splitting things
into two trials. He may have his reasons, but I adamantly don't
want to do this.

James quickly glances at me. Then, tentatively, "Or he's calling
us in to tell us it's over?"

I scoff, but my mind catches. Dare I?

I glance back at him and we lock eyes. Dare we?

"More likely it's another offer," I counter out loud, "and I'll tell you what – I'm going to be ticked off if he's pulling me from work to tell me to consider another 'amazing' offer."

We agree it's probably about the video and having to push the trial to the spring, and James encourages me to be open-minded. "Whatever it takes" has been our family motto this entire time, and we have a second mortgage against our house and multiple maxed-out credit card balances to prove it.

I pack my Box of Proof in the backseat of my car just in case. I listen to the same meditation that got me to court every morning of the April trial, but I listen with fresh ears, as if hearing the words for the first time.

"I am thinking thoughts that are filled with positivity…I am allowing myself to be in sync with life…I am motivated and inspired to make choices for my highest good and the highest good of everyone involved…"

When I get to the parking garage, I decide to leave the Box in the car. After a moment, I decide to leave my laptop, too. I *am* daring to hope, it turns out. I pay extra attention to my surroundings as I make my way into the building. I look myself in the eye in the mirrored elevator wall. I straighten my ponytail. I smile. I study my soft brown leather boots, my grey Levi's, the black and mustard yellow houndstooth blouse with billowy sleeves, and my cropped black leather jacket. I am carrying the white purse I bought myself as a congratulations present after the first trial, and I fiddle with the leather piping along its edge as the elevator carries me up to the second floor.

The elevator doors open and as I walk down the hall towards my lawyer's office, I notice that for the first time in the two years I have been walking down this carpeted stretch, every hallway light is finally working. The hallway is lit up brighter than I've ever seen it. It gives the space a different vibe and feeds into my growing anticipation. I daresay I have a bit of a spring in my step.

The first person I see when I walk through the door is my lawyer's partner through the open door of his office. He breaks into a grin as he stands up to greet me, and it is then that I know.

"It's being dismissed," he says when he reaches me.

I reflexively hit him on the shoulder as my eyes widen and an involuntary cuss word flies out of my mouth. The whole world stops. He's still grinning, and I start to grin back, tears forming in my eyes as the realization of what is happening begins to register.

It's being dismissed.

This all started on a Thursday, and now it's ending on a Wednesday. It's actually ending, like *for real* ending. I can remove this brave face, this cape of courage, this weighted vest of false accusations, this armor of ick.

My lawyer shows up minutes later with flowers for me. I hug both of them. I pace back and forth, my hands pressed to my cheeks. I cannot stop smiling.

I read the dismissal letter, then read it again. They are dismissing "in the interest of justice," which we assume to mean that their investigation ultimately showed there wasn't sufficient information to warrant a trial. There never was.

I'd be furious if I wasn't so overjoyed.

I am going to be able to breathe again, I realize. Fully and completely and independently, and go where I want, when I want, and with whom I want. I am staggeringly giddy with the sudden availability of these simple freedoms.

One more court date for the official dismissal, and then it is finally, finally *over*.

Thank you, Universe. Thank you, again.

I call James the minute I get back into the car. "Crack open the champagne!" I squeal into the phone. I call my sister next, and then my parents. I can hear their cheers from a thousand miles away.

When I get home, James and I do indeed toast with champagne, then I set about reaching out to everyone I can think of, one by one, just like I did two years ago to ask for letters, only this time I get to spread the good word over and over again to every kind soul who has hung in there with me.

It's being dismissed! They did an investigation and they are dropping the charges!

They are the happiest phone calls I've ever had the pleasure of making, the very best texts I've ever had the privilege of sending, and I smile for the rest of the evening.

I am so proud of myself.

I did not give up, and I did not give in.

October 29, 2018

I meditate. I sleep. I pray. I stomp.

Surely goodness and mercy shall follow me all the days of my life, and I will dwell in the house of the Lord forever.

The sun is shining and I am bubbly as I record an Instagram story during my morning walk with the dogs. I am walking on air.

"I've been engaged in a battle not of my choosing for a few years now," I chirp into the camera, "and y'all? Today it's over! I did it! I stood up for myself. I had truth on my side, and I kept love close, and I won!"

I cannot stop smiling.

I smile when I spot a cloud in the shape of a heart in the sky as James and I drive to the courthouse. I smile as I hold the elevator for strangers. I smile as I over tip the barista at the café.

Some friends once again graciously carve time out of their busy lives to be here with me for this glorious day, and I smile as I greet and hug each of them in turn. We are all smiling and making cheerful small talk as we wait for the room to be called to order.

Today is a docket day, and the room is full of random people also waiting to appear before the judge. Everybody here will bear witness to my case's dismissal. I smile at them all.

Both district attorneys enter the courtroom, followed by the original DA assigned to my case. She is here coincidentally for an entirely different reason, and while I certainly was not expecting to see her, I kind of love how she happens to show up in my world today. It brings me so much joy to smile right in her face as she passes by me to find a seat. She does not smile back.

She's not the only one not smiling. The X family have asked to address the court today, as is evidently their right. I'd been told to expect a speech from Loretta, but it is Angus and Rose who speak, instead. Neither Loretta nor Ivy are anywhere to be found. Angus lectures the judge about his disappointment in the system, and I get it – the system did *all* of us wrong here. Had they executed a proper investigation to begin with, this wouldn't have wasted nearly as much of our collective time. I begin mapping out celebration party details in my head as he elaborates effusively.

Then Rose takes her turn. She is *so* passionate and *so* melodramatic that it almost looks like she's auditioning for something, and again – I get it. She's been led to believe that her sister was harmed under her very nose, and now it seems that nobody is being made to pay for that. It must feel confusing and unfair. Believe me, I can relate to confusing and unfair. During her speech, I listen as she re-states all the allegations against me, recounts highlights of her own testimony, and leans into the microphone while looking right at me when she uses words like *molest, abuse,* and *pedophile.* She really gives it her all. I feel a pang of recognition in the way she wants to publicly process her pain.

Then she is done, and I am smiling again. Now it is really over. The truth mattered. Love won.

I am free.

November, 2018

For my birthday this year, I host an online fundraiser. I ask everyone I know for donations to "Proclaim Justice," a non-profit organization that provides legal representation and advocacy to win freedom for victims of wrongful convictions. After the past two years of my life, I'm convinced it happens All. The. Time.

I'd first learned of the non-profit at a concert I attended a few weeks before my arrest in 2016. I'd been so moved by the cause – intuitive foreshadowing, anyone? – that I'd actually purchased a Proclaim Justice t-shirt at the show that night. When my own personal criminal justice battle began just a couple weeks later, I quickly came to regard that yellow t-shirt as part of my unofficial uniform (see also: my grey "Fierce like Frida" t-shirt and my white "Love Wins" t-shirt.)

On my birthday fundraiser platform, I explain to my audience that I'd recently learned firsthand how our country's justice system is alarmingly broken. Like, off the charts broken. I describe how it's set up to make you buy back your freedom after a false accusation, and how justice is only an option if you can afford it.

I point out that people are spending their lives behind bars simply because they cannot afford to stand their ground for the time it takes to defend their innocence. Because I had the privilege of that luxury, I declare that it's time for me to reach back and help others, and donating to this cause is one way I am choosing to do that.

I set a fundraising goal of $250, which I plan to match. It is both exciting and satisfying to raise almost five times that amount, making the total donation just shy of $1,500.

I vow it is only the start.

***

I post a final update in my beloved online group.

"Hello, my gorgeous, beautiful, wonderful friends…let's chat!

It took two years, one month, and twenty-nine days, but 'in the interest of justice,' all charges have finally been officially dropped! The case has been dismissed!

These past two years (and one month and twenty-nine days) have not been easy, but I can hold my head high and look myself square in the eye for the rest of my life because for all my many flaws, I know without a doubt I am fundamentally a good, decent person with strong values and a heart of motherfucking gold, and shame on anyone who tries to make me feel otherwise, you know what I mean?

Thank you for showing up for me.

Having support like the support I've had - actual, physical friends who I could quite literally lean on – sent such an important message to the opposition (and the jury!) that people love, care about, and believe me. It matters more than I ever would have guessed or even expected. So thank you. I truly couldn't have sustained this alone. I believe in karma, and I know yours will be beautiful.

In the nutshelliest of nutshells, the prosecution finally did an investigation this past summer – after they arrested me, locked me up, ankle monitored me, took me to trial resulting in two acquittals and an 11-1 jury in my favor on the other five charges – and ultimately concluded that they were unable to proceed to a second trial 'in the interest of justice.' Meaning if they had done the investigation before arresting me like they are supposed to, it's likely I'd never have been arrested at all. Better late than never?

We went to court on October 29th for the official dismissal and it was a happy, relief-filled day.

The case has been sealed. It was dismissed 'without prejudice,' meaning it's possible for the remaining five counts to be tried again, but not probable. They'd need a smoking gun, and there simply isn't one.

I'll tell you what - if I never see anyone from the X family again, it'll be too soon.

I'm focused on slowly but surely shaking this all off and rising up out of the muck like I know I am bound to do. My first order of business is quitting my god-awful job as soon as possible. As most of you know, working for Regina has been an almost equally horrible experience in its own way, but I suppose what they say is true – when it rains, it pours.

I've accepted that perhaps I needed these past couple of years to be as heavy as possible. A masterclass in adversity, if you will. In any case, I am now gravitating towards people and experiences that bring light and safety and happiness to my heart.

What does feel good is that I'm writing. I want to tell this story. I want to explain every last confusing detail around how it went this far, I want to show how this false accusation could have happened in the first place, and how terrifyingly simple it was for people with a lot of power to be very lazy about it. I'm going to use the conversations and information found in this group while I write. This treasure trove of dates, developments, questions, answers, timelines, and technicalities will be as valuable a resource as I could ever hope to have, and I thank you for contributing to it like you have.

We're looking to start traveling again, as economically as possible. This means we're likely eyeing your guest room. Expect an email.

Speaking of guest rooms, James and I have a cozy one at our house that loves to be occupied, and we operate this place kind of like a bed and breakfast. Come see.

Speaking of me and James, we came out the other side of this so much stronger; I'm proud but not surprised. Not all of my relationships fared quite as well, but that is the nature of catastrophic events – they change things and we can choose to let it bum us out or we can decide that it's for the best. I have decided it's for the best.

Speaking of dissolving relationships, so many folks we quite frankly don't like anymore were so integrated in our original wedding party (and therefore littered throughout all our wedding photos) that we are calling for a re-do. We dream of a more intimate affair for our ten-year vow renewal, one that more accurately reflects our circle, everything else to be determined.

Many thanks and so much love to each and every one of you for holding me in your thoughts, keeping me in your prayers and wanting good things for me throughout this. I hope to see you soon. Keep the faith!"

***

We celebrate the dismissal a few times, because when something of this magnitude ends, it feels so good to celebrate!

The first celebration is immediately after we leave the courthouse on dismissal day. My legal team buys the group of us brunch at a nearby diner, where we drink mimosas and bloody Marys and eat pancakes and eggs. The mood is merry as all nine of us pour over nuances that made the ending extra sweet.

"Did you see that the original district attorney was there today?"

"I did! What are the odds?"

"I can't believe neither Loretta nor Ivy showed."

"I can."

"What did you all think about Rose's speech? Delivered with such theatrics! If she's not in her school's drama program, she has missed her calling, that's all I have to say about that."

We discuss the major turning points of the case, filling everybody in on how weeks passed without so much as a peep from the judge after he said we'd hear from him "sooner than later" with his rulings. I wonder out loud if he had a private word with the district attorneys, or if their supervisor had finally stepped in, or what.

My lawyer surmises anything is possible. "I mean, I'm fairly certain the judge knew our next move would be a Rule 21, so I suppose it's possible that he conveyed something to the district attorneys if he thought they were ultimately on a sinking ship. But it is also possible that their boss put the kibosh on it, or even that they came to the conclusion themselves."

And finally, we speculate over the many still-unanswered questions – *If there was no Facebook message, how did Ivy come to learn about Loretta's stories? How does someone with no sense of smell get triggered by scents? Was Loretta abused by someone else? If so, who?* – and I effusively and repeatedly offer my gratitude to everyone at the table.

The entire rest of the day, I savor the feeling of standing my ground when I knew I was right. The victory is sweet and allows for the realization that it is finally time to let my own childhood trauma heal. I stood up for that version of my inner child, and now that she's been acknowledged, heard, and defended, she can begin to let go, even forty years after the fact. She deserves closure, and so do I.

The second celebration is a festive, light-hearted pizza party at our house the following Friday night. My sister and nieces come from Wisconsin, and we fly giant helium letter balloons in the front yard that spell out, "YAY!" Friends, neighbors, and my legal team all come together to eat pizza and drink champagne and toast to truth, friendship, resiliency, and new beginnings. The kids play freeze tag and Ghost in the Graveyard while the adults gather around the fire in the backyard and the food on the back porch. There is laughter and cheer and easy chatter and sighs of contentment.

And finally, a few weeks later, I get on an airplane (without asking permission, what what!) to go see my parents for one more celebration with them, because the need to see my mom and dad in person right now is undeniable. Neither of them were in perfect health when the legal case began, and these past couple of years haven't been especially easy. They not only grappled with their daughter struggling through her toughest life challenge to date, but they also did it while contending with new-to-them knowledge that their little girl had been abused by someone else's hand all those years ago. My parents have loved and supported me tirelessly through both the trial and my life in general, and they deserve to commemorate this sweet relief of closure, too. I am only there for two nights but it is plenty of time to laugh and cry and feast on steak and cake, relishing the victory of successfully making it out alive to the other side, together.

***

As you may recall, I always play Solitaire on my phone when I fly.

And so after I climb aboard that flight back to Wisconsin to visit my folks, I click my seatbelt, pop in my ear buds, and pull out my phone to settle in for a couple hours of solid Solitaire saturation.

When I first open the app, it takes a moment to update, and when I win my first game, I immediately notice the update has changed the game-winning message. It's different than the one I've been using as moral support for the past couple of years.

The winning message used to tell me, "You Win!"

Now, as the graphics dance across the screen, it says, "You Won!"

My eyes grow wide as I smile at this wink from the universe, and I press "Play Again."

Epilogue

"Write hard and clear about what hurts." –Ernest Hemingway

2019

Healing from trauma doesn't happen overnight. Ask me how I know.

Even once the source of trauma is removed – say, the case gets dropped, or you stop working for the lying narcissist – there is all the untangling of sticky energy and learned behavior that comes in the aftermath. The "epilogue" is what my friend Amelia calls it.

It may not be surprising to hear that I have spent a considerable amount of time since September 1, 2016 trying to piece together how this situation could have happened at all, let alone made its way to a trial. I have so many theories. Here's one of them.

As a freshman in high school, Loretta dated an older boy, a junior at her school. According to Ivy and Angus, the breakup turned Loretta into a mess at the end of freshman year and the following summer. She stopped showering or changing her clothes. She stopped eating anything of nutritional value. She stopped doing her schoolwork. She'd obviously been badly hurt by this boy, at the very least emotionally, and perhaps otherwise as well.

When she is a sophomore, he is a senior, and she is still trying to process the pain of whatever went down between them. She begins to dissociate more often than not. By the time she is interviewed by the police, she'll say she does it "almost all the time."

When a buddy of hers shares his past experience of childhood abuse, something catches in Loretta's brain – *wait, she wonders, why is there something familiar about that? Didn't something like that happen to me, too?*

She rummages around in her memory and something about babysitter abuse niggles at her from somewhere in the back. The more she thinks about it, the more she seems to remember and the more a story starts to take shape.

When my face simultaneously appears in her mind's eye, she's not sure why because she doesn't remember the conversation we had when I told her and her sister about the abuse I experienced as a child.

So she takes that story – *my* story – and tries to make sense of it the only way she can, by assuming she was the abused child. That would make me the abusing babysitter.

She tries the idea on for size. She tests the story in conversations with her friends, gaining some sympathy and attention for it. She realizes it can be used as an outlet to process the real pain and trauma caused, perhaps, by the older ex-boyfriend.

As she becomes more familiar with the narrative, she starts using it to explain more about the parts of herself she either doesn't understand or doesn't want to own. She begins integrating pieces from our actual, factual friendship to fill in details. *We visited Alex in Santa Barbara, so I think it happened there. And then she lived with Connie... I think it happened there, too. I also remember that moldy basement apartment with the colorful walls. Let me think, let me think...you know what? I can remember sleeping over there, so I bet it happened there! Maybe even twice?* So on and so forth.

In the psychology world, *cognitive dissonance* refers to a situation where conflicting attitudes, beliefs or behaviors produce a feeling of mental discomfort, and this discomfort consequently leads to an alteration in someone's attitudes, beliefs or behaviors in an effort to reduce the discomfort, restore emotional balance, and re-create a sense of safety in their world.

For example, let's say when Loretta first experiments with telling someone she'd been abused by a babysitter, she feels the dissonance of knowing that the story she's telling might not be entirely accurate, but she receives an emotional charge from the reaction she gets when she tells it, so she tells it again.

When Ivy somehow catches wind of it, she wants to run with it because it relieves her own self of being the reason our friendship imploded. If I abused her kid, then it's my fault, and if it's my fault, it can't be hers. She won't have to hold the responsibility anymore. What relief she must feel.

Loretta initially puts up a ton of resistance to her mother's tunnel vision around this. She won't even look at Ivy when she brings it up, let alone talk to her about any of it, because at her core, Loretta knows what she's been saying to her friends might not be 100% true. Her memories are admittedly fuzzy and confusing and only come to her in bits and pieces, and she's trying to stitch them together as best she can, but she is certain of nothing.

So she hems and haws through almost three months of therapy appointments, trying to weigh the pros and cons of coming clean versus steamrolling ahead, her mother on Team Alex-is-the-Enemy all the while.

At this point Loretta may be thinking something like, *what's the actual harm in just sticking with this story? I don't know if what I'm telling people actually happened or not, but either way, I can just substitute Alex as the villain of my story instead of my ex-boyfriend who I still have to see in the halls every day at school. Alex is a safe projection target because she isn't even in our lives anymore – she abandoned me when she got married. Plus, all this attention from my mom feels nice, too.*

This dances on the edge of what's known as "forced compliance." Forced compliance occurs when an individual performs an action that is inconsistent with their beliefs. When someone is forced to publicly do something they privately really don't want to do, like, say, talk to a therapist and then the police about fabrications they'd been using to gain sympathy and attention from their peers, dissonance is created between their cognition (I didn't want to do this) and their behavior (I did it).

The behavior clearly can't be changed because it already happened, so now a person's resulting dissonance needs to be reduced by re-evaluating their attitude about what they have done.

For decades, research has shown that when people are forced to comply with behaviors that create dissonance, they will later decide the behavior was actually more favorable than they originally said or thought. By changing their opinion of their behavior, they experience less internal conflict.

Once Loretta lies, the lie gets away from her and takes on a life of its own, eventually consuming her to the point of affecting her own mental health.

The only way to justify the catastrophe she'd created is to commit 100% to the story she'd been telling. Otherwise, the dissonance, discomfort, and disparity between fact and fiction will be too heavy to bear.

My best guess is that somewhere along the way, her survival instincts flipped the switch for her, turning her lies into truth in her mind and guesses into fact in her re-tellings. By doing so, she saved herself – for the time being, anyway – from having to reckon with the amount of damage she's caused.

Of course, this is only a guess.

***

I also think a lot about a particularly interesting twist to the story that didn't even see the light of day during the trial.

Remember the printed Instant Messenger conversation we presented to Ivy during her cross-examination? My lawyer talked then about how it showed Ivy asking me to share my story of childhood abuse with her children. But threaded into that same conversation and printed on that same piece of paper was also the reason she asked me that question that day, stemming from a troubling conversation between Ivy and my spiritual advisor, Saida, with whom Ivy had also worked in the past.

During a phone call session, Ivy expressed concern to Saida about Loretta, and was shocked to hear Saida's premonition. Saida had a vision of dark, male energy wanting to hurt Loretta, and she stressed the importance of not allowing Loretta to attend sleepovers at houses where older brothers or random uncles lived.

Upon being advised to watch a talk show episode about pedophiles, Ivy had reached out to me in a slight panic, asking more questions about my past situation, wanting to know more details about my decision to keep it from my parents, and ultimately asking me to tell her kids my story.

I'd often thought about that particular set of circumstances over the years, wondering if Ivy adhered to Saida's advice of keeping Loretta away from homes with older brothers.

Something tells me she did not.

***

Getting through a traumatic event is one thing, but healing from it is another thing entirely. The former is a show of strength and a study in perseverance, whereas the latter is a practice in resilience, forgiveness, endurance, and faith that as you put the pieces back together, they'll be stronger than you'd ever dreamed they could be. Healing takes patience and a dedicated stubbornness to find gratitude for the blessings, even when they come disguised as Regina.

But I find that right now, gratitude (and my trust in karma) can only take me so far toward my goal of forgiveness. I come to discover I actually have a lot of anger to deal with first.

In the months immediately following the case dismissal, I experience an overwhelming desire to scream at people, some more than others. I fight almost debilitating urges to circle back around to certain folks, to rub my freedom in their faces. *Oh, you weren't willing to stand by my side? Turns out I didn't even need you, you big jerk.*

I feel ill-equipped to rise above these petty yet powerful inclinations. I don't know how to scratch that itch without sinking to a much lower energetic vibration. And where, exactly, am I supposed to put all this overflowing emotion?

At first, I spend more time than I care to admit drafting nasty letters, fingertips hovering dangerously over "send" buttons after seeking out the haters on social media. Time and time again, my sister talks me off a proverbial ledge.

"Alex, listen to me. Take that emotion and channel it into your book," Mona says. "Do *not* send that email. Deep down, you do not want to put that out into the world."

She is right.

After all, I do not need to be the cause of anyone else's suffering. *They* are the cause of their suffering, just like I am the cause of mine.

The recurring refrain of "don't get angry" from my childhood demands my attention now, as I work to dislodge the embedded directive from the inner workings of my psyche. I need to see what happens when I allow myself to get angry.

On her website, The Holistic Psychologist, Dr. Nicole LePera explains that we tend to be protective and defensive around our childhood experience, but the truth is we have a unique opportunity to heal and consciously choose different behavior as adults. We can choose to provide ourselves what we didn't have as a child and to teach ourselves what we wish we'd been taught. It's not easy, but it's possible. This doesn't have to be done out of anger or aggression towards our parents, either. It can be addressed with compassion and an understanding that our parents did the very best they could do given the circumstances they had to navigate, including how they'd been raised.

This process is called re-parenting, and as a self-awareness junkie with a degree in Early Childhood Education, I find it fascinating.

Years of therapy have taught me to differentiate between my initial reaction to something, which is indicative of my early childhood conditioning, and my next response, which is usually more aligned with the educated, multi-faceted human being I have evolved into, a person with an entirely different set of priorities, values, beliefs, and behaviors than I had during my first five years of life.

I was not granted permission to express anger as a child, even though I had good reason to be angry. So now, instead of blindly listening to my knee-jerk reaction of "don't" when I feel anger bubbling up, I switch to a response of "come in."

It'd been too risky to let my anger lead during the legal battle. I needed to follow my faith in love so I could stand up for my abused inner child more than I needed to experiment with releasing emotion in the name of healing her. But a baseline of safety has been restored to my daily life since the case was dropped, and it would seem that my faith is leading me back to my anger. Now it is time.

With a beginner's mind, I clumsily and awkwardly ask the emotion to come in and stay a while. I am tentative with my invitation, but it does not need to be asked twice. My anger swoops in like it owns the place and immediately begins to re-decorate.

Its sudden, all-encompassing presence is white hot and suffocating, like pinpricks of fire blazing up my spine while sucker punching me from behind. It shreds my common sense and makes me feel slightly sick to my stomach almost all the time. It rages at me for trying to understand it and mocks the boundaries I try to enforce.

The anger shoves itself into practically every interaction of my life, creating epic waves of self-doubt and self-hate like I have never experienced before. I don't want to see anyone, go anywhere, or engage in anything, for fear of doing it wrong. I find I cannot trust myself in social settings to use appropriate verbal filters; it's as if learning to stand up for myself has erased my understanding of what "appropriate" even means.

My confusion is reinforced when my husband and I meet out-of-town friends for an afternoon drink in a bar, and an off-handed remark I make as a joke about the slippery nature of perpetual victimhood causes one of them to literally jump out of her chair and furiously retort, "Fuck you, Alex! You've demanded so much time and attention these past few years, and guess what, princess? This world does not revolve around you." I am aghast and my husband is livid; for all intents and purposes, the friendship dies right then and there, in that dingy bar on Broadway Avenue.

Such is the cost of trauma: Not all relationships survive.

I am desperate for different outcomes in any and all relationships going forward rather than what feels like the suffocating, inevitable repeat dynamics of mean girls who become frenemies who become holes I try to avoid on strolls down memory lane. The pattern is of course reflective of where I, myself, need a course correction, and I know that if I want a different outcome, it is up to me to set wheels of motion in new directions. The realization mentally paralyzes me.

From a psychological perspective, none of this is especially surprising. In his book "My Grandmother's Hands," author Resmaa Menakem points out, "Trauma hurts. It can fill us with reflexive fear, anxiety, depression, and shame. It can cause us to fly off the handle; to reflexively retreat or disappear; to do things that don't make sense, even to ourselves; or sometimes, to harm others or ourselves."

It's been said that your beliefs form your thoughts, and your thoughts prompt your words, which lead to your actions, which create your habits, which illustrate your values, which become your destiny. In theory, destinies can be altered by shifting any piece along that continuum. I am willing to make changes, but I am floundering in a sea of confusion over which changes are the ones I need to be making. I turn in metaphorical circles, bumping up against uncertainty at each pause. I can't decipher which beliefs, thoughts, words, actions, habits, and/or values are the ones that lead me to the sour friendship dynamics, and which ones are responsible for the good stuff.

Because after all, my lifelong propensity for prickly friendships like the one I had with Ivy is actually balanced by a long string of strong, beautiful, enduring friendships like the ones I share with people like Carys, Amelia, and Jules, to name just a few. A lot of amazing people have loved me for a very long time, warts and all, so it can't be that I *only* make terrible friendship decisions, or that I'm the only one who does. I'm so upside down in my perspectives and new to understanding what appropriate levels of anger feel like that I can't tell which gut instincts I should still trust and which ones I should be examining closer in an effort to potentially dismantle. It's jarring and disheartening.

"You've unleashed the kraken!" my husband laughs when I bemoan how my changed perspectives feel like Pandora's Box – the more anger I try and process, the more I seem to find to be angry about. He is joking, but I fear he might be right. I thought my emotion just wanted to be heard, but some days I'm not so sure. This anger is so raw and wild and unpredictable that it feels like it might swallow me whole, but not before it leaves a path of destruction in its wake. I second-guess *everything*, especially my decision to do this shadow work in the first place.

One day my anger and I are shopping in Costco when a gently smiling man approaches me. "Excuse me," he says, "do you drive a black Honda? I think someone just hit your car in the parking lot, right as you walked in."

Goddammit, I think to myself as I distractedly thank him and make my way back out of the huge warehouse. Something feels off, but I can't figure it out right away. I'm parked in a back corner of this sprawling lot – how did this guy see my car get hit but I didn't? I reach and examine my car. It is untouched.

As soon as I see this, I am humiliated with a realization. Not ten minutes earlier, in an effort to make my way into the proper entrance turn lane for the Costco parking lot, I'd boldly chosen to aggressively accelerate and merge in front of a slow-poke car to my left, causing that car's driver to flip me off in response. I'd laughed and given them a sarcastic thumbs up. *Way to be a jerk about a turn lane*, I'd thought. Was this that guy?

I make my way back into the building, not quite willing to believe that a stranger deliberately sent me on a fools' errand but trembling with a quiet rage nonetheless. When I spot him a few minutes later, he is literally pointing at me and laughing. It was a prank. "Maybe stop cutting people off," he sneers as his wife averts her eyes and quickly pushes their cart in the opposite direction.

I am fuming, incredulous. I cannot form words. I am seeing red.

And then, suddenly, I am not. Suddenly, I am crystal clear on the connection between this black cloud I carry around with me all the time and the negative interactions that seem to be multiplying in my life. By giving this anger permission to express itself carte blanc, these types of terrible interactions with friends and strangers alike have no choice but to show up in my life. It's where I'm vibrating. It's what I'm attracting. It's what I'm subconsciously expecting so it's what I'm creating.

My game of angry hot potato screeches to a halt with the understanding that I can just stop playing. I don't have to lob it at someone else to be relieved of its burdens. I can just let it drop to the ground and walk away. I can make a different choice.

The stranger in Costco is my tipping point. I realize I've been a disciple of love for so long at the expense of my anger that I'd forgotten they can co-exist. They aren't mutually exclusive emotions, and allowing my anger to have a seat at the table doesn't negate my desire nor my ability to lead with love. Neither does it erase my desire to use forgiveness as one of my healing tools, however abstract the concept still feels to me. Emotional forgiveness work will have to wait, though, as other forms of healing force their way onto my calendar.

As often happens when people experience chronic levels of traumatic stress, my body retaliates. In addition to my being continuously exhausted all the time, my heartrate is erratic and my whole body sporadically twitches when I read in bed at night. My body temperature fluctuates drastically, suddenly and often, leading me to assume it's perimenopause. I regularly black out when

I stand up and when I practice yoga in the backyard. I attribute it to the heat or my lack of breakfast or the moon.

Maybe this is just what healing from trauma is like? I've never done it before, so I genuinely am not sure.

Halfway through the year, in July, I seek out a new doctor to have a few innocuous moles removed and a full blood panel done, "just to check." Days later, I am diagnosed with a common blood disorder, anemia, and an overactive thyroid leads to another diagnosis of Grave's Disease, an autoimmune disorder.

I am grateful to have an answer but alarmed at this doctor's lack of guidance around healing through anything not involving a prescription. Her initial (and only) course of action is to push multiple pills down my throat without so much as a question about my lifestyle or diet or exercise or health goals.

As a certified health coach, I am aware of the very real power of non-pharmaceutical options and educated just enough to know that a doctor's suggested course of prescriptive action is but one prong to a multi-faceted approach to healing no matter what ails you. I understand how the quality of what I put in, on, and use around my body all have a significant impact on my health. I understand that processing my trauma is also a component in my quest for a clean bill of health.

I ask, "Are there nutritional pieces I should be adjusting? Supplements I should explore? Lifestyle practices I should begin or stop?"

This new doctor only stares at me blankly. I am offered a prescription, and then another prescription to counter the possible side effects of the first prescription. She tells me she will not approve my request to use my Health Savings Account funds to pay for Reiki, something within her power but not her comfort level. *"What's Reiki?"* she'd asked me when I'd initiated the request, thinking it'd be a no-brainer.

She asks now if I have any other questions, and it is my turn to take a moment and a breath as I stare at her. I am not going to find what I need here, so I do not bother with any more questions. I thank her, leave the office, and immediately locate a different doctor in an entirely different practice who is better aligned with my belief in a bigger picture for healing beyond a laundry list of prescription drugs.

What have these past few years been for if not to teach me how important it is to advocate for myself?

I feel fortunate that I'm formally trained in how to bridge the gap between a doctor's order and the creation of a sustainable habit. I become my own health coaching client. After all, I have dubbed this "The Year of Healing," so what better way to walk my talk. I decide to do some of my own research and armed with scientific studies, I begin to craft a personalized healing plan.

Within days of my new diagnosis, my body decides it has more to say. Muscles in my lower back spasm to the point of rendering me practically immobile. I can hardly walk; I can barely sit. The pain makes it tough to breath and hard to think. I'm in rough shape as I call around to nearby chiropractic offices, begging to be seen by a female practitioner ASAP. This is how Dr. Lauren comes into my life.

I quickly come to regard Dr. Lauren as a bit of a genius. Dr. Lauren has extensive medical training and an intuitive intelligence similar to Saida's; she both knows things and *knows* things. X-rays reveal I'm suffering not only a significant misalignment throughout my lower back and pelvic floor but a dangerous lack of curvature in my neck as well. I can use my Health Savings Account here, so I am able to begin a focused care plan. I will receive adjustments through early December and be assigned physical therapy exercises as my body begins to re-align.

I am so lucky.

I am also willing to show up and do the work.

But a few weeks into my care plan, I feel only marginally better. Dr. Lauren suggests my lingering pain may be indicative of one of two things: either a need for an anti-inflammatory diet or a need to address stagnant emotional pain. If my problems were strictly physical in nature, she says, I'd be feeling better by now.

She is right on both counts, and I know it, so I agree to alter my eating habits and adopt a daily affirmation practice, even if reciting "I am" statements into the bathroom mirror feels silly at first. I stick with it and soon feeling silly morphs into feeling stronger. Our mindsets really do matter; what we tell ourselves genuinely alters what we believe.

I also renew my focus on finding forgiveness because I recognize it as the only way out; I cannot expect peace in my own life if I am spending my emotional currency on wishing ill will towards others. I find a free online course about the spiritual nature of forgiving that includes a few practical suggestions, and I subsequently begin reciting a Forgiveness Prayer each morning, rotating my focus between Loretta, Ivy, Rose, and even Regina, who'd, almost predictably, been a real pill about my quitting. I repeatedly own up to my responsibility and think long and hard about the role I played in the demise of each relationship. I pray for release, for flow, for compassion, for peace.

The Year of Healing, indeed.

I can come to a place of forgiveness easily enough for Loretta and Rose. I once loved those children as though they were my own even if I had no business doing so, and when our friendship ended, my heart broke, and I grieved them, as though they had died. Yes, they contributed to hurting me in a devastatingly excessive way these past few years, but they ultimately did not break my spirit. If anything, I feel sorry for them. They are children, at least one of whom seems to have a significant mental illness, and children do what their parents train them to do, whether they realize it or not. I continue to include them in my prayers at night. I pray they can find healthy paths to self-forgiveness when they come to understand this hellish situation was actually of their own making, not mine.

It is Ivy for whom I have the most trouble finding forgiveness. Objectively, I can empathize with her. If someone believes their child has been harmed, they're obviously going to cross any mountain necessary to see that the person who caused the harm is held accountable. A parent *should* advocate tirelessly for their child. It is a parent's role to not only protect but also teach their child how to survive their own inevitable journeys across life's mountains. But when you do not take the time to do your due diligence, to collect all of the pertinent facts or ensure you understand the full story before proceeding, it's like modeling how to cross a mountain in a blizzard by wearing a bathing suit and holding a cup of coffee. You are modeling ill-equipped choices to survive the endeavor, and it is your child who is going to suffer for it.

When Ivy asked me to tell her kids about my own childhood abuse, she said she would never forgive herself if something like that happened to them right under her nose. She created what's known as a "self-fulfilling prophecy," which is a sociological term used to describe a belief or expectation that an individual holds about a future event that the individual will then cater to through either behavior or beliefs to make sure it comes true. She was so worried about missing signs that her children were being hurt "right under her nose" that she later chose to believe she had. A false nightmare of her own creation.

Neither Ivy nor Angus were willing to consider anything but Loretta's version as the truth, even after they expressed concern about her state of mind, even after her stories didn't add up, even after I told the prosecution that I could show how the lion's share of Loretta's claims couldn't have happened.

Rather than take a beat to consider the likelihood that Loretta's memory – not me – had betrayed her, that family came after me with all their torches blazing, ready to ruin my life. From where I stand, it looks less like Ivy wanting to help Loretta and more like Ivy wanting to watch me burn in a pile of her own insecurities.

But what Ivy also didn't account for is that truth is fireproof. Try as you might, you can't burn truth to the ground; you can only burn away the layers that hide it.

And so I earnestly chip away at forgiving Ivy – like the rest of us, she, too, is only doing the best she is capable of – although the process has me continually bumping up against the uncomfortable fact that the longer Ivy digs in her heels blaming me, the longer Loretta goes without the professional help she so desperately needs. It may even be a completely missed boat by now.

As for my nightmare of a boss, I land on seeing her as a blessing wrapped in barbed wire. With a sustained and concentrated effort, I can forgive her because she is another perfect example of the phrase "hurt people hurt people." I am only half-kidding when I say working with Regina gave me more PTSD to muddle through than the legal debacle did, and I wouldn't wish her on anyone, but I can easily identify the silver linings of her oozing into my life, even beyond the obvious ones like the paycheck. I made a few great friends through my association with her and met a slew of other fabulous people, besides. Regina herself was a stunning reminder that you shouldn't trust everything you see on the internet. I also consider it a gift to have had so many relatively inconsequential opportunities to practice standing up for both myself and others when I witness something unethical, unjust, or straight-up unkind. That kind of education will benefit me forevermore.

Sometimes we can get fooled into believing forgiveness equates total emotional healing, and moving on is simply a matter dusting oneself off and choosing "good vibes only." In my experience, this is false. Casting a healing net goes so much wider and deeper than being willing or even able to forgive.

Real healing takes both time and genuine soul work, and that can get messy. Healing includes accepting and integrating painful experiences from the past in an effort to re-shape emotional patterns moving forward. It can feel daunting but daunting doesn't stop me anymore.

I primarily rely on my mindfulness practice to help me do this. When painful memories surface, I give myself the gift of pausing to recognize any negative thought spiral for what it is: a learned pattern that I have the ability and power to release.

I remind myself that the point of life isn't to avoid conflict or complicated situations, it's to navigate them without losing myself in them.

Next, since emotions need to be expressed to be processed, I use a multitude of outlets to do exactly that. I journal my thoughts without censoring them; I ring my sister for one of our epic phone calls; I talk things out with my husband as we walk around the lake. The lake walks are a favored method because they combine emotional release with physical movement, a well-known recipe for successful trauma healing.

Finally, as an act of kindness and self-care, I work on exchanging harsh self-talk for gentle, compassionate self-understanding. I stop shaming myself for being "such a bitch" or "such an idiot" in how I showed up in past experiences, instead reminding myself "I still had so much to learn," "I did the best I could with what I was working with at the time," and "I've been fortunate to have had so many opportunities for growth!"

My husband and I begin exploring the possibility of relocating. At first we're just entertaining a desire to get out of our house, to live in a fresh dwelling that neither Loretta nor Ivy, Rose nor Regina have ever been. One conversation leads to another, and suddenly we find ourselves comparing the merits of Atlanta vs. Dallas, Chicago vs. Salt Lake City, Charleston vs. St. Louis.

I practice directing my energy to my faith, my self-care, and my writing.

My faith is born from the understanding that what's to come is better than what's already been. At this point, I am counting on it.

As for my self-care, I find that while the need for it is universal, the finer details remain personal. In other words, self-care in the name of healing is unique to each person who undertakes it. For me, it looks like following my doctors' orders as one prong of my plan while trusting my own intuition to expand and extrapolate steps towards healing both my childhood trauma and present day ailments.

I read a multitude of scientific studies and begin to change my daily self-care behaviors in addition to taking my prescription. Scented candles are out; essential oil diffusers are in.

In fact, we slowly but surely undertake a slew of new lifestyle practices in our home, building on our new habits as time passes. What could easily feel overwhelming – making changes is disruptive and can be a slippery slope for feelings of shame when you realize how long ago you could have learned to be healthier – is distilled by pragmatism. I just spent a considerable amount of time and money protecting the freedom of my existence, so it follows I will do everything I can to care for the body that houses my existence. The decisions are congruent; they go hand in hand and are reflective of the person I want to continue being – someone who actively stands up for herself and others in light of a situation's truth. Now that I know more truth about how my particular health conditions can be handled, I can (and do) choose to act accordingly.

I go back to the basics of caring for my body, mind, and soul on fundamental levels. I start tracking *everything*. How much water did I drink? How much sleep did I get? When did I last shower? What am I grateful for today? When did my last cycle start? How consistently am I exercising? When is the last time I actually got on my yoga mat?

Writing it all down helps me find patterns, make sense, and take action. As a result, both my mental and physical health slowly improve through this dedication to self-care.

But here in the second half of my epilogue year, true self-care goes deeper still. It is now that I begin to really address my own problematic tendencies as I continue to remove hurtful people from my life. I acknowledge my need to hold myself accountable for myself.

I was so angry at the world for a while, and now I find I'm not as much anymore. How liberating it is to catch more consistent glimpses of following my own path again, lovingly guided by my own intuition.

With each passing week, I find with firmer footing my way back to the proverbial sunshine. I follow the signs I find from the universe. I envision, and then get to work creating the next version of my life. In my mind's eye, she's glorious.

Since September 1, 2016, I have come so far and worked so hard. I have learned so much about both who I am and the role I play in the world. I am infinitely grateful for all the ways I've been able to fine tune the kind of life I want to be living and the business I want to be building and the company I want to be keeping and the message I want to be sending.

I hire a book coach. I begin to write my story.

I want to tell this story because I am a justice-driven individual, and it feels extremely important to me to ensure both sides of the story have their place in print, not just the lopsided version of Loretta's false allegations immortalized in the news media. I want to tell this story to show the mountain can be moved, pent-up anger can be handled with care, and stale friendships can and should be released once they run their course. I want to show the world that faith can triumph over fear, that truth matters, and that love wins.

I continue to let myself feel my feelings and learn from my missteps, and I'm better at honoring myself with boundaries without blame or anger because it's actually a gift, getting that time, space, and energy back.

***

It is the gift of time that allows the diligence to my health to pay off. When I return to my endocrinologist for another round of bloodwork at the end of the year, he is impressed by the improvement in my numbers. He decreases my medication by a third and tells me to keep up the good work with all the ways I'm supporting my health. He says with progress like mine, it's likely I'll be one of the rare cases who goes into complete remission within two years. Three months after that, he cuts my dosage in half and tells me I'll likely be off medication completely just nine months after my initial diagnosis. He's amazed.

Hearing this pleases but doesn't surprise me, not after the past few years of beating the odds, achieving what was considered impossible, and surprising a lot of folks along the way.

I no longer doubt what I can do once I decide it must be done.

***

My husband and I ultimately conclude that Colorado has indeed run its course for us, so we pack up and move a thousand miles east to start a fresh new chapter. It turns out to be the third best decision of my life, after marrying him and not taking a plea deal.

***

I am a spiritual person, and I view these past few years of struggle as a main bullet point of my spirit's Soul Contract. This is precisely why a baseline of love throughout the whole ordeal was necessary – it felt like a spiritual test from the start, an invitation to gather what this life has taught me and apply it.

Of course it happened in plain sight in the physical realm for all to see, so of course I had to contend with actively engaging everything the physical realm entails, including but not limited to a confusing and expensive criminal justice system, intimate lessons in angry mob mentality, the sharp edges of the arbitrary importance placed on associations and reputations, and conscientious maneuvering through an inherently racist and patriarchal system. While the race and socioeconomic class I was born into influenced my success in some of these things far more than my personal beliefs or who I actually am as a person, the experience has nonetheless been difficult, demoralizing, and downright exhausting.

Regardless, life continues to be just as much – if not more – about its width and depth as it is its length. I find that when riding the inevitable wave between hurting and healing and hurting again, it helps to remember the process isn't meant to be linear or fair.

Whether we view them as unfair struggles or opportunities for growth, life is overflowing with situations we weren't necessarily expecting. I've long been an advocate for the idea that you will always experience what you choose to believe. In other words, the universe will always throw you the bone you expect to find, which is why I am choosing to move forward with an intentionally positive mindset. I'm choosing a mindset that treats the rest of my life as a gift, a mindset that sees my time on earth as a continuous experiment in how to raise my energetic vibration, come what may. I will always choose to see the curveballs as opportunities for growth, just like I will always choose to reach back and use what I've learned to light the way for others to do the same.

None of us know what we're doing, not really. We are all making life up as we go along, and we have no idea how long we get to do it, exactly why we're doing it, or what comes next after we're done doing it. We hope for the best and learn as we go.

So what have I learned from this? Having the truth on my side only matters if I'm willing to stand up for it, love wins every time when I'm patient enough to let it, and karma doesn't miss a single beat.

Acknowledgements

"If I could reach up and hold a star for every time you've made me smile, the entire evening sky would be in the palm of my hand." - Anonymous

Elisabeth - I could write another book just about all the ways you make my life better, but for now, please know I appreciate who you are and how you show up in the world more than you'll ever know. I would not have made it through this without you, and unequivocally terrible situation aside, I had the time of my life fighting dragons with you.

My undying gratitude will forever belong to:

- the entire **Truth Matters, Love Wins** group, especially the **Love in Action** contingency, (and especially Emily) for their steadfast belief in me and commitment to taking beautiful care of my heart and my soul during my darkest hours and lowest lows.
- everyone who came to support and/or testify for me in court, especially those who traveled from out-of-state or out-of-town to do so, and especially my dad, Ron, and my stepfather-in-law, Gary, the two who were there every single day without fail.
- everyone who contributed to mitigating the substantial financial burden this created, especially my Aunt Karla for Dr. Loftus, my parents for their unrelenting generosity in ways too numerous to list, and Elisabeth, Sarah, and Emily

for organizing multiple fundraising efforts that eased both financial strain and worried minds.

- everyone who wrote me a letter of support, sent a kind word my way, and/or stood up for me in conversations I was not a part of.
- Doug, Todd, and Bonnie – working with all of you was worth every penny, and I hope I never have to do it again.
- Saida – you are a gift and a blessing to me in all directions of time and space.
- Simon and Ingrid – to be unconditionally loved like that is a treasure.

I could not have written this book without:

- the gentle kindness of Lisa Sherman, my book coach.
- the encouraging support and generous wisdom of Sara Connell, my Thought Leader coach.
- the dedicated expertise of Rob Price, my Author Manager at Gatekeeper Press
- the gift of time, diligence, and influential feedback from my early readers: Elisabeth, Emily, Caryn, Danielle, Hannah, Heather, James, and Margo. You each made it better.

Most of all, thank you to my husband, James, forever my always. You are the very best kind of human being. I love you, I like you, and I'll never finish being grateful for you or the beautiful life we've built together.

Appendix A: Truth Matters, Love Wins Playlist

Music has served as both an outlet for my strong emotions and a source of inspiration and strength throughout my entire life. This situation was no different. I created the following playlist based on the suggestions from my friends, and every time I did, it felt like a giant hug.

o   I'll Let You Go (Live): Jessica Allossery
o   Moment of Forgiveness: Indigo Girls
o   Dearly Departed (feat. Esme´ Patterson): Shakey Graves
o   Call It Heaven (feat. Esme´ Patterson): Shakey Graves
o   Pansy Waltz: Shakey Graves
o   I Know: Shovels & Rope
o   1200 Miles: Shovels & Rope
o   Birmingham: Shovels & Rope
o   Botched Execution: Shovels & Rope
o   St. Anne's Parade: Shovels & Rope
o   Buffalo Nickel: Shovels & Rope
o   Rise: Katy Perry
o   Roar: Katy Perry
o   Merry-Go-Round: Antje Duvekot
o   Things Happen: Dawes
o   Ho Hey: The Lumineers
o   Ophelia: The Lumineers
o   Won't Go Back: Steve Martin and Edie Brickell
o   I'm By Your Side: Steve Martin and Edie Brickell
o   Riptide: Vance Joy

o   America's Sweetheart: Elle King
o   Never Gonna Let You Down: Colbie Caillet
o   Good To Be Alive (Hallelujah): Andy Grammer
o   Sunnier Days: Diego Garcia
o   Shake It Off: Taylor Swift
o   Look What You Made Me Do: Taylor Swift
o   Bad Blood: Taylor Swift
o   Little Bit of Love: Katie Herzig
o   Be Okay: Oh Honey
o   Brave: Sara Bareilles
o   I'm Alive (Life Sounds Like): Michael Franti & Spearhead
o   Fighter: Christina Aguilera
o   Stronger: Kanye West
o   O Haleakala: Trevor Hall
o   Boardwalks: Little May
o   Chateau Lobby #4 (in C for Two Virgins): Father John Misty
o   The Place That I Call Home: The Infamous Stringdusters
o   Hell No: Ingrid Michaelson
o   Celebrate: Ingrid Michaelson
o   You and I: Margaret Glaspy
o   No Matter Who: Margaret Glaspy
o   Heavy Metal: Miles Nielsen
o   Strangers: Miles Nielsen
o   Think of You: MS MR
o   The Wolf: Mumford & Sons
o   Kansas City: The New Basement Tapes
o   When I Get My Hands on You: The New Basement Tapes
o   Born: Over the Rhine
o   Welcome Home: Radical Face
o   The Island: Skipinnish
o   Wait So Long: Trampled By Turtles
o   Victory: Trampled By Turtles
o   You and Me: You+Me

- o Break the Cycle: You+Me
- o Live Life: Zayde Wølf
- o Don't Lose Your Love: Ivan & Alyosha
- o Shine Like You Mean It: Clooney
- o Broken White Line: Kris Delmhorst
- o Count On Me: Bruno Mars
- o House of Gold: Twenty One Pilots
- o Me Too: Meghan Trainor
- o Beautiful Thing: Grace VanderWaal
- o Inner Demons: Julia Brennan
- o Million Reasons: Lady Gaga
- o Don't Kill My Vibe (Acoustic): Sigrid
- o Long Walk to Never: Jaymay
- o Bastards: Kesha
- o Praying: Kesha
- o Rainbow: Kesha
- o Hymn: Kesha

Appendix B: Box of Proof Timeline (for Ivy)

Loretta originally named May 2008 through May 2010 as the window of time her abuse happened. I lived in California for 14 of those months, so due to geography, her 2-year timeframe naturally whittles itself down to the 39 weeks between mid-August, 2009, when I moved from California back to Colorado, and early May, 2010, when her appointed window ends.

This appendix summarizes the documentation in my Box of Proof to show where I was, what I was doing, and with whom I was doing it for each of those 39 weeks, one folder per week.

White columns are weeks I lived at Connie's; grey columns are weeks I lived in the moldy basement apartment. Bolded columns are weekends when both girls (or just Rose) stayed the night.

You'll notice I extended the timeline well past the 39 weeks in question. I did the same with the folders in the Box of Proof. In fact, I extended all the way through July of 2011 – a full fourteen months past her alleged dates – to when the X family left for a month-long vacation in Puerto Rico and I moved from the moldy basement to a sunny, third floor apartment across town, a place Loretta never mentioned.

You'll also notice that even with this drastic extension, there were zero nights that Loretta stayed with me by herself in the moldy basement apartment.

The bottom line is that Loretta did not tell the truth.

Week	1	2	3	4	5
Weekend dates	**8/15-16/09**	8/22-23/09	8/29-30/09	9/5-6/09	9/12-13/09
What I did that weekend, where I did it, and with whom:	**hosted Loretta (Lo) and Rose (Ro) for a long weekend at Connie's; did an obstacle course race with Ivy on Sun in Boulder**	Rockies game in Denver with Alice	Connie's birthday party outing to Blackhawk Casino with Connie and her friends	watched all three X kids - Lo, Ro, and Slater - at their house	watched all three X kids at their house
Did Loretta sleep by herself at my house?	**no**	no	no	no	no
Documentation includes:					
Picture	x	x	x		
Ticket Stub	x	x			
Blog	x			x	x
Diary			x		x
Calendar					
Chat	x				x

Week	6	7	8	9	10
Weekend dates	9/19-20/09	**9/26-27/09**	10/3-4/09	10/10-11/09	10/17-18/09
What I did that weekend, where I did it, and with whom:	traveled to Aspen, CO, with Connie	**saw Cirque with X family, hosted Lo and Ro for surprise sleepover afterwards; met Ivy for breakfast next morning**	stayed close to home except Sat afternoon with X family for kids' school function	hosted out-of-town friend, Danielle	amusement park with X family on Sat; home on Sun
Did Loretta sleep alone at my house?	no	**no**	no	no	no
Documentation includes:					
Picture	x		x	x	
Ticket Stub		x			x
Blog	x				x
Diary	x	x	x		x
Calendar					
Chat		x			

Week	11	12	13	14	15
Weekend dates	10/24-25/09	10/31-11/1/09	11/7-8/2009	11/14-15/09	**11/21-22/09**
What I did that weekend, where I did it, and with whom:	traveled to Sun City West, Arizona, to spend a long weekend with Grandma Joan	stayed at X house Fri, trick or treat w/ kids Sat, then costume party in Denver	Mona/family visiting from Wisconsin; X family comes to our family dinner party at Connie's	traveled to Breckenridge, CO for my birthday with Ivy, Alice, and Grace	**host Lo and Ro at Connie's house for the weekend**
Did Loretta sleep alone at my house?	no	no	no	no	**no**
Documentation includes:					
Picture		x	x	x	x
Ticket Stub					
Blog	x	x	x	x	
Diary	x			x	x
Calendar					
Chat					

Week	16	17	18	19	20
Weekend dates	11/28-29/09	12/5-6/09	12/12-13/09	12/19-20/09	12/26-27/09
What I did that weekend, where I did it, and with whom:	celebrated Thanksgiving w/ X family at their house	travel to San Francisco to visit Amelia	attend concert Fri night with friends; stay home Sat night	dog sit for housemates' dogs at Connie's	in Wisconsin with my family for the holidays
Did Loretta sleep alone at my house?	no	no	no	no	no
Documentation includes:					
Picture	x	x	x		x
Ticket Stub			x		
Blog		x	x	x	x
Diary	x	x			x
Calendar					
Chat					

Week	21	22	23	24	25
Weekend dates	1/2-3/10	1/9-10/10	1/16-17/10	1/23-24/10	1/30-31/10
What I did that weekend, where I did it, and with whom:	accepted invitation from X family to spend New Year's in Breckenridge, CO	walked around Sloan's Lake in Denver with Alice; 2-hour Sat night phone conversation with a high school friend, Pat	lazy, cold weekend at Connie's	meet Ivy and girls in a park in Denver on Saturday afternoon; Alice spends the night on Saturday night	traveled to Wisconsin to visit Mona and spend time with Pat
Did Loretta sleep alone at my house?	no	no	no	no	no
Documentation includes:					
Picture	x				x
Ticket Stub					
Blog	x	x	x	x	x
Diary	x	x	x	x	x
Calendar					
Chat					

Week	26	27	28	29	30
Weekend Dates	2/6-7/10	2/13-14/10	2/20-21/10	2/27-28/10	3/6-7/10
What I did that weekend, where I did it, and with whom:	Ro's birthday party; took Lo to 10:05pm movie in Denver; Lo sleeps over at Connie's	spent time at X house	traveled to Wisconsin to visit Mona and spend time with Pat	still in Wisconsin	move into the moldy basement in Denver; host Lo and Ro Fri; X family helps me move on Sat
Did Loretta sleep alone at my house?	yes	no	no	no	no
Documentation includes:					
Picture	x	x	x	x	x
Ticket Stub	x				
Blog	x				x
Diary	x				x
Calendar					
Chat	x				

Week	31	32	33	34	35
Weekend Dates	**3/13-14/10**	3/20-21/10	3/27-28/10	4/3-4/10	4/10-11/10
What I did that weekend, where I did it, and with whom:	**dinner with Ramona and Alice; Ro and I to planetarium on Sat, hosted all 3 X kids Sat night**	Missy's birthday party in Denver	travelled with Lo and Ro to my parents' house in Georgia for spring break	Jules/family in town; watched March Madness at Leigh and Eric's house in Denver	Rockies game with Alice in Denver; Sat afternoon at X house
Did Loretta sleep alone at my house?	**no**	no	no	no	no
Documentation includes:					
Picture	x		x	x	x
Ticket Stub			x	x	
Blog	x	x	x		
Diary	x	x	x		x
Calendar					
Chat	x				

Week	36	37	38	39	40
Weekend Dates	4/17-18/10	4/24-25/10	5/1-2/10	5/8-9/10	5/15-16/10
What I did that weekend, where I did it, and with whom:	travel to Salt Lake City, UT with Alice and Ivy to run a half-marathon	Rockies games with Alice on both Fri and Sun; hosted my housewarming party on Sat night	A quiet weekend at home by myself: yoga; house projects; cook dinner	Spent weekend at X house to celebrate Lo's birthday	dinner at Melting Pot with X family
Did Loretta sleep alone at my house?	no	no	no	no	no
Documentation includes:					
Picture	x	x			x
Ticket Stub					
Blog	x	x			x
Diary	x		x		
Calendar		x	x	x	x
Chat					

Alexandra J. Kuisis

Week	41	42	43	44	45
Weekend Dates	**5/22-23/10**	5/29-30/10	6/5-6/10	6/12-13/10	6/19-20/10
What I did that weekend, where I did it, and with whom:	**Hosted X kids overnight at my house in Denver**	worked with an organizing client, had a massage, spent time at X house	traveled to Wisconsin to visit Mona/family	traveled to California to visit friends and family	hung with Alice in Denver, saw a movie with X family
Did Loretta sleep alone at my house?	**no**	no	no	no	no
Documentation includes:					
Picture	x		x	x	x
Ticket Stub		x			x
Blog		x			x
Diary		x			
Calendar	x	x	x	x	x
Chat	x				

Week	46	47	48	49	50
Weekend Dates	6/26-27/10	7/3-4/10	7/10-11/10	7/17-18/10	**7/24-25/10**
What I did that weekend, where I did it, and with whom:	spent time at X house; babysit a school family in Denver	hung with Alice in Denver; volunteer at Cherry Creek Arts Festival	X family's house Thurs-Fri; babysat for the Nanny Family in Denver Sat	wine tasting tour in Denver with Meg	**hosted Ro for the weekend - one night in the Moldy Basement, one night at the Nanny Family's house**
Did Loretta sleep alone at my house?	no	no	no	no	**no**
Documentation includes:					
Picture					x
Ticket Stub					
Blog					
Diary	x	x			
Calendar	x	x		x	x
Chat					

Week	51	52	53	54	55
Weekend Dates	7/31-8/1/10	8/7-8/10	8/14-15/10	8/21-22/10	8/28-29/10
What I did that weekend, where I did it, and with whom:	Hosted Lo at Nanny Family's house in Denver 7/28 after Angus's 40th b-day; took Lo to airport 7/29; Boulder on Sat	finished organizing projects at X house while Ivy and kids out of town	attended a Rockies baseball game Fri night in Denver; traveled to Steamboat Springs, CO, Sat-Sun	babysat Nanny Family on Fri night; took Lo and Ro to water park on Sat afternoon	volunteered at the Shambhala Mountain Center - a Buddhist retreat center - in Red Feather Lake, CO all week
Did Loretta sleep alone at my house?	Yes (Nanny Family's house)	no	no	no	no
Documentation includes:					
Picture	x		x	x	x
Ticket Stub			x	x	
Blog	x		x	x	x
Diary	x				
Calendar	x	x	x	x	x
Chat	x			x	

Week	56	57	58	59	60
Weekend Dates	9/4-5/10	9/11-12/10	9/18-19/10	9/25-26/10	10/2-3/10
What I did that weekend, where I did it, and with whom:	watched X kids while Ivy and Angus traveled	camped in Deckers, CO with friends	traveled to Philadelphia, PA for a half-marathon Girls' Weekend with Helen and Amelia	Rockies baseball game/drinks in Denver to celebrate Alice's birthday	hosted Lo and Ro on Fri; school function on Sat afternoon, home alone Sat night
Did Loretta sleep alone at my house?	no	no	no	no	no
Documentation includes:					
Picture	x	x	x	x	x
Ticket Stub					
Blog	x	x	x		x
Diary					
Calendar	x	x	x	x	x
Chat					

Week	61	62	63	64	65
Weekend Dates	10/9-10/10	10/16-17/10	10/23-24/10	10/30-31/10	11/6-7/10
What I did that weekend, where I did it, and with whom:	happy hour in Denver on Fri; dinner and Paula Poundstone show with Ivy in Denver on Sat, she stays over	hosted an out-of-town friend, Joe; Ivy and kids over for picnic/hot tubbing on Sat	hosted out-of-town friend, Joe	Spent time at X family house	babysat Nanny Family on Fri; attended a work party in Denver on Sat
Did Loretta sleep alone at my house?	no	no	no	no	no
Documentation includes:					
Picture	x	x	x	x	
Ticket Stub	x		x		
Blog	x			x	
Diary				x	x
Calendar	x	x	x	x	x
Chat					

Week	66	67	68	69	70
Weekend Dates	11/13-14/10	11/20-21/10	**11/27-28/10**	12/4-5/10	12/11-12/10
What I did that weekend, where I did it, and with whom:	happy hour with colleagues on Fri; celebrated my birthday in Denver with a group of girlfriends on Sat	traveled to Wisconsin to visit Mona/family	**Michael Franti concert with Lo and Ro on Sat afternoon; hosted all 3 X kids Sat night; errands with Ivy and kids Sun**	traveled in Thailand with Joe	traveled in Thailand with Joe
Did Loretta sleep alone at my house?	no	no	**no**	no	no
Documentation includes:					
Picture	x	x	**x**	x	x
Ticket Stub			**x**	x	x
Blog	x	x			
Diary			**x**		
Calendar	x	x	**x**	x	x
Chat					

Week	71	72	73	74	75
Weekend Dates	12/18-19/10	12/25-26/10	1/1-2/11	1/8-9/11	1/15-16/11
What I did that weekend, where I did it, and with whom:	traveled in Thailand with Joe	traveled in Thailand with Joe and visited in San Francisco with Amelia	celebrated the New Year at home in Denver; watched football with Alice	spent time with entire X family at their house	happy hour in Denver on Fri; work party/football playoff games in Denver on Sat
Did Loretta sleep alone at my house?	no	no	no	no	no
Documentation includes:					
Picture	x	x	x		
Ticket Stub	x	x			
Blog			x	x	
Diary			x		x
Calendar	x	x		x	x
Chat					

Week	76	77	78	79	80
Weekend Dates	1/22-23/11	1/29-30/11	**2/5-6/11**	2/12-13/11	2/19-20/11
What I did that weekend, where I did it, and with whom:	babysat a school family in Denver	attended a concert at Swallow Hill and a party at the Dirty Duck in Denver; redeemed Groupon for snowboarding lessons at Arapahoe Basin, CO, on Sun	**hosted Ivy and kids Fri night in preparation for REI sale Sat morning; work party on Sat night; Super Bowl party on Sun**	visited with Annie; attended the school's fundraising Gala in Denver	volunteered with Alice at Single in the City event in Denver on Fri; spent time with X family at their house on Sat
Did Loretta sleep alone at my house?	no	no	**no**	no	no
Documentation includes:					
Picture		x	**x**	x	x
Ticket Stub					
Blog			**x**		
Diary					
Calendar	x	x	**x**	x	x
Chat			**x**		x

Week	81	82	83	84	85
Weekend Dates	2/26-27/11	3/5-6/11	3/12-13/11	3/19-20/11	3/26-27/11
What I did that weekend, where I did it, and with whom:	happy hour with work friends in Denver on Fri night; engagement party in Denver on Sat night	Mona/family arrived in Denver Fri; Ivy, Ro and Slater met us for dinner; traveled to Arizona with Mona/family Sat	return from Arizona on Sat, meet friends at a bar to play pool	happy hour Fri; with X kids at their house on Sat; drop off to Eileen on Sun	with X kids at their house on Thurs while Ivy and Angus in Costa Rica; fly to Arizona to visit Grandma Joan
Did Loretta sleep alone at my house?	no	no	no	no	no
Documentation includes:					
Picture		x	x		x
Ticket Stub				x	
Blog		x			
Diary	x			x	x
Calendar	x	x		x	x
Chat				x	x

Week	86	87	88	89	90
Weekend Dates	4/2-3/11	4/9-10/11	4/16-17/11	4/23-24/11	4/30-5/1/11
What I did that weekend, where I did it, and with whom:	attended Rockies game Fri, Alice's housewarming party Sat, Rockies game Sun, all in Denver	attended a work party Fri night; first date on Sat in Denver	volunteered at Doors Open Denver; happy hour, second date in Denver on Sat	babysat in Denver on Fri; third date to see Lauryn Hill in Denver on Sat night; flew to Arizona for Grandma's funeral on Sun	painting class with Ivy, stayed at X house on Sat; took Slater to Rockies game on Sun then to Lo and Ro's cotillion
Did Loretta sleep alone at my house?	no	no	no	no	no
Documentation includes:					
Picture	x	x	x		x
Ticket Stub	x		x	x	
Blog	x		x		
Diary		x			x
Calendar	x	x		x	x
Chat			x		x

Week	91	92	93	94	95
Weekend Dates	5/7-8/11	5/14-15/11	5/21-22/11	5/28-29/11	**6/4-5/11**
What I did that weekend, where I did it, and with whom:	met Ivy and kids on Pearl Street in Boulder for Lo's birthday on Sat, back to Denver on Sat night	ran errands and completed house projects; volunteered @ Colfax marathon in Denver Sun at 5am	traveled to Wisconsin to visit Mona/family	X house for Lo's 5th grade graduation; out with friends in Denver Sat night; babysit School Family on Sun in Denver	**Stay home Fri and Sat; hosted Ro on Sun night in Denver**
Did Loretta sleep alone at my house?	no	no	no	no	**no**
Documentation includes:					
Picture	x		x	x	**x**
Ticket Stub					
Blog	x				**x**
Diary	x				
Calendar	x				
Chat				x	

Week	96	97	98	99	100
Dates Sat/Sun	6/11-12 /11	6/18-19/11	6/25-26/11	7/2-3/11	7/9-10/11
What I did that weekend, where I did it, and with whom:	babysat on Sat; Rockies game on Sun	Mumford and Sons concert with Cecily on Thurs night; happy hour on Fri; Pride in Denver on Sat	organizing client in Denver on Fri night; babysat in Denver on Sat; X house on Sun to visit	dinner date Fri in Denver; happy hour Sat in Denver; Rockies game on Sun	traveled to Aspen; X family left for Puerto Rico, where they remained until I moved out of the moldy apartment
Did Loretta sleep alone at my house?	no	no	no	no	no
Documentation includes:					
Picture	x	x	x	x	x
Ticket Stub	x	x		x	
Blog					
Diary	x			x	x
Calendar	x	x	x	x	x
Chat					x

References

A Note from the Author

- National Association for the Advancement of Colored People website, https://www.naacp.org/criminal-justice-fact-sheet/
- Kate Antonovics & Brian G Knight, 2009. "A New Look at Racial Profiling: Evidence from the Boston Police Department," The Review of Economics and Statistics, MIT Press, vol. 91(1), pages 163-177, 09.
- Fryer, Roland G., 2016. "An Empirical Analysis of Racial Differences in Police Use of Force." Journal Bureau of Economic Reasearch. NBER Working Paper No. 22399 https://www.nber.org/papers/w22399
- Starr, Sonja B. "Racial Disparity in Federal Criminal Sentences." M. M. Rehavi, co-author. J. Pol. Econ. 122, no. 6 (2014): 1320-54.
- Shamena Anwar & Patrick Bayer & Randi Hjalmarsson, 2012. "The Impact of Jury Race in Criminal Trials," The Quarterly Journal of Economics, Oxford University Press, vol. 127(2), pages 1017-1055.
- Abrams, David S. and Bertrand, Marianne and Mullainathan, Sendhil, Do Judges Vary in Their Treatment of Race? (May 28, 2013). Journal of Legal Studies, Vol. 41, No. 2 (June 2012), pp. 347-383, Available at SSRN: https://ssrn.com/abstract=1800840

Chapter 1

- https://www.apa.org/research/action/polygraph
- https://www.trutv.com/shows/adam-ruins-everything/articles/adam-ruins-forensic-science

Chapter 2

- https://www.atlasobscura.com/articles/
  communal-sleeping-history-sharing-bed
- https://evolutionaryparenting.com/
  bedsharing-beyond-infancy-the-question-of-independence/
- Okami P, Weisner T, Olmstead R. Outcome correlates of parent-child bedsharing: an eighteen-year longitudinal study. *Developmental and Behavioral Pediatrics* 2002; 23: 244-53.
- Keller MA, Goldberg WA. Co-sleeping: help or hindrance for young children's independence? *Infant and Child Development* 2004; 13: 369-88.

Chapter 5

- https://www.shouselaw.com/colorado/CO_plea_bargains.html
- https://www.westword.com/news/
  colorado-prisoners-by-the-disturbing-numbers-11050425
- https://www.courts.state.co.us/userfiles/file/Administration/
  Planning_and_Analysis/Annual_Statistical_Reports/2014/
  Annual%20Statistical%20Report%20FY2014%20FINAL.pdf

Chapter 6

- https://www.reiki.org/faqs/what-reiki
- https://metoomvmt.org/

Chapters 7 and 8

- https://www.mind.org.uk/information-support/
  types-of-mental-health-problems/
  dissociation-and-dissociative-disorders/about-dissociation/

- Loftus, Elizabeth F, and Katherine Ketcham. *The Myth of Repressed Memory: False Memories and Allegations of Sexual Abuse.* New York: St. Martin's Press, 1994. Print.
- Loftus, Elizabeth F. Planting misinformation in the human mind: *A 30-year investigation of the malleability of memory.* Cold Spring Harbor Laboratory Press, 2005. Web.
- Loftus, Elizabeth F. *How Reliable is Your Memory?* Ted Global 2013. Web.

Epilogue

- https://www.psychologytoday.com/us/basics/cognitive-dissonance
- https://yourholisticpsychologist.com/ what-is-reparenting-and-how-to-begin/
- https://www.ncbi.nlm.nih.gov/pmc/articles/PMC4807731/
- https://www.sciencedirect.com/science/article/abs/ pii/0022103170900569
- Menakem, Resmaa. *My Grandmother's Hands: Racialized Trauma and the Pathway to Mending Our Hearts and Bodies.*, 2017. Print. p42

Made in the USA
Monee, IL
05 May 2021

67863503R00163